A Collection of Letters to Nuns

by
the Optina Elder and Director of
HIEROSCHEMAMONK AN.

*Published in
Russian by the Kozelsk Optina Hermitage of
the Entry of the Theotokos
Holy Trinity - St. Sergius Lavra Press
1910*

**Translated by Holy Nativity Convent
Boston, Massachusetts**

First Printing: 1993
Second Printing: 2003

Holy Trinity Monastery
Printshop of St. Job of Pochaev
Jordanville, New York
2003

Printed with the Blessing of Archbishop Laurus of Syracuse
and Holy Trinity Monastery.

Published by Holy Trinity Monastery,
Jordanville, N.Y. 13361-0036
ISBN 0-88465-053-7

Translated from the Russian by Holy Nativity Convent,
Boston. Copyright 1991, all Rights Reserved.

TABLE OF CONTENTS

Saint Anatoly of Optina

FOREWORD

These letters to nuns which we offer to the reader's attention were written by the Optina Elder, Director of the Skete, and Confessor, Father Hieroschemamonk Anatoly, a contemporary, disciple, and friend of the Elder Father Hieroschemamonk Amvrosy.

Father Anatoly, in the world Alexis Zertsalov, came from an ecclesiastical calling. He finished the course of studies at the Kaluga Ecclesiastical Seminary, and in 1853 at 29 years of age he joined the brotherhood of Optina Hermitage under the guidance of the Elder of that time, Father Hieroschemamonk Makary (Ivanov) who, while himself also guiding the young monk, entrusted him to the immediate care of his close disciple, and subsequently his successor in eldership, Father Amvrosy (Grenkov).

Thus, Father Anatoly matured spiritually under the direct guidance of two great instructors in the monastic life, and from them he diligently absorbed spiritual wisdom.

In 1874, after the death of Father Ilarion, the Director of the Skete, Father Anatoly, at the Elder Father Amvrosy's bidding, was appointed Director of the Skete and simultaneously Confessor of the Optina brotherhood.

From this time until the very time of Father Amvrosy's repose in 1891, these two strugglers labored together hand in hand in the work of spiritual guidance, both of the monks of Optina Hermitage, and of the nuns of numerous convents who turned to the Elders, and also of lay people.

Their cells were located next to each other, separated only by the Holy Gates of the Skete, and everyone coming to Father Amvrosy also went to Father Anatoly to receive his blessing. The Elders were closely united by their identical spiritual training, by profound mutual understanding and sympathy, and by their common goal in life, consisting in the struggle of tireless self-perfection in Christ, tireless prayer, and service to their neighbor.

When Father Amvrosy founded the Shamordino convent, he entrusted Father Anatoly with being the confessor of the Shamordino sisters as well.

Over the years, with Father Amvrosy's blessing, Father Anatoly came to have numerous spiritual ties and relations resulting in a sizeable correspondence on his part, part of which namely, his letters to nuns, we now offer to the reader's attention.

We will not find in Father Anatoly's letters the variety of content and answers to different kinds of practical questions with which Father Amvrosy's letters abound.

But Father Anatoly's letters have their own remarkable qualities. Living a purely inner life, being an experienced doer of mental prayer, Father Anatoly left in his letters the impress of his soul, highly attuned with Christian thoughts and feelings. Filled with profound living faith, having come to know by experience the winding and thorny path of inner, spiritual Christian growth, a zealot of monastic struggle in the spirit of and according to the testament of the great Elders Paissy, Theodore, Lev, Makary and Amvrosy, as well as the great instructors of old, Abba Dorotheos, John of the Ladder, Isaac the Syrian, and others — to the depth and wealth of his spiritual knowledge Father Anatoly joined a tenderly loving heart, a soul of childlike simplicity, and an amazing capability for inclining others to his own bent, for pouring his own spiritual makeup into their souls.

He knew how to touch in an affectionate, tender, fatherly way every ailing, distraught human soul, which understood neither itself or others, — how to soothe it, clear before it the path of the spiritual life, and show it where and how to go. And in all justice one may term him, as well as his contemporary and friend, Father Amvrosy, a true healer of souls in affliction and perplexity.

Father Anatoly's letters teach the knowledge and love of God; they clarify the lofty goal of the Christian and the monastic life; they provide encouragement in the struggle of battling against passions and weaknesses; they teach the Prayer of Jesus; and in general they contain many useful lessons for anyone seeking the spiritual life. Thus we think that not only Father Anatoly's former spiritual children, for whom each word of their unforgettable Batiushka is holy and precious, but also all Russian nuns will read Father Anatoly's letters with joy and with great benefit to their souls, and make them their handbook alongside the works of the Fathers and Teachers of the Faith and of Christian life.

Some of the letters presented here were printed in the periodical *Soul-Profiting Reading* in the years 1902-1906, but a substantial majority of them appear here in print for the first time.

Father Anatoly survived Father Amvrosy by three years and reposed in 1894. After Father Amvrosy's death and prior to his own repose, he shared his labors as Elder and Confessor with another close disciple of Father Amvrosy, now the Optina Elder Father Hieroschemamonk Joseph.

If God blesses, a detailed biography of Father Anatoly will be published in the near future.

Protopriest Serge Chetverikov
July 19, 1909

THE LETTERS OF SAINT ANATOLY OF OPTINA TO NUNS

Icon of the Optina Elders

LETTERS TO A.Th.

1. ACCEPT REPROACHES AS BEING DESERVING OF THEM

November 6, 1875

I received your letter, A., sister in the Lord, and I was glad that the Lord has arranged for you a comfortable nook. Wrongly do the sisters reproach you for being without an obedience; your obedience is the most precious one there is and also the simplest: accept reproaches as being deserving of them, and pray to God for those who reproach you. It is concerning this blessed obedience that the Apostle Paul said in his epistles, *He became obedient unto death, even the death of the Cross. Wherefore God also hath highly exalted Him* (Phil. 2: 8, 9). This obedience is also precious in that it is not seen by others and is much nearer to humility than other obediences. And this precisely is what is precious for us. As for not having accepted my suggestion, do not grieve over it. The Lord Himself will arrange things, only have a sincere desire and have humility, which can take the place of any rule and of all struggles.[1] Peace to you, and God's blessing. I remain your well-wisher, the greatly sinful Hieromonk Anatoly. [P.S.] — You should always clearly indicate the date on your letters.

2. ONE OUGHT TO PLACE ONE'S HOPE NOT IN ONE'S VIRTUES
BUT IN GOD'S MERCY AND IN THE SACRIFICE OF THE SON OF GOD UPON THE CROSS

November 14, 1875

I received the letter from you, Sister A., and the scarf, and I thank you for it. But mostly I thank you for the thought, although I am sorry for you, that you are allotting your small amount of money for my health when you yourself are still sick.

As for your not going to Matins, your being lazy, your having neither humility nor patience — for all this you should reproach and

---

1. Podvigi, in Russian.

bemoan yourself. And what is more, you should thank the Lord for not giving horns to such a rambunctious cow![1] Because just look at how you are thinking — I am not doing anything — how can I be saved?" Why, can our miniscule virtues really save us? Don't you remember God's words, *all the righteousness* of man before God is as a filthy rag (cf. Is. 64:6)? Better seek mercy from our Master and not payment for labors. And you will be saved more easily than those who labor without discretion.

Now, that you are still shedding tears (kvasishsya[2]), that is not good from a worldly standpoint, but spiritually it is an adornment — precious necklaces around one's neck. And for you and me it is also a remedy against spiritual maladies and a protection against much that is unseemly. Give thanks to God for everything, and for being deemed worthy to serve the sisters by reading the prayers for them — but it is not good to think that this will be *credited to your account*. What will be imputed to us is the great sacrifice offered by our sweetest Jesus upon the Cross to Him Who is eternal Righteousness — we ourselves have nothing that is good. Labor according to your strength, but do not yourself appraise your merits, do not count up your virtues. Instead, look at and enumerate your weaknesses and your sins, and the Lord will never forsake you. . . Peace to you, and God's blessing and the blessing of our Fathers.[3] Sincerely wishing your salvation, I remain, the greatly sinful Hieromonk Anatoly.

Instead of my photograph, I am sending you my assurance that I think of you — and let that be enough.

3. ILLNESS IS BENEFICIAL FOR THE SOUL

January 1, 1876

I received your two letters, A., God-loving novice, much-enduring handmaid of Jesus and my sister in the Lord. Peace to you!

Peace to your spirit!

Peace to your ailing body!

Do not imagine that peace abides in a healthy body: there, toads and

---

1. Lit., "apt to butt." Perhaps what is meant is that if the Lord were to equip such an unruly soul with virtues, it would only fall further into destructive pride.

2. Kvásishsya — From the word "kvass," a fermented drink — hence more literally, "you are still sour," i.e., "things aren't going well."

3. I.e., the Elders Leonid and Makary.

leeches abide. No, peace abides only in our mortified flesh. And this precisely is the true peace, the peace of Jesus, *the peace. . .which passeth all understanding* (Phil. 4:7). And so, do not let it surprise you that I who love you do not grieve on hearing that you are sick and that your sister causes you suffering.

True, I am sorry that you have pain; but at the same time I am not sorry in spirit, knowing as I do for certain that your tribulations are for you an eternal treasure. . . Now, as regards N__, you must never forget her in your prayers. She is your great benefactress, your true unmercenary doctor. Just look how unselfish she is: physicians and pharmacists demand rubles and rubles to help you in your illnesses — and even so, they just might take your money and not help you any. Now this one does not take a kopeck, and yet she heals chronic illnesses of the soul, incurable leprosy — our sins. So be patient; be condescending with N__; be thankful to God; and I believe that you will receive a hundredfold in this age and thousands of thousands of times over in the future, endless, eternal one. Thank you for your greeting; I greet you with the new year. May God grant that you may attain also to that year[1] which is succeeded by neither fall nor winter — where is eternal spring, eternal gladness, where is the unceasing feast and the sound of them that keep festival (Ps. 41:4). Desiring this for you and for me, and ever prayerfully remembering you, I remain, the greatly sinful Hieromonk Anatoly.

4. WHEN YOU ARE BY YOURSELF, YOU SHOULD PRACTICE SAYING THE JESUS PRAYER

February 12, 1876

I received your letter, much-ailing Sister A. . . You write with some distress that when the others go to church, you sit in your cell feeling imprisoned. This means, Matushka, that you forget my desire and my reminder to you, that you should practice saying the oral Prayer of Jesus as much as possible — and especially when you are left all alone. That is the most advantageous time to root it in your memory. So, instead you wander mentally — no wonder you become despondent. The Prayer of Jesus, on the contrary, gladdens the heart. . .

With regard to your poor manner of life, do not lose heart but humble yourself, and the Lord will look upon your humility more than upon great struggles performed without humility. Peace to you, and the blessing of the Lord.

Greatly sinful Hieromonk Anatoly

---

1. Or, "that summer."

5. WE MUST LIVE NOT ACCORDING TO OUR OWN WILL BUT ACCORDING TO GOD'S

March 17, 1876

Different people are worn down by many and various troubles — but as for you and me, sister, we bear about with us troubles of our own making. We keep wanting to chant in the choir, and the Lord keeps wanting us to humble ourselves and resemble Him, the humble and meek One and, like Him, to endure tribulations, although not such as those He bore for our sins, but little ones, a thousand times smaller. However, we do not at all want what God wants, but we want our own way instead, no matter what, even if things turn out worse. Now, nowhere has the Lord said that He loves good chanters or healthy young women, but whom does He love? The meek! *Upon whom shall I look*, He says, *but upon him that is humble and meek and trembleth at My words?* (Is. 66:2)

So now you have sorrows for your brother as well — they want to take him into the Christ-loving army for our own defense and that of the fatherland. You and I are not terribly brave, yet we wish to live in security. We do not want enemies to come and disgrace us and slaughter us — but still, do not go, brother, just sit with us and wait for our foes to catch us. Where is the logic and where Christian love?. . . What to do?. . . Just forget it and do not meddle in situations unasked. Do not seek out tribulations for yourself which you are not obligated to seek out, but seek and earnestly seek Him Whom we are obligated and urgently obligated to seek: seek Jesus, our Bridegroom, our Nourisher, our Hope, our Life and the Light of our eyes! And we will not be put to shame.

I know that without being accustomed to it, it is difficult to call upon Him constantly, very difficult indeed! But then, who demands that you repeat this prayer tirelessly? Labor according to your strength, labor with humility and self-reproach, and you will form the habit, and you will come to love it so much that they will not be able to tear you away from it by force. Because it is sweet and joy-making. *I remembered God and I was gladdened* (Ps. 76:3). So be at peace. Never hesitate to write to me; I will receive it all with love and answer as I am able. Now, you probably will not have a chance to write before Holy Week, and so I wish that you may meet this radiant feast in peace and tranquility. And in good health, too, if it is pleasing to God. But still we should remember that our true Pascha is there, in the unsetting light, with myriads of myriads of angels and saints, and with the Source of light, our sweetest Jesus.

Unworthy Hieromonk Anatoly

6. BEFORE YOU ADORN THE SOUL, YOU HAVE TO CLEANSE IT

August 12, 1876

Most reverend Matushka A., at the last minute, when I had just answered some letters I had to answer, yours suddenly turned up! Although I read it long ago, I have not answered it yet. True, it is not urgent, but I cannot help hurrying to set your mind at rest with my reply, because you have set my mind at rest. And you have set my mind at rest because you thank God for the consolation He has given you at Optina, you remember our love for you, and thus you comfort yourself!

Glory be to God for all things!

May God bless you to read the commemoration. As for the full prostrations which are made with it, you may do them as your strength will allow — they are not required of one who is ill.

As for the clothing. . . I told you. . . But these things are not important. Here is what is important: to adorn the inner dwelling! But before adorning it, we who are passionate must cleanse it. And there is only one tool for cleansing it which is available to us: "Lord Jesus Christ, Son of God, have mercy on me." So there you have a Matins![1] Peace to you! Save yourself![2] I remain with sincere best wishes, the unworthy Hieromonk Anatoly.

7. THE ENEMY WILL NOT FORGIVE THOSE WHO COME TO LOVE THE JESUS PRAYER

December 20, 1876

I remember receiving your letter, G.,[3] but I cannot remember whether I answered it or not, and I cannot find the letter. I do remember you wrote that the Jesus Prayer stays with you more. If that is so, glory to Thee, O Lord! Keep on with it and devise ways to hold on to it more tightly. A better time than this you will not find. When the time for trading is over,[4] you can wave your arms all you want, but it will be too late.

---

1. See Letters #2 and 4.
2. An expression signifying, "Struggle!"
3. Probably Grusha, a nickname for Agrippina. See Letters #11 and 13. The use of nicknames accounts for varying initials in many letters.
4. Lit., "when the market breaks up." See Matthew 25:14-30.

Only, G., remember the ancient saying. Be prepared to encounter tribulations.[1] For the enemy will never leave anyone who comes to love the Jesus Prayer alone without getting even. Without fail he will incite older people against you, or younger people, but one way or another they will make trouble for sure.

I do not know where your M.S. saw this photograph. In all of Russia I have given one to only three nuns, including yourself. Now, if you will patiently endure trials, show love for your neighbor, and with humility practice saying the Jesus Prayer as much as you are able, then I will give you another photograph.

Unworthy Hieromonk Anatoly

I greet you with the approaching feast of the Nativity of Christ. God has now become man so as to make us men gods. This I earnestly desire for you and for all who pray for us. Glory to God in the highest, and on earth peace!

8. ONE MUST HUMBLE ONESELF, BE PATIENT, AND PRAY

January 9, 1877

Matushka A., I think I have already received two letters from you. And I will answer them briefly, as I am going away soon. . .

I will send you the photograph, but don't you go getting conceited. . . Humble yourself rather, and pray to God for me and for yourself! G., you are enough to make me laugh, you and your choir. Just like a hen with an egg.[2]

---

1. Cf. Sirach (Ecclesiasticus) 2:1: "My son, if thou come to serve the Lord God, prepare thy soul for temptation."
2. See Letter #5. To chant in the choir seems to have been a common ambition among the sisters (see also Letters #45, 193 and 222). In an account of the Elder Anatoly's life, we read, "During the chanting of 'Make steadfast, O holy Theotokos. . . all them that form a company and gather for to praise thy name. . . deem them all worthy of glory's crowns' during a service, one sister got the idea that only chanters will receive a reward, and she became grieved that she was not a chanter. With these thoughts she went to see the Elder. Upon meeting her, he asked her three times, 'Do you chant?,' and on receiving a negative response, he said, 'That's what the problem is — there is no chanting down here,' and he indicated the heart, thus signifying that everything depends upon the inner disposition of the soul as one performs an obedience, and not upon the character of the obedience itself." From *Russian Strugglers for Piety of the 18th & 19th Centuries*, ed. Russian Monastery of St. Panteleimon, Mt. Athos, July Volume, (Moscow, 1908), p.98.

With regard to your not being good at patiently bearing trials and illnesses, reproach yourself, but do not despair. You are still a learner, a novice.

Yes, M.S.'s end is very edifying. As for you and me, let's learn at least a small lesson from her death: first, do not lift heavy things,[1] as she herself enjoined you; and the second lesson is, don't ask for photographs, or you will die. As soon as she got to asking for one, she died right away. Seek rather that photograph on which is written, "Lord Jesus Christ, Son of God, have mercy on me, a sinner."

Unprofitable Hieromonk Anatoly

9. IT IS BENEFICIAL TO FEAR DEATH, BUT ONE SHOULD NOT BECOME DESPONDENT

July 6, 1878

My dear reverend Matushka, . . .

I received all your letters. That you fear death is very correct and beneficial. Anyone who has even a few sins cannot help but fear death. But you, Matushka, are not reckoned among the desperate sinners — you belong to the good flock of those who repent and reproach themselves and feel contrition for their sins. So do not lose heart! I am a hundred times worse than you. Yet I keep crying out: Thou, O Lord, didst come to save sinners, and not to call the righteous to repentance (Cf. Mark 2:17). And therefore, save me also who am a sinner!

You pray like this, too! Peace to you!

Hieromonk Anatoly

10. WE MUST SERVE GOD WITHOUT EXPECTING A REWARD IN THIS LIFE

October 18, 1879

Skete of Optina Hermitage

Peace to you and the blessing of the Lord! Are you still as lazy as ever? Are you still as impatient as ever? If so, correct yourself! I spoke with your D. about various matters, but after some discussion, it turns out that many things are hard to correct. Most important, you would then have nothing to endure patiently, and your labor would lose its value.

---

1. This may have either a literal or a figurative meaning.

And one should add: the servants of lay people work for money and for ease — often they even try to find work, and they cannot find it. . . Are we monastics also after pay and gratitude and esteem?. . . What if you are recompensed with all these things in abundance, and when the time comes, they say, *Thou in thy lifetime receivedst thy good things?* (Luke 16:25). . .

11. WE MUST BE PATIENT, AWATING RECOMPENCE IN THE FUTURE LIFE

December 9, 1880

[My] bitter, albeit reverend, G.,[1]

. . . Do not be angry that I have not written to you for a long time, and do not think I have forgotten you! You are at the very top of my list of the ailing who await the moving of consolation.[2] I have not answered you because generally I have been writing little, and there were many whose infirmity was greater than yours. Greet with a bow for me the entire Christ-loving assembly struggling and suffering for Christ, their Bridegroom. There, everything will be brought out into the open, everything will be weighed in the balance, everything will be valued at its worth, everything will be made up for a hundredfold — sicknesses and animosities and infirmities — and even those people will be recompensed, to whom I wrote briefly and rarely in answer to their long and frequent and devoted letters.

The Lord will remember you and S. and P., the little carper! And you will come to love all this.[3] You will come to love it terribly! But now be patient! And do not demand an accounting from me, the sinner and slothful one! — although, I did not notice from your letters that they required an immediate answer. Peace to you, and the blessing of the Lord.

Unworthy Hieromonk Anatoly

---

1. Grusha, a nickname for Agrippina, means "pear."
2. The Slavonic wording here suggests John 5:3, waiting for the moving of the water at Bethesda.
3. I.e., the monastic life.

12. CONCERNING ORDER IN COMMUNAL WORK
November 13, 1886

Reverend Mother A., I asked Mother S. and Mother A. to teach you embroidery. Learn while teachers are easy to come by. But make sure you behave yourselves properly while you work. If anyone gets out of order, let the senior ones put her to do prostrations. While you work, the sisters should take turns reading aloud.

Of course it is difficult to read continually, so alternate — but read for no less than an hour each day. Visitors should not come during work time, except for superiors. But if anyone from the upper class should come, they should not stay for very long. Right then and there you can read to them from the Ladder or St. Ephraim the Syrian[1] concerning idleness and how harmful it is to roam around from cell to cell. . . For your sessions I am sending a pound of tea, five pounds of sugar, half a pood[2] of bagels, and a measure of apples. . . Only, be good. If I come and find disorderliness, I'll disband you all.

Hieromonk Anatoly

Peace to you, and success in your pure and holy work.

13. ONE MUST SUFFER WITH CHRIST IN ORDER TO BE GLORIFIED WITH HIM[3]

I received your two letters, A., sister in the Lord. . . I am very sorry that the unkind sisters have hung you on a cross. But perhaps our Lord Jesus Christ Himself has commanded them to do this so that you would come to resemble Him. And whoever resembles Christ in being crucified will resemble Him in resurrection and ascension into Heaven as well. That is certain. So do not wait for me to say to you, *Come down from the cross* (Matt. 27:40). For when the Jews said this to the Lord, He did not listen to them. Hang a little longer upon the cross, our G.— you will ripen

---

1. Perhaps St. Isaac the Syrian is meant here.
2. Pood — Approximately 36 lbs.
3. This English translation is faithful to the sequence of letters in the printed Russian collection (1910). Usually, the dated letters to a particular individual are in sequence; the undated (or partially dated) letters follow at the end, and may be quite out of sequence.
This translation is also faithful to the paragraph structure of the original, so sometimes there are sharp subject transitions within paragraphs.

and become a sweet fruit for the heavenly Bridegroom![1]

Hieromonk Anatoly

14. INSTRUCTION CONCERNING THE JESUS PRAYER

I have gotten completely scrambled up in my correspondence, Sister A., and I do not know whether I answered you or not.

One can practice mental prayer in illness and infirmity, amid people and at work. Only sometimes one's head aches from this, but what to do? But to make up for this you will come to love it. A thousand times over you will come to love it. Try to keep your thought with Jesus not actually in your head, but direct it somewhat to your bosom. Then, of course, your chest will start to ache, but that cannot be helped. *Our God is a consuming fire* (Heb. 12:29), and where we are impure, there it hurts. This pain is sent because of our unworthiness, but with time it will pass. . . Your unworthy suppliant before God, Hieromonk Anatoly.

15. CONCERNING THE SAME, ON THE DAY OF CHRIST'S NATIVITY

I greet you, A., sister in the Lord, with the celebration of the Nativity of our Saviour Jesus Christ. On such a day, I can fulfill your request to give you a word of instruction: this day Jesus Christ was born to bring peace on earth. And so if you want to have peace, have Jesus — if not in your heart, then at least on your lips, as I have enjoined you personally. . . . Peace to you, and the blessing of the Lord! I remain your sincere well-wisher, the greatly sinful Hieromonk Anatoly.

16. WE MUST PATIENTLY ENDURE TRIBULATIONS

Reverend Matushka A., *Rejoice in the Lord! Praise is meet for the upright!*(Ps. 32:1). This praise is meet for you on two counts: in the first place, you say that you grieved those who were sick and considered yourself to be in the right — and in the second place, you acknowledge that on account of this you yourself are now meetly and rightly enduring tribulations. Looks like on all counts you are right, and praise is meet for you! Only, Mother, be patient. . . *and the Lord is near! Him whom the Lord loveth, He chasteneth. And He scourgeth every son whom He receiveth* (Heb. 12:6). So it follows that you are a favorite of the Lord's and are sitting at His very feet.

Hieromonk Anatoly

---

1. Grusha, a nickname for Agrippina, means "pear."

17. ONE CANNOT GO THROUGH LIFE WITHOUT EXPERIENCING DEPRESSION

February 19

I have received your many letters, G. . . Why you have been attacked by this depression I cannot even guess. But at some point long ago I wrote to you that a monastic can never go through life without ever being attacked by depression and despondency, and occasionally even by a bit of despair. . .

Hieromonk Anatoly

18. THE RISEN CHRIST RESURRECTS ALL

April 14

Christ is risen, G.! Risen is Christ, and there is not one dead in the tomb.[1] If there is not one dead, can there possibly be anyone who will be sick? No!

We celebrate the death of death, the destruction of Hades, the beginning of a new and everlasting life. And with leaps of joy we praise the Cause thereof.[2]

But what about Sasha? And Masha? And everyone else who is ill? This question the Lord Himself answered when the Apostles, hearing of Lazarus' illness, began to grieve — that is, they understood in a human manner. But He Who is eternal Truth said, *This sickness is not unto death, but for the glory of God. I am glad for your sakes* (John 11:4,15).

Hieromonk Anatoly

Serve the sick with love. Jesus said, If ye have served these little ones, ye have served Me (Cf. Matt. 25:40)!

19. ONE MUST ASK PATIENCE OF GOD

October 24

[You say] I reason with you to have patience, but I myself do not give you any. Why, what am I supposed to do if I myself do not have

---

1. From the Catechetical Homily of St. John Chrysostom read at the end of the Paschal Matins.
2. From the Paschal Canon.

any? Now, here I sit, and I do not reproach you for not giving me any [patience]. . . How many times have I told you to ask God; He has plenty of everything. And if you would please beg a little bit of it for me, too. Because as it is, you do not have any either for yourself or for me. It is time we corrected ourselves. He who comes to recognize his infirmity is better than he who has seen angels.[1]

Hieromonk Anatoly

20. ON PATIENT ENDURANCE OF ILLNESS

March 6

My Matushka,
I have buried myself in letters and I will never dig through to yours. . . I thank you for the scarf. . . Thank you even more for trying to say the Jesus Prayer. That will prove very, very useful to you. Only, please humble yourself!. . . I rejoice even more that you bear your illness patiently. Not always, of course, but to make up for it we repent, humble ourselves, condemn ourselves. For our poverty, even that is sufficient. Glory to Thee, O Lord, for Thy mercy and longsuffering towards us! As for prostrations, we won't even put you to do them. Just lie there and lie there as long as you want, only do not forget Jesus. . . Peace to you, sister! Be patient, await God's mercy, pray, and above all humble yourself. Your sincere well-wisher, Hieromonk Anatoly.

As for people disturbing you — that is, run here, fetch there — that is beneficial for you: [this way], thoughts will sully you less.

21. MORE CONCERNING THE JESUS PRAYER

September 6

Peace to you, Sister A.! You wish to receive a line from me — here are five for you! If you want to show gratitude, reward them with five words — #1 Lord, #2 Jesus, #3 Christ, #4 Son, #5 of God. To these add "have mercy on me, a sinner." And keep repeating. And thus you will please God, and thank me, and save yourself.

Unworthy Hieromonk Anatoly

---

1. Cf. *The Ascetical Homilies of St. Isaac the Syrian*, Homily 64, p.317.

22. ON PATIENT ENDURANCE FOR THE SAKE OF CHRIST WHO IS BORN

December 24

Peace to you! Christ is born, give ye glory![1] Now, each is commanded to give glory in whatever way he can: one by labor, another by chanting — and you and I by patience. Christ will receive this too, just as He did the praise of the angels, which they rendered to the One Who was born, as He, the King of kings and Lord of lords, lay small, weak, and newly born in a manger, out in the cold, in the field. . . And what awaited Him in the future? Tribulations, hunger, thirst, revilings, wounds, blows, scourging, and finally, being nailed to the Cross and a shameful death. All of this the Lord beheld as a man — a child lying in the manger, wrapped in swaddling clothes. Let us also patiently endure for a little while for the sake of the Lord Who died for us, that we may also be glorified together with Him.

Hieromonk Anatoly

II. LETTERS TO T.

23. THE INNER PARADISE IS FOUND THROUGH PATIENCE AND HUMILITY

May 27, 1875

I received your letter of May 22, sister in the Lord and prosphora baker, T. I rejoice that you liked our Optina so much that it seemed like Paradise to you. However, our Paradise depends upon ourselves: be patient, humble yourself, and you will find Paradise within yourself. As one saint says, "Seek neither Rome nor Jerusalem,[2] but rather make ready the house of your soul, and then not only Peter and Paul will come to you, but the Lord Himself with His Most Pure Mother and with a multitude of angels and saints." And so do not be discouraged that you have not yet attained to this, but try and begin, not from the top but with the

1. From the Katavasis of the Nativity of Christ.
2. This rhymes in Russian — "ni Ríma, ni Ierusalíma."

bottom step — that is, with humility, with self-reproach. Say to yourself, "I am unworthy to live in Paradise during my life — deem me worthy, at least after my death, to inherit Thy Paradise together with the wise thief."

I would write more, but I am ill; I do not go out and I do not receive anyone. Now don't you hesitate, write when you like and what you like and I will lay it all to heart. Only I do not promise punctual answers.

May God keep you and set you and establish you upon the way of truth. Your sincere well-wisher, the greatly sinful Hieromonk Anatoly.

24. CHRISTIAN PERFECTION IS ATTAINED GRADUALLY
July 22, 1875

I received your letters, novice of God,[1] reverend prosphora baker, T., and I marvelled at your brilliance. How in the world did you manage to praise me so highly? Of course, even someone who is unlearned can render praise where praise is due — but you succeeded in extolling one who is worse than everyone else. But I won't argue with you, since I fear Him Who said, *He that receiveth a righteous man in the name of a righteous man shall receive a righteous man's reward* (Matt. 10:41). Instead, in return for your acclamation of me, I want to scold you: where did you get the idea that I will be burdened by your letters — how can you write, "I will bother you with my sins?" Not I, but the Son of God Himself says, *I came not to call the righteous, but sinners to repentance* (Mark 2:17). As for me — I am telling you, I am worse than anyone else.

And so how can I shun those who sin but then repent — won't the Lord turn away from me if I forsake someone? So now, forget this unreasonable doubt; write everything, and I will always receive it with heartfelt sympathy. I think I already wrote to you about this before. As for your not being patient, reproach yourself for this, but do not be disturbed. You came to the monastery to learn, and so learn patience, humility, and the other virtues which adorn the crown of monasticism. Does someone who is learning a craft right away pick up an awl, a wax-end[2], or whatever — an axe, a paintbrush — and right away make a shoe, a cupboard, a picture? If this cannot happen in real life, how is it that you want to learn the science of sciences all at once? For monasticism is higher than all knowledge — it teaches the heavenly, angelic way of life.

---

1. The Russian word for "novice" signifies "one who is under obedience."
2. Wax-covered thread used by shoemakers.

And so here too, just as with a craft, a sinful person who enters a monastery in order to prepare himself for the eternal life does not become a saint right away, but before this falls into sin many times, ruins the work he has begun, and because of this receives rebukes or chastisements from others, especially his superiors. And that is how he lives, learning and humbling himself. And later he grows unnoticeably *unto the measure of the stature of the fullness of Christ* (Eph. 4:13). I say unnoticeably, because if someone begins to notice that he has progressed, that already is bad and ruin is near at hand for a monastic.

So be prudent and attentive, and the Lord will not forsake you. Peace to you, and God's blessing!

Greatly sinful Hieromonk Anatoly

25. *EVERYTHING SHOULD BE DONE WITH A BLESSING*

August 11, 1875

Now I will write to you, humble T., exactly according to your wish — one little line. I am very pressed for time. I approve of your prudence, that without a blessing you do not have any dealings with others. If you continue this way, it will be the easier for you to preserve and save yourself. Peace to you. Guard your conscience, preserve peace, labor according to your strength, pray always: walking, lying down, eating — and in time you will come to resemble a nun, and the Lord will abide with you forever.

Greatly sinful Hieromonk Anatoly

26. *THE UNDERSTANDING WITH WHICH ONE SHOULD RECEIVE THE ANGELIC SCHEMA*

February 22, 1876

On receiving your first letter of February 13, I was comforted that the Mother Abbess intends to clothe you in the angelic schema. And I planned on the eve of Saturday, in our usual litany for health [and salvation], to commemorate the novice Tat., and on the eve of Sunday, the former Tat., the nun. But your second letter of February 14, which it grieved you [to write], or rather, which revealed your faintheartedness, gave me no joy either. The Apostle Paul writes to his disciples, Who is he then that loveth me, but the same which is made sorry by me (Cf. II Cor. 2:2)? But as for you, it looks like you do not love your spiritual father very much, since you became so grieved that you fell into depression and became ill. Why, what after all did I write? I did not accuse, I did not reproach; I merely reminded you of the necessity for sincere frankness, which is something I have need of as well as everyone else. But you understood in another way.

But peace — let's forget about it. I was convinced of your sincerity and your feelings, and I still am. And that should be enough for you. As you come to receive the angelic schema, approach this holy work with understanding. This is not some earthly distinction and honor, but the most utter humility. The way[1] of true monasticism is sincere humility, and St. Isaac the Syrian calls humility the raiment of the Godhead. Read for yourself his 53rd homily. The little angelic schema is a betrothal to our heavenly Bridegroom, our sweetest Jesus. And so, as soon as they clothe you with this garment of humility, you will be obligated always to have on your tongue the name of Jesus, and as a betrothed bride to have before your eyes the portrait of your Bridegroom. Peace to you. I forgive your unreasonable and unfair grief, and I will commemorate your name as I promised. Ever your sincere well-wisher, the greatly sinful Hieromonk Anatoly.

27. HUMILITY — THE FOUNDATION OF THE MONASTIC LIFE

March 13, 1876

I congratulate you, sister in the Lord, most reverend Mother T., with the reception of the sacred angelic schema. Do you know that this schema is the sign of your betrothal to the heavenly Bridegroom, Jesus? As it is chanted in the troparion to a virgin martyr, "Thee do I love, O my Bridegroom," and so on — and according to the teachings of St. Theodore the Studite, every nun is a martyr. So remember to Whom you have betrothed yourself!

You ask directions and edifying instruction lest you stray from the right path? Begin with humility, continue with humility, and end with humility, and you will be appointed a place with the saints. This path, that is, the path of humility, is the safest one, and as the Fathers say, it is "impossible to fall from. For where can the humble person fall to when he considers himself to be worse than everyone else?"[2] Moreover, how can one fail to humble oneself when Jesus, the God of gods and Lord of lords, humbled Himself *unto death, even the death of the Cross*? (Phil. 2:8).

---

1. Or "schema."
2. Cf. St. Barsanuphius, Answer #161.

The Astonishment of angels,[1] the One more comely in beauty than all the sons of men (Cf. Ps. 44:2), died a shameful death for us — and will we who are sinful and infirm refuse to see our sins, our infirmities?

As for proud thoughts, flee them as you would fire. *Every one that is proud in heart is an abomination before God* (Prov. 16:5). Before Him, the Pure One and Holy, "the heaven itself is not pure" (Cf. Job 15:15). And what is all our righteousness? The Prophet Isaiah valued it at its worth long ago: it is *a cast-off filthy rag*! (Is. 64:6).

You ask how you can avoid straying from this path? Listen not to me, the corrupt one, but to Him Who is eternal Truth incarnate, to Jesus: *No man looking back is fit for the Kingdom of God* (Luke 9:62).

This means that everyone who wishes to attain to Christ's Kingdom should not look back and recall his great virtues, and especially not his proud thoughts, but look upon the struggles and the glory of the saints — and then we will be with them! And look upon your own infirmities, your sins, the going forth of the soul [from the body] and the terrible torments then — and you will not sin (Cf. Sir. 7:36). Peace to you, Mother T.

Greatly sinful Hieromonk Anatoly

28. A PASCHAL ENCOURAGEMENT FOR ONE FAINTHEARTED

April 22, 1876

Christ is risen, sister in the Lord, Mother T.!

See how the sisters have honored you: they have given you a nice name. The gazelle,[2] or the mountain deer, always skips about the heights, bounds across gorges, flies about like a bird upon the mountain cliffs — but our gazelle cannot get across a slice of bread, cannot swim across a cup of tea, is listless in everything, is tripped up everywhere. A young struggler who has only just entered upon the spiritual life, and already she is exhausted! What a pity!

All right, let us forget the past. With this new year let us begin again to live according to the Gospel in a truly monastic way. God will forgive you for having been lazy, for you repented, and you felt remorse, and you berated yourself. But now you must make a beginning. Let us prepare — at least little by little — a dowry for our Bridegroom. He is not demanding but longsuffering: while you and I put together and adorn our wedding garment, thread by thread, in order to meet Him — He will

---

1. From the Akathist to our Sweetest Lord Jesus Christ.
2. The name Tabitha "gazelle" in Hebrew.

keep waiting, He will keep knocking at the door (See Rev. 3:20) of our heart until we open the house of our heart to Him, the Holy and Pure One. Only, do not sleep much so as not to oversleep and miss your Bridegroom, because we do not know when He will come to us: in the evening, in the morning, or at cockcrow (Cf. Mark 13:35). Now, we chanted not long ago, and we are still chanting, "The godly-wise women followed after Thee (the Bridegroom) in haste with sweet-smelling myrrh. But Him Whom they sought with tears as dead, they joyfully adored as the living God."[1]

Thus, to our dead works and to our mortified flesh, the risen Jesus is able to give both life and power. Only, let us worship Him as dead — that is, in our leanness and our nothingness[2] — and then we will be able to behold within ourselves the living God. Now let us hasten as the Magi to worship Him and bring to Him the myrrh of mercifulness to our neighbor and of humility, "and let us make lamentation and cry aloud in exclamation: Arise, O Master, Thou Who dost grant resurrection to the fallen."[3] Peace to you, T.!

Greatly sinful Hieromonk Anatoly

29. THE ALTERNATION OF JOYS AND SORROWS IN LIFE IS INEVITABLE

July 5, 1876

Most reverend Mother and sister in the Lord, T.,

Peace to you!. . .It seems you regret that it is not as pleasant for you at N— as it is at Optina. But at Optina you were a guest, and one cannot be a guest perpetually. Then you would have to demand from nature, too, that it would not send us unpleasant snows, winds, rains, bad weather — but then we would have no bread, no kasha, no clothes, no shoes: everything would dry up and be scorched as a result of those perpetually clear, warm days. No, everything is good at its proper time.

Without winter there would be no spring, without spring there would be no summer. It is the same in the spiritual life: a little consolation and then a little affliction, and so, little by little, the path of salvation unfolds. . .

No, one cannot become accustomed quickly to saying the Jesus Prayer. Only try not to forget God, and repent of your forgetfulness and distraction. . .

---

1. From the Paschal Canon.
2. I.e., in abstinence, poverty, humility, etc.
3. From the Oikos following the Kontakion of Pascha.

It is all right to be sick as much as you like, for that is very beneficial for us, but to be sad only from time to time, for you have no reason to be. Instead, better thank God for His mercies to us the infirm ones. . .If because of your keeping to yourself they consider you proud, you should rejoice. If they disturb your prayer, do not be discouraged, but humble yourself.

Greatly sinful Hieromonk Anatoly

30. IT IS INEXPEDIENT FOR A MONASTIC TO LIVE IN RETIREMENT

August 7, 1876

Peace to you! I spoke with Batiushka[1] about your distressing cir-cumstances, but he does not much approve your living in retirement. The communal obedience is a great rampart for the monastic against many temptations. So be at peace and rest assured, bearing in mind that we remember you at Optina and are trying to perfect your path to salvation — only do not be in a hurry; just sit by the seaside awhile and wait for fair weather.[2]

31. ONE MUST PATIENTLY COLLECT ONE'S THOUGHTS

September 9, 1876

Matushka T., you grieve that you become distracted — so what is the problem: collect your thoughts and you will be a wise merchant. But if during prayer your thoughts become scattered, that is normal; it is impossible for beginners not to become distracted. As for your becoming disturbed because of your thoughts, there is only one remedy: patience and humility. Peace to you!

Greatly sinful Hieromonk Anatoly

32. ON THE JESUS PRAYER, ITS ACTION AND ITS FRUITS

December 20, 1876

Reverend Mother T., You truly comforted me when you wrote that prayer is no longer as difficult for you as it was before. I am referring to

---

1. Father Amvrosy. (This footnote is from the Russian text.)
2. I.e., "be patient." This expression occurs frequently in the letters.

the Jesus Prayer. Glory to Thee, O Lord, Who condescendest to our infirmities!

You may not say it continually as yet. For until a person tastes *that the Lord is good* (Ps. 33:8), it is difficult to have Jesus unceasingly in one's heart. But thanks be to God just for what you do have! And so while the prayer remains, do not leave off. Most important, during the time of prayer, bemoan yourself as unworthy to pronounce the name which is ceaselessly glorified in Heaven and on earth by angels and by men. As for afflictions, gather them as you would a treasure, for this greatly helps the Jesus Prayer. [This prayer] is the reason why the enemy perverts and incites everyone who can possibly harass you. I warned you long ago that the more a Christian says this prayer, the more he antagonizes the Devil, who cannot endure the name of Jesus and who attacks such a person through other people, even near ones. I knew a young woman whom her own father came to hate so much that he wanted to kill her. Only she practiced mental prayer, which you may not do as yet.

With regard to your not having acquired patience, do not be discouraged, but try to acquire it little by little. And with regard to your flesh being exhausted, that is good: *though our outward man perish, yet the inward man is renewed day by day. . .* (II Cor. 4:16). Be merciful to the sisters if they provoke you. As for their considering you angry because you are silent, that means nothing, absolutely nothing. Peace to you and blessing from our sweetest Jesus.

Unworthy Hieromonk Anatoly

33. THE MORE PAINFUL AFFLICTIONS ARE, THE MORE THERAPEUTIC THEY ARE

December 1, 1878

Do not be discouraged, T.! Wait patiently a bit. I said before and I will say again that you make your own troubles. Remember that all the saints walked this way — that is, the way of afflictions — and they reached the gates of the Kingdom. There is no other way. True, your sorrows seem to you to be too much, but this again is because of your lack of understanding. That is why sorrows are sorrowful — because they are painful. They grab you by your very heart. . .But the more painful they are, the more therapeutic they are. Peace to you.

I wish you both spiritual and bodily health, and I remain, Hieromonk Anatoly.

34. DO NOT SEEK FRIENDSHIPS

November 24, 1879

Skete of Optina Hermitage
Peace to your reverence!

In order to be at peace, do not seek anyone's friendship! Sit in your cell and it will teach you everything![1] Everything good, that is. But other people's cells always teach everything evil.

Your sincere well-wisher, the greatly sinful Hieromonk Anatoly.

35. EARTHLY AFFLICTIONS WILL BE RECOMPENSED

January 4, 1881

Skete
Reverend Matushka T.,

That you have pain, yea, I believe it! But, my Matushka, just do not go too far, do not be foolish. Is there anyone for whom the burden of trials is light? How great before God is St. Isaac the Syrian, and he, too, says, "There is no man who will not find the time bitter wherein he is given the virulent potion of trials to drink"[2] . . . And so you too, squeak a little and a little more, and then be quiet! It will pass! Yea, it will pass, and it will not be remembered! But the fruit of these pains will grow and ripen and be embellished. And how sweet it will be! How fragrant! How it will sparkle with all the colors of the rainbow, with all the lovelinesses of precious stones. Every drop of sweat, every sigh will be recompensed a thousand times over by our compassionate Setter of the contest, Jesus. Wait on the Lord; be thou manful. *Let thy heart be strengthened*! (Ps. 26:16). Save yourself, peace to you!

Hieromonk Anatoly

36. ONE MUST WORSHIP THE FATHER IN SPIRIT AND IN TRUTH

I received yet another letter from you, T., sister in the Lord — the one of August 25. I see your devotion to me, the unworthy one, and to our monastery, and I also believe your desire to visit us. But I have to tell

---

1. A saying of St. Moses the Ethiopian. See *The Paradise of the Holy Fathers*, Vol. II, p.16.
2. *The Ascetical Homilies of St. Isaac the Syrian*, Homily 61, p.296.

you that you are thinking just like that Samaritan woman at the well of Jacob, who was ready to dispute with the Lord regarding the place of worship: our fathers worshipped "in this mountain," etc. — read it in John, chapter 4. But how did the Lord answer her? "Neither in this mountain, nor yet at Jerusalem worship the Father. . . The true worshippers shall worship the Father in spirit and in truth." That is what our worship should be like! Let our minds and hearts be directed to this, and believe me, we shall find mercy and eternal life. We are spiritual people,[1] and so our communication should be in spirit — and that is true Christian unity, which unto the ages will not be broken, in Christ Jesus our Lord, as it is chanted in the canon, "O great and most sacred Pascha, Christ — O Wisdom and Word and Power of God! Grant that we may partake of Thee fully in the unwaning day of Thy Kingdom."[2] Seek after this, and the peace of God will come to you of itself. As it is now, you seek a place and people. Everything holy is holy, and everything pure is pure, I will not argue — but a monastic's greatest attention should be directed to that which is most needful and most profitable — and what can be more needful and more profitable than the Kingdom of Heaven? And where is it? Listen to God Himself Who proclaims, *The Kingdom of God is within you* (Luke 17:21). So attend to yourself! If your patience runs out, do not become discouraged. All the saints walked by this path, and with them I wish that you may abide eternally. Peace to you, and God's blessing.

Greatly sinful Hieromonk Anatoly

37. IT IS BENEFICIAL FOR A MONASTIC TO READ BOOKS

I received your letter. . . To read books is essential for a monastic if he wishes to be a monastic not in his clothing only but in deed and in truth. But without books not only will you not be a monastic, but you will not even acquire an understanding of true monasticism. You should not despair on account of your lack of good deeds; at least you will judge yourself. But if you were not to read books, you would not even know that you do not have anything good in yourself. In your foolishness you would think that you were living correctly. And you would turn out like the Pharisee of the Gospel. But we chant, "O Lord, number me with the publican."[3]

Now, old people the Lord Himself commends, when He receives

1. I.e. monastics, clergy.
2. From the Paschal Canon.
3. Cf. Sessional Hymn of Compunction, Monday, Grave Tone.

those coming at the eleventh hour, that is, at twilight. The merciful Master of the house not only does not deprive them of all reward, but even makes them equal with those who came in the morning and bore the labor and heat of the day. You likewise are right in not liking people who are curious. Read in the book, *Ears of Wheat Gathered*[1] the little article, "Advice of the Mind to the Soul." I can give you no better advice than this.

May the Lord bless you and direct your path.

Greatly sinful Hieromonk Anatoly

38. DO NOT BE DECEIVED BY YOUR SUPPOSED HUMILITY

August 20

I do not know, Matushka, who these sisters are who have discovered in you such an abyss of humility that they wonder how in the world you can patiently endure such terrible oppression on the part of your [spiritual] mother. It seems to me that it is the enemy who teaches them to say such things and marvel at your patience. Better humble yourself rather, sister, and reproach yourself, but only yourself and not anyone else. I keep repeating my line, which is that illnesses and sorrows are for you a great mercy of God, or else your mischief would come down on your own head. As regards a trip home for treatment — may God bless. Only, be careful — watch yourself. God watches over those who watch over themselves!

39. REFLECT MORE OFTEN UPON FUTURE BLESSEDNESS AND FUTURE TORMENT

That is exactly it, Matushka — how sad it is to be parted from one's near ones, even for a season! But what will happen to those who at the end of time will stand on the left of their Saviour and God, when unto the ages, irrevocably, hopelessly, our Joy, our Light, our Life — our Saviour, encompassed by eternal glory, by countless multitudes of angels and saints, will enter through the gates of Paradise into the Jerusalem on high? And when they will behold the choirs of the saved and their jubilation, but will themselves go down into the abysses, and mountains will

---

1. *Ears of Wheat Gathered as Nourishment for the Soul*, a Paissian anthology published by Optina hermitage in 1849.

cover them, through which not even the smallest ray of light will ever penetrate, not even the smallest echo of our sweetest Jesus? . . . Reflect on this! If you will reflect upon it more often, you will not be so irritable and so fretful. And you will be kinder to the sisters!

III. LETTERS TO N.Z.

40. LET US REPROACH OURSELVES IN TEMPTATIONS
January 16, 1874

I received your letter, Sister N. You complain of temptations and imagine that I will not believe how hard it is for you to battle against the passions. I believe it, Matushka N., I believe it. Even though you are already 23, those temptations still will not leave you alone — of course that is not pleasant! But here I, Matushka, have been in the monastery 23 years now, and still I labor under Pharaoh's yoke. What to do? Shout the alarm? No, dear, you will not get anywhere that way. . . Let us reproach ourselves instead, as the sinful publican contrived to do, and he left the temple justified rather than the righteous Pharisee. However, all your sins are the sins of a novice, and a novice comes to learn the spiritual life. So what is so surprising if she does make mistakes? Peace to you!

41. THE SAD STORY OF THE CHOIR DIRECTRESS OF N—
November 6, 1876

I received your many letters, Sister N. . . I received them, I read them, and I thought, can it be that our N. has not heard the story about the N— choir directress? Although I heard this story and read about it in publications and in letters, still, I found out about it also from the N— sisters themselves. Here is this story for you in brief. In N—, at the convent, there was a young choir directress. A certain man, married, kept coming and listening to the chanters, and he kept looking at the choir directress. One rather foggy evening the choir directress disappeared. Ten days later, they brought back her corpse for the funeral at the convent. The Abbess and the sisters did not permit her to be buried in monastic clothing but buried her in lay clothing.

And that nice ruiner and seducer of the reposed one attended the funeral as if nothing had happened. Do you see, our N., how some people live — like cats, dogs, sparrows and the other animals? They have darkness in their minds and in their hearts, and like insane people they do not think, why, they do not know, they do not believe that God exists, that eternity exists, that there exists death, both physical and spiritual! And so they live and they die like brute beasts and worse. But we, we — I am telling you, our N., you and I believe and confess that God exists, that eternity exists, that demons exist, that angels exist — and you and I, Sister N., have been dedicated (obreklís), or clothed (obleklís), as angels — in the angelic schema. The entire world (except for corrupters and the Devil) looks upon us as saints and calls us blessed, and in comparison with us calls itself wretched. And really and truly, every maiden who has consecrated herself to God is the bride of Jesus Christ, is the likeness of the Mother of God herself. . . *The virgins that follow after her* (the Mother of God) *shall be brought unto the King* (Jesus Christ); *they shall be brought with gladness and rejoicing.* . . They shall be brought into the temple of the King. . . (Ps. 44:13,14). And you, our N., you want to exchange our high monastic lot for the pleasure of a moment, pleasure proper to beasts, cattle, and the rest of the animals!. . . Really, N., how peculiar you are! However, I know and I know well that you do fight against temptation. And I have spoken only to warn you. So keep fighting, our good struggler, keep fighting, and the Lord will number you in the choir of the martyrs!

42. HAVING GROWN WISER, YOU HAVE STARTED TO SPEAK OF DEATH

March 8, 1880

Well now, Matushka, truly you have comforted me. You are not even expecting an answer because I am so busy. So just for that I have constrained myself [to write]. But since in your long letter there is much that is interesting, I will put it off until a more convenient time. For now, I will just commend you on having grown wiser, that is, you have started mentioning death. Be wise in your dealings with others, and spare N—. And God will spare you. Remember Abba Ammon who covered his brother with a vessel![1]

43. SAVING TEMPTATIONS

Do not be discouraged, Sister N. The temptations you describe in your letter of August 16 are all human ones.[2] What you should fear is to fall prey to demonic ones! Pride is the culmination of the demons' scheme. But He *Who will have all men to be saved and to come unto the knowledge of the truth* (I Tim. 2:4) permits the Devil and people to humble us. . . Since, Matushka, in God's first blessed instrument intended for your healing you do not wish to recognize God's hand, therefore temptations are sent to you. . . If you are not made wiser, yet more temptations or afflictions will be sent to you, greater than the first.[3] But let us hasten to humble ourselves, and it will all blow away like dust in the wind. And until we do learn to humble ourselves, let us endure patiently, guarding ourselves with the fear of God. . .

Regarding vacations, I, too, say that they are not profitable for anyone, and for you doubly harmful. . .

44. UNDERSTAND YOUR TEMPTATIONS

N., you yourself sense that your urge for prayer to St. Sergius,

---

1. "On one occasion Abba Ammon came to a certain place to eat with the brethren, and there was there a brother concerning whom evil reports were abroad, for it had happened that a woman had come and entered his cell. And when all the people who were living in that place heard [of this], they were troubled, and they gathered together to expel that brother from his cell, and learning that the blessed Bishop Ammon was there, they came and entreated him to go with them. Now when the brother knew [this], he took the woman and hid her under an earthenware vessel. And much people having assembled, and Abba Ammon, understanding what the brother had done, for the sake of God hid the matter. And he went in and sat upon the earthenware vessel, and commanded that the cell of the brother should be searched, but although they examined the place they found no one there. Then Abba Ammon answered and said, 'What is this that ye have done? May God forgive you,' and he prayed and said, 'Let all the people go forth,' and finally he took the brother by the hand, and said unto him, 'Take heed to thy soul, O my brother,' and having said this he departed, and he refused to make public the matter of the brother." See *The Paradise of the Holy Fathers*, Vol. II, p.92.
2. See St. Mark the Ascetic, "On the Spiritual Law", #46: "Better a human than a demonic sin. Through performing the Lord's will, we overcome both." The Philokalia, ed. Sts. Nikodimos and Makarios, trans. G.E.H. Palmer, Philip Sherrard, and Kallistos Ware, (London: Faber & Faber, 1979), Vol. I, p.113.

together with a journey to him, is a temptation. And I will add that these years, this temptation is one of the links in the chain of temptations[1] which have been hounding you. It is only these links that keep changing. All of them have the same root: "I," she says, (N., that is), "am awfully smart and know what's what." It follows that if you humble yourself and acknowledge your weakness, all your temptations, the whole chain of them, will fly right off you.

45. AWAIT FUTURE GLORY, ENDLESS LIFE

Christ is risen! I greet you, Sister N., with the bright feast of Christ's Resurrection! I wish that you may spend these holy days in joy in our risen Saviour, and that you may prove worthy of celebrating that great day which is called the Eighth Day, when the true Pascha, Jesus, will be manifested in the glory of the Father, not in riddles and figures, but clearly and in actuality. And we will see Him face to face. And we will enter in to Him, not as sinners, as unprofitable servants, but as friends, "Ye are My friends, if ye have love one to another" (Cf. John 13:35; 15:14) — as children, "I will be a Father unto them, and they shall be My sons and daughters , saith the Lord Almighty" (Cf. II Cor. 6:18). And greater still, *Holy Father, keep through Thine own name those whom Thou hast given Me, that they may be one, as We are* (John 17:11). Behold what manner of sublime and awesome and ineffable life awaits us! Ponder this especially during the days of Pascha. And thank our Saviour and Bridegroom Jesus Christ. And await His mercy, keeping your lamp perpetually burning. It may be that the Bridegroom will not tarry for long, and those virgins who are ready will enter with Him into the marriage. Let us keep vigil!

I sent you the music. . . And you chant to the glory of God (and not

---

3. (from previous page) See *The Ascetical Homilies of St. Isaac the Syrian*, Homily 74, p.362: "But if, on the contrary, we become stiff-necked in our afflictions and do not confess that we are the cause of these and are worthy to suffer things even greater; if, instead, we blame other men, sometimes the demons, sometimes even God's justice; if we maintain that we are innocent of such deeds; and if we continue to think and say this without comprehending that God knows and understands more than we, that His judgments are throughout the whole earth, and that a man is not chastened unless He gives His command: then everything that comes upon us will cause us constant sorrow, our tribulations will become very vehement, and we shall be handed over from one to another as in a chain. Thus it will be until we come to know ourselves, we humble ourselves, and we perceive our iniquities (for unless we perceive our iniquities, we cannot be corrected). . ."
1. See Footnote #42, Letter #43.

to your own), and do not forget that there is another kind of chanting as well: "Rejoice, O ye heavens, and let the foundations of the earth be shaken. Cry out with gladness, O ye mountains: for behold, Emmanuel hath nailed our sins to the Cross and hath raised up Adam"[1]

O Thy divine and beloved and most sweet voice! Thou hast truly promised that Thou wouldst be with us unto the end of the world, O Christ![2]

O great and most sacred Pascha, Christ! O Wisdom. . . grant that we may partake of Thee fully in the unwaning day of Thy Kingdom.[3]

Why is this day unwaning? Because its Sun is not a creature but Jesus Christ. This Sun will rise once, and unto the ages and endless ages will never set, will never be darkened, no little cloud will ever block It, Its rays will not burn! There is unwaning light! Unspeakable glory! Ineffable beauty! Eternal gladness! Amen!

46. ON CELEBRATING WISELY

N. the choir directress "could not wait to greet [me with the feast]"; as for me, even though I can "wait," still I greet you with the feast of the Nativity of Christ. And I will keep repeating: celebrate this great feast with the understanding. . . for celebration with the understanding is as far from ostensible, unfeeling celebration as Heaven is from earth. One who celebrates with the understanding will not sin even if he were to wish it. But one who celebrates externally, even though he may be preserved from falls not a little by the splendor of the festival, is not[4] immune from them. So I wish that you may celebrate with the understanding, at least a little. (St. Dimitry of Rostov has much wisdom concerning this feast.)

47. KNOW WHOM YOU ARE SERVING!

Christ is risen! I thank you for your greeting. And I greet you with the Pentecost season we are in! You, I think, understand at least a little what it means when you chant the words, "A mystic Pascha!"[5] Does that mean the one we celebrate is not the real one? No, it is not the real one!

---

1. Cf. Resurrection Stichera for "Lord I have cried", First Tone.
2. From the Paschal Canon.
3. Ibid.
4. The word "not" appears to be indicated here but is not in the Russian text (this is a double negative in the Russian and one part could easily have been dropped).
5. From the Stichera of Pascha.

Now if you were to be shown that real one, you would break everything in rushing to that Pascha, where is the eternal sound of them that keep festival (Ps. 41:4), where is eternal gladness! But you and I are so wise and farsighted that we are ready to sell mountains of gold for a lump of clay to the first seductive demon we happen to see. You pray "without fervor and only out of obedience to me," and you think that that is not good at all! Silly! Both in books and in verbal admonitions I think you have heard a thousand times: *Obedience is higher than fasting and prayer!*

Do not worry about your mother; she can be saved without you. And do not dwell on how she is thinking about you! You came to the convent to serve God and not someone else. And so await great rewards from Him, and from Him alone!

It is true that there is plenty of money in Moscow, but too little, too little — and absolutely nothing to redeem the souls that have been swallowed up by Moscow.

IV. LETTERS TO D.

48. HOW A NUN SHOULD CONDUCT HERSELF

December 7, 1876

Sister in the Lord D., Peace to you and the blessing of the Lord!. . . In answer to your letter, you may write everything, only try to make it brief and legible. You do not need any particular skill here. Just write what you have done as you have done it. The main thing is, do not lie and do not hide anything, even if something is not nice, for I, too, am an exceedingly sinful person. And so, there is no one to be ashamed in front of. All the weaknesses you have confessed in your letters are unimportant — except that they are important in that if you cater to them, you will come to grief, and then you will struggle, but it will be too late. Better stand your ground now. We do not forbid you to eat — only be moderate. In church, when the Devil stops up your ears and closes your eyes, try to say the Jesus Prayer. Pay attention to the kathismata as much as you can, and later they will become sweet to you. In them there is much beauty and sweetness which will drive away sleep and despondency. . . To look at men is a sin for a nun. As for your laziness in chanting, that is from your negligence and from the Devil. . . Say the Jesus Prayer at this time. And look into the *Ladder* more often. Especially read the 14th, 19th, and 6th instructions.[1] In church do not be disorderly, that is, do not talk and do not let your eyes wander, or God will permit the Devil to pollute your house too [as you have polluted His]. The notion that you will live a long time yet is a trick. Satan has tricked many thousands with this thought — but our true, eternal Bridegroom has said clearly, *In such an hour as ye think not the Son of man cometh. . .* (Matt. 24:44). Say the Jesus Prayer as often as possible.

49. SEEK NOT TEMPORAL BUT ETERNAL JOY — SEEK CHRIST

March 1, 1877

My Matushka D., I read your letter. And how I pity you, that you grieved so because your sunshine had been dimmed and its light had completely gone out! Why, what are you and I to do? After all, we live in a world where by God's command the sun must set without fail and rise again. So what is so strange about it if your sun has set? Now when the Lord sends us a joyous morning, again your dear sunshine will rise and shine on you and warm you. Only do not be despondent, do not be faint-hearted. Why, we are monastics, brides of Christ. He, Jesus, is our real Sun. Let us seek after this One. If It should illumine and warm a person, he is deemed worthy of unspeakable joy and delight."And this joy no man taketh from you" (Cf. John 16:22). But the joy which is in this world, be it great or small, is always temporary. However, I trust that D. will receive both the one and the other. Only, let her learn to be patient. Because an impatient nun is like a rotten melon. I repeat, do not be despondent, you will see both suns; only struggle, humble yourself, obey whom you ought to obey. And we will be together there. And here, too, you will see your sunshine. . .

---

1. Lit.,"words." In Russian, as in Greek, the "steps" are called "homilies/talks/instructions": "Step 14. On that clamorous mistress, the stomach;" "Step 19. On sleep, prayer, and psalmody with the brotherhood"; "Step 6. On remembrance of death". See *The Ladder of Divine Ascent.*

50. DO NOT BE DECEIVED BY THE ALLUREMENTS OF THE WORLD, REMEMBERING THE ETERNAL GLORY OF THE FUTURE LIFE

December 10, 1878

You write that life is difficult for you! Why, you have doomed yourself to this! Unwise D.! You look at the tiny things and overlook the big ones. You foolishly envy the peasant women who enjoy the good things of country life — husbands, songs, dances, etc. But it never even crosses your mind that you are walking the path envied and sought out by rich women, famous ones, princesses and queens! Remember the holy Great Martyr Barbara! Remember St. Euphrosyne. Remember those who even enjoyed and were sated with worldly enjoyments, the most beautiful and wealthy Pelagia and Eudokia. Was there anything they did not have? Chests full of gold and pearls! Princes waiting on them! But as ones wise, they forsook everything and went forth to fasts and afflictions in monasteries. So you too, endure patiently and believe that with them you will inherit the eternal Kingdom with Christ and with all the saints!

51. LIVE IN A GODLY MANNER AND YOU WILL BE SAVED

September 15, 1879

Peace to you, D.! I received your letter which was sent to me about two months ago.

You keep complaining that I have forgotten you, whereas I remember you always and pray for you. So see how dense you are! Live in a godly manner, be meek and kind to the sisters, have remembrance of God as much as you can, and you will be saved. And I will always be with you in spirit. And now I bless you mentally.

52. BE PATIENT ABOUT HOUSING INCONVENIENCES

March 12, 1891

I cannot but pity you, D.! I can believe that it is distressing for you, and I would sincerely like to help you! But what can I do? I cannot make the Superior give everyone the room she wants. She provides for you and looks after your needs as far as possible; as for me, how can I help you when you have woes and sufferings? Explain the situation carefully to Matushka, but I would not advise you to make any hasty plans. Peace to you! Remember, we must through *much* tribulation enter into the Kingdom of Heaven (Cf. Acts 14:22)!

53. DO NOT SEEK A NEW DWELLING. WHY YOU BECOME DEPRESSED

Christ is risen! I received your letter, D. I read it all, and I reread it. And having read it and having given it some thought, I could not help concluding that you are a silly little girl, very much so. Come on, how can one fail to see God's mercy covering you? A convent that is one of the best in Russia, a convent well disposed to Optina, very good sisters, a most kind spiritual mother — no, it is something else she wants. . . Come on, silly, where is your brain? Even if because of your devotion to me, you would like to live closer to Optina, that is not profitable either. I am not saying that I do not love you, but do you know why and for what purpose we became acquainted? You would like to be saved, for it is on this account that you left your homeland and everything dear to you on earth! And I also desire, and desire greatly, for you to be saved, for you to become an angel in time! If in time you attain to this — there is all your happiness, all your joys, all your life. And I will be pleased, too, that D., such a silly little girl, is so happy! So beautiful! A bride of my God and Lord Jesus Christ! And she was called a daughter of mine! And when I present you to our true Bridegroom, won't there be fulfilled in me the words read at the Liturgy not long ago, *He that hath the bride is the bridegroom: but the friend of the bridegroom, which standeth and heareth him, rejoiceth greatly because of the bridegroom's voice: this my joy therefore is fulfilled* (John 3:29). But you think in a childish way. If only I could live closer to the Elder! Why, the spirit is higher than the body, and he is more devoted to his Elder who is devoted in spirit, and not in body. Judas was physically closest to the Lord, and he did not see eternal life — whereas Abgar had never seen the Lord but was wholeheartedly devoted to Him and invited the Lord to come and live with him, promising Him everything necessary. But although the Lord greatly loved Abgar, He did not go to him. And why? So as to fulfill the will of His heavenly Father.

And you should do likewise. Although your thought impels you to move closer to your Elder, you keep repeating, "I came to the convent not in order to be my Elder's favorite, but in order to be the beloved of my Bridegroom Jesus Christ. If my Elder helps me in this, then I love him also, but if he hinders me, then I deny him." So, D., be at peace and be sensible. I have faith that if you do your best to pay heed to yourself, the Lord will always be with you. And thus you will give joy also to me, a sinner, who love you. Therefore, constrain yourself in the monastic life as you are able, especially in the Jesus Prayer. I tell you a thousand times over, you will come to love it.

I would not at all wish to send you my mug shot, because even at Optina only Batiushka and a couple of close people have one but for the sake of your devotion to me, the unworthy one, and in the hope that you will not show me to anyone, and especially that you will not hang me (although I deserve it), I am sending you a photograph.

. . . You become depressed because you do not remember Jesus Christ. . . One cannot quickly become accustomed to saying the Jesus Prayer. If it were so, then everyone would say it, but the price is too high.

The godly-wise women followed after Thee in haste with myrrh. . . they joyfully adored the living God. . .[1] And if, like the myrrh-bearing women, we hasten after our Bridegroom, we will overtake Him, we will see Him, we will embrace Him. And He will be with us unto the ages!

54. A NUN IS THE BRIDE OF CHRIST THE SON OF GOD

Wrongly, D., do you take such a gloomy view of your life and of others. [You say] people look at you as though you were in jail? Silly girl! Day and night you should be dancing for joy that the Lord has led you *out of darkness and the shadow of death* (Ps. 106:14) and brought you to a sacred convent of virgins who have consecrated themselves to the King of kings and Lord of lords, as — not servants, not friends — but as brides.

He Who is more holy than all the saints[2] did not disdain us, but betrothed us unto Himself as a virgin bride, pure and blameless. And He is the Son of God. . . That same Son of God Who is the Creator of Heaven and earth, did not disdain to take upon Himself the form of a servant, that is, the likeness of a man, and was *obedient unto death, even the death of the Cross* (Phil. 2:8), — that is, the most shameful of deaths.

And what is so burdensome for you? That you are following in the footsteps of your beloved Bridegroom? That you are walking by the same path which He also walked — He, One of the all-holy Trinity? For our Lord and God walked not in the way of glory but of ignominy, humiliation, weakness, and death! But now, what about you and me? Our rassa of muhoyár[3] is not a joy to us but rather a disgrace?!... Just

---

1. From the Paschal Canon.
2. From the Akathist Hymn to the Theotokos.
3. Muhoyár — An ancient Asiatic fabric made of cotton with silk or wool. Being inexpensive, it was a standard fabric for making monastic rassas and a symbol of monastic simplicity (see also Letter #362).

look how far you have gone off!. . . Some nun you are!. . .

But may God forgive all your whims. You are still young but mostly just plain silly! And so one cannot demand anything of you. Just live peaceably; look at your sins and weaknesses, humble yourself, and thank the Lord that He has numbered you with His chosen ones!

55. PATIENTLY ENDURE TRIBULATIONS FOR OUR SWEETEST JESUS

You are wrong, D., in thinking that I have forgotten you. I remember you a lot. And I would like to write to you often and much, but my wanting to is not enough. One feels for others as well. There are many poor ones who receive scarcely one letter a year. And they grieve also.

Many afflictions make you despondent; if you had known about this, you would not have come to the convent. But then would I have become acquainted with you? And would our Lord Jesus Christ have accounted you as His beloved, as one chosen? And would you be concerning yourself over the salvation of your soul — or only over cows, pigs, house, husband, children? What a silly little thing you are!

Wait on the Lord, be thou manful and let thy heart be strengthened. And *wait on the Lord* (Ps. 26:16). Why, it is for Him that you are enduring afflictions, for your Bridegroom, our sweetest Jesus, and not for earthly happiness! So be a wise virgin! Have confidence! I assure you, you will be an heir of the eternal Kingdom of Heaven!

Do not grieve over your dresser and other trivialities. Guard your house — it is more precious than Heaven and earth, sun and stars and all the visible world, beautiful though it is — but you do not understand this. You have impure dreams at night. . . When this happens, you must make fifty prostrations and read the psalm, Have mercy on me, O God. Write letters always, in whatever way you can — I will receive all with love. You may write down your thoughts, the ones that bother you the most. Peace to you and blessing from the Lord, from Batiushka Amvrosy, and from me, a sinner!

56. YOU ARE NOT AFRAID TO HAVE REMEMBRANCE OF WRONGS

That is just it, D., you became frightened of a red sky, but you are not afraid to have remembrance of wrongs. Our Heaven is not this one, but the Heaven of heavens, above the heavens (Cf. Ps. 148:4)! Where God Himself is, eternal Love, eternal Joy! Eternal Light! But this sky will burn up. And all the elements will burst into flame (Cf. II Pet. 3:10). But *our conversation is in the Heavens* (Phil. 3:20). Have patience, humble yourself — and you will be there.

57. YOUR ELDER WILL NOT FORGET YOU

May God forgive you, D., for your faintheartedness. You tell me over and over again to give you my assurance that I am not angry with you. But I did assure you that I never forget you. Isn't that enough for you? So relax. Rest assured. Sometimes even the saints are permitted to experience the kind of heaviness you feel in church. And you and I are not saints as yet. Be patient. Reproach yourself, and it is enough. Keep writing letters — don't hesitate. I am pleased to receive your letters. Of course your chest demands a rest, but who is going to chant? Who is going to work? Sigh to the Lord and continue your work, and when convenient explain the situation to Matushka.

58. THE MONASTIC LIFE IS THE VERY SWEETEST ONE!

Christ is risen! Peace to you and the blessing of the Lord!. . . The monastic life is hard — that everyone knows; but that it is the highest one, the purest, the most beautiful, and even the easiest — what am I saying, just the easiest: it is inexpressibly captivating, most sweet, gladdening, radiant, shining with eternal joy — this few people know. But the truth is on the side of the few and not of the many. That is why the Lord said to His beloved disciples, "Fear not, My little flock! For it is God's good pleasure to give you" (Cf. Luke 12:32) — What? Happiness, do you think? Wealth? Enjoyment? No! A *Kingdom*! And what a Kingdom! In which there are not only all good things, all possible treasures, but also beauty, and glory, light, joy, ardent love, divine life, and eternal gladness. This *Kingdom is the Kingdom of all the ages* (Ps. 144:13), before which all the greatest kingdoms of this world are smoke and stench! And it is in this Kingdom of light and gladness that there is prepared for you a royal palace, and for all who have loved the Lord Jesus. *The virgins that follow after her* (the Heavenly Queen) *shall be brought unto the King* (Ps. 44:13). Only be patient, and you will receive all this with interest.

59. ALWAYS ONE CAN PRAY

. . . D., you keep complaining about afflictions — but the great Elder Father Seraphim of Sarov said, "He who has no afflictions, has no salvation."

You say it is awkward for you to get up for prayer and reading. So don't get up, and don't light a candle — just lie there and maybe cover your head with the blanket, but keep repeating, "Lord Jesus Christ our God have mercy on me, a sinner." And that will be very good and even better [than getting up].

60. RULES FOR YOUR LIFE

. . . Read what is blessed for you to read, even if without attention. God will recompense every effort. When you read the Psalter for everyone, you need not read it at home.

Read the *Ladder* in its entirety. Eat a little less, and if you load your plate too much, reproach yourself. You do not have to go to trapeza[1] if you do not wish to eat in the evening. If you go to the early one, you may drink tea.

Peace to you!

Unworthy Hieromonk Anatoly

---

1. Trapeza — Communal meal, and in monasteries also the refectory.

V. LETTERS TO E.K.

61. IT IS NOT THE BUSINESS OF MONASTICS TO CONCERN THEMSELVES ABOUT LAY PEOPLE

August 26, 1876

. . . With regard to your brothers, I explained to Batiushka concerning them, but do not you worry about them any more. It is not the business of monastics to think about and concern themselves over lay people, even relatives; the Lord has said plainly, *Seek ye first the Kingdom of God, and His righteousness; and all these things* (that is, the good things of this world) *shall be added unto you* (Matt. 6:33). To go to your Matushka Abbess to say your thoughts[1] is a good work, and may the Lord help you in this! Only you should know that the demons do not at all like people who make it their practice. Read chapters 40, 41, 42, 43, and 44 of Theodore of Edessa in the *Philokalia*.[2] May the Lord help you!

62. GO TO SAY YOUR THOUGHTS

November 14, 1876

Sister E., you *are* amazing! You write that you do not understand my words, when you have been told clearly that not only do I wish that you go to Matushka to say your thoughts, but that I even entreat God con-

---

1. Rooted in ancient Christian and monastic tradition, the practice of "saying one's thoughts" (or "disclosing one's thoughts," or "revealing one's thoughts") consists in the confession of one's sins — including and especially one's sins of thought — and of one's perplexities, to an elder or eldress for the purpose of receiving spiritual counsel. Absolution is not given.

This ancient practice had fallen into oblivion in Russia, and its restoration by the Elder Leonid had occasioned charges of heresy against him. Eldresses hearing thoughts were accused of assuming the prerogatives of the clergy — and this despite the fact that confession to a priest, along with absolution read only by him, was practiced simultaneously by the nuns.

Probably at the time these letters were written, disclosure of thoughts was still viewed as an innovation by some, and many of the nuns were not used to the idea (see especially Letter #62). Hence the Elder Anatoly tries to encourage his spiritual children in this saving practice.

cerning this. But if it is my personal blessing you want, then I say to you clearly: May God bless you to say your thoughts. And do not be troubled; everything is good that we do for the sake of God. No wonder you

---

2. Ch. 40. When you have taken up your dwelling with a spiritual father and find that he helps you, let no one separate you from his love and from living with him. Do not judge him in any respect, do not revile him even though he censures or strikes you, do not listen to someone who slanders him to you, do not side with anyone who criticizes him, lest the Lord should be angered with you and blot you out of the book of the living (cf. Exodus 32:33).

Ch 41. The struggle to achieve obedience is won by means of renunciation, as we have learned. He who seeks to be obedient must arm himself with three weapons: faith, hope, and divine and holy love (cf. I Cor. 13:13). Thus defended, he will *fight the good fight* and receive *a crown of righteousness* (II Tim. 4:7-8).

Ch. 42. Do not judge the actions of your spiritual father, but obey his commands. For the demons are in the habit of showing you his defects, so that your ears may be deaf to what he tells you. They aim either to drive you from the arena as a feeble and cowardly fighter, or simply to terrify you with thoughts that undermine your faith, and so to make you sluggish about every form of virtue.

Ch. 43. A monk who disobeys the commands of his spiritual father transgresses the special vows of his profession. But he who has embraced obedience and slain his own will with the sword of humility has indeed fulfilled the promise that he made to Christ in the presence of many witnesses.

Ch. 44. From our own observations we have clearly perceived that the enemies of our life, the demons, are exceedingly jealous of those pursuing the ascetic way under obedience to a spiritual father. Gnashing their teeth at them and devising all sorts of schemes, they do and suggest everything possible so as to separate a monk from his spiritual father's care. They propose plausible excuses, they contrive irritations, they arouse hatred against the father, they represent his admonitions as rebukes, they make his words of correction seem like sharpened arrows. Why, they ask, since you are free, have you become a slave — a slave to a merciless master? How long will you wear yourself out under the yoke of servitude and not see the light of freedom? Then they make suggestions about giving hospitality, visiting the sick and caring for the poor. Next they extol above measure the rewards of extreme stillness and solitude, and sow all sorts of evil weeds in the heart of the devout warrior, simply to cast him out of the fold of his spiritual father; and having unmoored him from that untroubled haven, they drive him out to sea, into the fierce and soul-destroying tempest. Finally, when they have enslaved him to their own authority, they use him according to their own evil desires." See *The Philokalia*, Vol. II, p.21.

did not understand St. Theodore of Edessa! That just means you did not put his teachings into practice. Now, if you will faithfully go to say your thoughts, then you will understand!...

63. THE ENEMY WILL DO US NO HARM
IF WE OURSELVES DO NOT CONSENT

March 10, 1879

F., you still will not understand! Why, you yourself see that for years the enemy has been scaring you but has accomplished nothing so far.

And he cannot, because you are living not on your own but under Matushka's protection and that of the reverend sisters. Here is what Batiushka Father Amvrosy said concerning you, "She should not despair, but trust in God's mercy." The enemy only suggests thoughts; he can accomplish nothing without God's permission and unless we ourselves consent. And so, do not consent and he will not hurt you.

64. EVERYONE SHOULD REJOICE
ON THE DAY OF PASCHA

April 12, 1883

Skete of Optina Hermitage

Reverend Sister E., Christ is risen!... What ails you? Why are you despondent?

In gladness Heaven and earth glorify the Giver of life Who is risen from the grave — and you, be glad also, if so be that you are heavenly! And be glad likewise if you are earthly. Now are all things filled with light — heaven and earth and the nethermost regions of the earth.[1] Now there is gladness even in the nethermost regions, for the eternal Light, Christ our God, has shone forth there.

Be glad even if you have not fasted! Believe that the Most Merciful One will recompense all your afflictions. If anyone [have labored] from the first hour, let him celebrate. There, too, will be he who has labored

---

1. From the Paschal Canon.

from the sixth hour, and from the ninth, and even those who came at the very last moment will not be deprived of their reward. The Lord is merciful to the first, and to this one He giveth, and He praiseth the intention. Wherefore, enter ye all into the joy of our Lord![1]

65. ONE CAN ENTRUST ONE'S SOUL ONLY TO AN EXPERIENCED ELDER

March 12, 1891

Peace to you and God's blessing, reverend Sister E. I received your letter of March 6. As usual, it consists entirely of complaints and murmuring, as if out of negligence I show no concern for you and for the others. But what can I do? One thing I wish all of you — patience, and to entreat God that He Himself would soothe you and order your life aright. You managed to find a pretext for murmuring, in that Batiushka Amvrosy and I forbade you to have anything to do with N— . . . Why, if you and others like you had a drop of sense, you would not even think of walking right into a snare. How in the world are you going to entrust your soul and your entire life to a man you do not really know? And how in the world can this newly-made[2] elder take you on? What is he going to teach you when he himself has no understanding of the path of eldership? How is it that you will not give any thought to so important a matter? Just try giving a coachman some lace to make. He will make you some all right — and ten real elders will not be able to untangle it! And all the lacemakers will go out of their minds! You know how the reposed X— nearly tracked down an elder for you — and what happened? You scarcely managed to get rid of him!

Humble yourself!. . . I do believe that it is hard for you and for G., but aren't there similar cases here too, where we have elders? Yea, there are plenty of them, and what can one do to help when God permits it? After all, it is not for our destruction that He permits us to have temptations, woes, afflictions, and illnesses — for otherwise, nowhere could

---

1. See the Catechetical Homily of St. John Chrysostom, read at the end of Paschal Matins. Part of the text in the letter is quite unclear. The homily reads, "He is merciful to the last and provideth for the first; and to this one He giveth, and to that one He showeth kindness. He receiveth their labors and acknowledgeth the purpose, and He honoreth the deed and praiseth the intention. Wherefore, enter ye all into the joy of our Lord. . ."
2. Lit., "newly-baked."

there be found any hope of salvation for us. And the Lord our Saviour, Who for our salvation died the shameful death of the Cross, would like to save all. He calls, teaches, threatens — and what do we do? We doze contentedly on the bed of slothfulness and self-deception; as for salvation, we have forgotten even to think about it. There is no time: we have to grumble a little, then we have to sleep, then we have to judge others some — and there are a lot of people to judge — and so there is no time to give any thought to our soul and to eternity!

66. BE MERCIFUL TO YOUR NEIGHBORS AND DO NOT CRITICIZE THEM

Well, how are you doing, Sister E.? I have not seen any letters from you in a long time. Does the Devil still trouble you with foolish thoughts? Humble yourself. Trust in God's mercy. Be merciful to your neighbors and do not criticize them, and the Lord will save you by His mercy and love for man.

67. OUR AFFLICTIONS WILL PASS

Peace to you! Do not be despondent. The Lord is near! I see the cloud of afflictions over you, but our life is not eternal. Both the sad things and the joyous things all pass away, but the righteousness of God abideth unto the ages (Cf. Ps. 111:8). *We must through much tribulation enter into the Kingdom of God* (Acts 14:22). The more tribulations, the more consolations! "According to the multitude of my sorrows, Thy consolations brought gladness unto my soul"(Cf. Ps. 93:19).

68. ONE MUST BE PATIENT

Sister E., For your illness, the prescription is one and the same: be patient. Spare the younger sisters. Call them to account only for being out of order or obstinate. And even then, wait a little.

Your emotional disturbance is already much less than before, and it will continue to ease up — only have patience. Peace to you!

69. MAKE A PRACTICE OF SAYING YOUR THOUGHTS

Sister E., do not grieve that the sisters are causing you pain. Right now this distraction is very beneficial for you, or else your thoughts would torment you to death. Be patient also with G. — she has a temptation. This will blow over if the Lord grants. I will write to her. As for you, go to Matushka [to say your thoughts]. The enemy wars against you because through Matushka you can escape his domination. And so do not listen to him. Go always! And keep better track of yourself. And pray to God for G.!

VI. LETTERS TO E.K.

70. OUR HOMELAND IS THE HEAVENLY JERUSALEM
November 11, 1882

Peace to you, D.! I am very sorry that they did not let you go home. But that is what monasteries are for, so that we do not do our own will but God's, that is, the will of those in authority. And when the time comes, you will receive everything. I myself do not like to make trips home, and I give my consent for others to do so only in case of need. For 30 years I never went home. Our home is there — the heavenly Jerusalem. There is our Father and our Bridegroom, our sisters, our brothers, and all our treasure and happiness!

71. DESPAIR IS A SIN UNTO DEATH
November 25, 1882

I am writing you a little line as a consolation, according to your wish, even though I am not certain that I will be able to console you. Despair is a sin unto death. Flee it. Instead, have faith in our merciful God and our Mediatress, the Theotokos, and the saints. They can do all things. But you must without fail humble yourself and endure patiently. Do not be despondent on account of tedium. One's monastic life is tried most of all by despondency. *But he that shall endure unto the end, the same shall be saved* (Matt. 24:13).

72. HOW TO CELEBRATE IN A HOLY WAY

Christ is risen! I greet you with this bright and joyous day. . . I wish that you may celebrate in a holy way, peacefully, reverently, and avoid socializing and laughter. And then you will feel joy. Otherwise, you will neither profit nor have joy.

73. THE SECRET OF SALVATION LIES IN PATIENCE

I read your whole long letter. It is evident that you are trying and that you desire to be saved — only you do not know how, you do not understand the spiritual life. Here the whole secret lies in patiently enduring whatever God sends. And before you know it, you'll be walking into Paradise. That you are depressed is not a disaster — it happens to everyone, but depression always goes away with time. Yours will go away, too. That you cry is good. *Blessed are they that mourn* (Matt. 5:4). After all, it is for the Lord's sake. But with all your might flee audacity, and do not be rude to the sisters.

74. WHY DO PEOPLE GO TO CONVENTS?

May God forgive you all the sins you have confessed, E.

The thought comes to you, why did you come to the convent? Why did all the saints go to convents? Daughters of kings, daughters of princes? And so you, too, have desired to walk by the same path, in order to endure patiently and suffer here just a very little — and for this to reign there with the Lord and with all the saints unto the ages and endless ages of ages! Peace to you!

VII. LETTERS TO A.K.

75. *YOU SHOULD THANK GOD THAT YOU ARE NOT RICH.*
HOW YOU SHOULD CONDUCT YOURSELF

February 13, 1878

See to what an extent you have become carried away with the world — you have even lost your mind: you say it is easier for rich people to be saved, whereas the Lord has said, How hardly shall they that have riches enter into the Kingdom of Heaven (Cf. Mark 10:23).

You should thank God that you are not rich. Do not say your thoughts to anyone except Matushka, or you will suffer for it. . . being put to shame. Stop looking at men, or you will get yourself such warfare that you won't even be glad of the monastic life. As it is, you sometimes grumble about having come to the convent. And that is terrible stupidity. The holy hierarch Tikhon of Zadonsk, as he was dying, gave special thanks to God that He had deemed him worthy of the monastic life.

76. *A REMEDY FOR UNCLEAN THOUGHTS*

February 19, 1882

I do remember about you always, G., only I cannot find the time to write. But if it were possible, I would write you two letters every day. It is a great pity that your Father Confessor is ill. The remedies against unclean thoughts are humility, self-reproach, abstinence, and above all, love of one's neighbors, one's sisters who are weak, infirm, ill, held captive by passions. However, St. Isaac the Syrian writes, "Watchfulness helps a young man more than works."[1] Peace to you, and salvation!

77. *THE HIGH LOT OF MONASTICS*

I greet you with the feast, G., and I wish you peace, zeal for the church services, and love for monasticism. Because the lot of nuns is very, very high — higher than the heavens and the stars of the heavens.

---

1. Cf. *The Ascetical Homilies of St. Isaac the Syrian*, Homily 51, p.249.

Their portion is with the angels. Only, one must have patience. And you never want to have patience — which means you do not understand where you are living. I am telling you, the Lord will save you, only have patience. If you have read the book of Abba Dorotheos, read John of the Ladder. Read the psalm, *The Lord is my light and my saviour!* (Ps. 26). And it will be easier for you to go to Matushka [to say your thoughts]. But I will not compel you. Peace to you!

78. BE HUMBLE AND NOT AUDACIOUS

I received your letter, I read it, and I am deeply sorry that G. will not listen to me, shows no respect for the older sisters, becomes proud and stubborn, will not ask forgiveness. And for this the Lord takes His help away from her, and the Devil pollutes her with impure thoughts. Now how I begged you to be humble, obedient, submissive — for such novices are beloved of the Mother of God and the Lord and of all good people. And submissive novices are loved by their superiors, and they always have such peace in their souls! But with audacious girls it is constantly jealousy, malice, irritability, anger, impurity, and everything unseemly. Correct yourself, G.— it is not too late. And you will comfort me. Peace to you and blessing from the Lord!

It is difficult for one who is proud to ask forgiveness. The Devil does not know how to ask forgiveness either, and does not like to do so. But the Devil is going on 8000, whereas G. is not even 18 yet. God will forgive you everything you have confessed.

79. BE PATIENT AND CORRECT YOURSELF

My sweet, ripe, fragrant G.[1] Still you grieve, and you cry, and you are depressed. Great are your woes: F. scolds you, she did not buy any sweets for the feast, and they hang awfully many other crosses on you — and you keep thrusting them away. That must mean Christ is not to your liking either — it is sweets you like, and nice clothes. . . Well, God will forgive you everything. Let us make a beginning of correcting ourselves. And then we will be happier, too.

---

1. Grusha, a nickname for Agrippina, means "pear."

Always the Jesus Prayer is burdensome at first and impure — but later it becomes gladsome.

80. BE SOBER-MINDED

I wrote to you not long ago, but your letter constrains me to write again. And first, I greet you with the feast of Pascha. Christ is risen! Second, you write that no matter how poorly you may be living, still you are living better than in the world. That is true. That I wrote to you. But do you know, G., that one can be harmed even by a good thing, and one can find a good use even for a bad thing. Many poisons heal illnesses, and good things harm a lot of people. For example, smart people have invented the knife for household use. But with a knife one can kill one's neighbor.

People lose their minds even from reading the Bible. Likewise with your situation: when the enemy wars against you, "Go on, sin!" and you say, "I am a nun! A bride of Jesus! And the heavenly Bridegroom will chastise me for being unfaithful to Him!" — the Devil will say, "Oh! Oh, you really are somebody special — a bride of Christ! One must esteem you as a saint!" But you must think, "I," she says, "not only do not dare to call myself a bride of Christ, but not even the least of His handmaids!"

81. DO NOT PAMPER YOURSELF WITH SWEETS

You self-indulgent little girl, just look what you have come up with: sugared water! Really? Why, rich people taste just a bit of sugar with their tea, and here she drinks sugared water! And it is not a sin for you? A young girl, she has come to save her soul, and she indulges herself like even rich fellows do not. Why, you have read the lives of the saints! Princesses, children of kings, came to monasteries, and nowhere does one see that they would drink sugared water! Is this the way of salvation? Self-indulgent one! And moreover you judge others? And you speak idly? Now after all this, is there any way thoughts are not going to pollute you? G., stop pampering yourself. Stop talking idly, be good, be a good nun; we will love you and concern ourselves over your salvation. Only humble yourself. Consider yourself worse than all, and you will be better than all. I do remember you. Write to me, hiding nothing. Because see how silly you are! You started pampering yourself with sugar — and during the fast yet! Are you a canary or something? But they do not even give canaries sugar all the time! I say this to you out of love and pity. Because he who loves sweets here will not enjoy the eternal, ineffable sweets. And I would like for you and me to be together there too, in the delights of Paradise. Desiring these for you, I remain your well-wisher. . .

82. ON ACCOUNT OF FAILURE TO DISCLOSE ONE'S THOUGHTS THE ENEMY TRIUMPHS

You grieve me, G., in that you keep opposing the older [sisters] and not listening to them. What demon has whispered to you that life in the world is better than the monastic life! Why, haven't you seen how many tribulations there are out there, how much want, wars, fights, contentions, drunkenness, disorders? You do not say your thoughts, Matushka — that is why the enemy triumphs over you. And this causes grief to all of us! Think it over, G.! You are a girl who is capable of monasticism; just do not listen to the enemy who wants to destroy you. And if you are patient, the Lord will help you, and the warfare will pass. Without this warfare, no one has been saved. Even the saints endured it. And God has not disowned you. He is always with you both day and night. He is in your heart and waits only for you to humble yourself in order to help you, and for you to call upon Him. And I do not forget you, G., and I often remember you in my prayers.

83. IF YOU LEAVE THE CONVENT, YOU WILL ALSO LOSE THE ETERNAL KINGDOM

Some people might be pretty sick of things, but G.K. is sickest of all! She is so sick of the convent that she would go and jump over the wall, but she just cannot get up the strength. Plus, they would see her. And even catch her. And then when I would come I would not find G.! And very likely there, too, in time — in the new, heavenly Jerusalem — on meeting the virgins, brides of Christ whom I have known, dancing and rejoicing, I would not find G.K. among them — she would have jumped right over the wall of Jerusalem. Which means that there, too, she would remain outside Christ's flock of elect children, of virgins beloved of God.

. . But since our G. did not leave the convent because everything was locked — why, that means we will see each other there often, very often, always even. For it is said that the royal gates will be opened and will never be closed again (Cf. Is. 60:11). However, you and I will see each other again here, too.

84. ON PASCHA YOUR SOUL SHOULD BE RADIANT

Christ is risen! "Now are all things filled with light; Heaven and earth and the nethermost regions of the earth."[1] But I do not know if there was brightness in your soul? It should be shining — you are a young girl, and moreover a chanter, and moreover well provided for! You do not go about barefoot, and you do not lie down to sleep hungry. And you get up just like a little bird and fly straight to Matins, to the doxology of God. No? Well, why not?

I should scold you, G., for having read the little note — but it is Pascha. God will forgive you!. . . Do not lose heart, G.! Let us make a beginning of correcting ourselves! I, too, wish to make a beginning!

VIII. LETTERS TO E.E.

85. THE LORD SENDS TEMPTATIONS FOR OUR SALVATION

December 23, 1876

I received your letter, sad and feeble D., and I was very sorry that such a bright little girl conducts her spiritual life in such an undiscerning manner. From your words, it is evident that you understand the spiritual significance of monasticism, but that in practice you fall short. Well, so what are we to do? Humble yourself, judge yourself for your weaknesses, and hasten to God with your petition for help. God will

---

1. From the Paschal Canon.

never permit those who have recourse to Him to remain in temptations beyond their strength, especially His young struggler. For He, the Friend of man, sees and knows well that it is for His sake, for the Holy One, that you are enduring from the Devil the assaults of the *passions of dishonor*,[1] but He waits to see our volition, and He exhausts us. But for what purpose? So that, in the first place, we would recognize our weakness and humble ourselves; second, so that having seen our own helplessness and the assaults of the enemy, we might turn to God, our *Helper in afflictions which mightily befall us* (Ps. 45:1); and third and most important of all, so that we might become practiced, having passed *through fire and water* (Ps. 65:12). For according to God's word, a man who has not been tried is unpracticed.[2] And God wishes to make you practiced and permits Matushka to scold you and frazzle you for a time. Yes, D., that is very beneficial. And it is a great help against carnal passion. St. Nilus of Sinai writes, "Turn not the tanners away though they beat and trample and stretch and scrape, for by this very means your garment is made radiant." You keep proclaiming[3] that your last hour has come. But after all, that is precisely what the Lord said, "Except a corn of wheat fall and die, it shall not come to life" (Cf. John 12:24). And so, the Lord sends you temptation. Your last hour comes in order that your passion, which is alive and well, might die. But according to God's word, "If we be dead with Christ, we shall also live with Him" (Cf. II Tim. 2:11).

May God forgive all your weaknesses — your slothfulness, distraction, carnal desire, vainglory, and other sins. And I, the unworthy one, do not judge you, for you are still young, untrained, and therefore also impatient.

As regards your feeling oppressed sometimes, examine your conscience: is there some little sin of which you have not repented?

When you complete your prayers or your rule, give thanks to God; when you do not, then berate yourself. Try not to accept blasphemous thoughts, and do not believe them, and the Lord will forgive you. When thoughts come, do not accept them, and do not repulse them, and especially do not exorcise or contradict them — that does not pertain to your measure! Instead, have recourse to the Lord with prayer and humility. Carnal thoughts and fearfulness are permitted on account of our pride.

---

1. Romans 1:26. In the King James translation, this is rendered "vile affections." "Passions of dishonor" is a more literal translation of the Greek (and the Slavonic); it is a phrase often encountered in the Fathers and in Church hymns.
2. St. Barsanuphius, Answer #255.
3. Lit., "trumpeting."

Reproach yourself and try not to look at the tempter — and the temptation will pass. We must honor the memory of the saints and look for
mercy from them. But in order to cast out the evil within — there is very,
very much that needs to be said. For now, just this is sufficient. . .

Write everything in whatever way you are able — do not hesitate; I
will always answer you when possible.

86. WHEN YOU SIN, REPENT IMMEDIATELY BEFORE GOD.
DO NOT DISDAIN YOUR SISTERS

April 29, 1878

If when you sin, you even immediately turn to God in repentance,
that is very good. That is the way it should be. And the Lord will forgive
you. If it is a serious sin, tell your Father Confessor or your Elder later. It
is a sin to look at people, especially men. Do not do this in the future.
You must love all of your sisters. In order not to disdain anyone, remember that your own face and chest and stomach will be corruption and
worms. And pray to God to give you understanding. You may read
books at any time. For your relatives you may read one kathisma.

87. A BLESSING FROM THE SAINTS OF THE KIEV CAVES

October 26, 1878

I have not written to you in a long time, D.! Peace to you! The holy
Fathers of the Kiev Caves, too, send all of you their blessing. I commemorated all of you there when I served in the Caves of St. Anthony where
his relics are. D., although you may grumble about life out of foolishness,
when I had a look at how many others are saving themselves, how they
endure want, malicious talk, labors — then I called your sisters blessed.
It is simply a breeze for them to save themselves. I trust that the Lord
will save you also, no matter how much the Devil may war against you.
But Jesus is stronger than he.

88. BE A WISE VIRGIN

March 29, 1879

I just read your letter, D., and I laughed not a little. You and I will absolutely see each other, if it pleases God. But for now I greet you with the feast of the Resurrection of Christ. And I wish for you, D., to be numbered among those wise virgins of whom we just chanted at Matins. For blessed is that servant, whom the Lord shall find watching. . .[1] *Watch therefore and pray, for ye know neither the day nor the hour wherein the Son of man cometh* (Cf. Matt. 25:13).

And what do we chant on Pascha concerning these wise ones? "The godly-wise women followed after Thee in haste with sweet-smelling myrrh"[2] — that is, as a beloved bride follows after her heavenly Bridegroom — and they overtake Him.

Only, one cannot speak much with you about this, or you will reinterpret everything in your own way; the surest means of salvation for you is one and the same: endure patiently whatever God sends, both good and bad.

It is difficult to give an answer to your funny questions not only in a letter but even in person. I have told you a hundred times that you will be saved —well, let that be enough for you. . .

89. PATIENT ENDURANCE MUST BE WITH DISCERNMENT: THE LORD BEHOLDS YOUR SOUL

June 1, 1879

My reverend martyr, sister in the Lord E.! May God forgive you all the sins you have confessed, my beloved child! I can see that you are struggling. According to your child's strength, you labor, you endure patiently, you suffer — at least a tiny bit — but still you constrain yourself. Believe that for everything you will receive your reward from our sweetest Jesus. Even a hundredfold you will receive it. Only be patient.

But even your patience should not be undiscerning, that is, cheerless, but patience with understanding — that the Lord beholds all your works, your very soul, as we behold the face of a loved one, that is, clearly, attentively. He looks and He makes trial: what kind of a person will you prove to be in afflictions? If you are patient, then you will be

---

1. Cf. Luke 12:37, and the Troparion of Holy Monday.
2. From the Paschal Canon.

beloved of Him. And even if you do not endure and you murmur, but afterwards you repent — you will be beloved of Him anyway.

90. THE LABOR OF MONASTICS IS NOT IN VAIN
December 1, 1879

Peace to you, D.! I have been wanting to write to you for a long time, but I haven't had a chance. You describe the difficulty of the monastic life. That is so, and it appeared difficult even to the holy Fathers. All the more so to us who are passionate. But the point is that the labor is not in vain, unlike the tribulations of those in the world. As for foolish people scaring you by saying that as you grow older your passions will multiply — that's not true. It is the Lord alone Who appoints tribulations for some at the outset, and for some in the middle, and for others at the end of their life. But you should labor and trust in God, that He sees all. And that He will reward you.

Every prayer to God is profitable. But exactly what the profit is — that we do not know. He alone is the righteous Judge, whereas we can mistake falsehood for truth. Pray, and believe. As for pride, it is fearful when we do not notice it: but if we notice it, and repent, and come to contrition, the Lord will not account it as sin.

As for impure thoughts, you cannot entirely repulse them as yet. . . Only the dispassionate are without thoughts. . . The Jesus Prayer cannot be without clouds of thoughts at first. But later, little by little, it is purified.

91. THE HOLY SPIRIT COMFORTS US IN TRIBULATIONS
February 19, 1882

No, fainthearted one, I haven't forgotten you! I do remember you, I remember you always! But to comfort you does not lie in my power. For our Comforter is the Holy Spirit. Turn to Him more often with your whole heart. And He will certainly come to you. Only, not when you yourself wish it and at the time you appoint. As for thoughts troubling you, and murmuring, and faintheartedness, that is the usual fruit of an incorrect and feeble manner of life. *But the hour is coming, and now is, when the dead* (in spirit, that is) *shall hear the voice of the Son of God, and they that hear shall live* (that is, by the Holy Spirit) (John 5:25).

92. HOW TO CELEBRATE PASCHA IN A HOLY WAY

April 4, 1889

Christ is risen! I greet you, D., with the all-joyous feast of the radiant Resurrection of Christ. I wish that you may celebrate it in a fitting way, that is, in a pure, holy, peaceful way. But in order to celebrate properly, here is what we must do: "Let us purify our senses and we shall behold Christ, radiant with the unapproachable light of the Resurrection."[1]

But no matter how much you may chant for one who is deaf, he will not hear. No matter what lovely things you may show to one who is blind, he will not be impressed. Let us purify our senses!

93. IT IS A SIN TO LAUGH. ABOUT THE FUTURE, ETERNAL PASCHA

Christ is risen! You greeted me with the beginning, and I greet you with the end of Lent and the beginning of Pascha! Peace to you! I read your letter, and I see you are struggling poorly. But still I haven't forgotten you, and I remember you often. I even told Batiushka Amvrosy that over there in K. there is a young girl named D., a very nice one because she promised me to live a good life. But when it came right down to it, D. went and let me down. All she does is sleep and laugh. How am I to tell Batiushka about you now? Well? Here's what, D.! For now I won't say anything about you to Batiushka. Meanwhile, you make a beginning of correcting yourself. I, too, wish to make a beginning. And so you and I will say we are trying according to our strength. Only listen, D., be truthful!

Laughing is a great sin. It is produced, laughter and familiarity, by the demon of fornication.[2] But you are a young girl, a bride of Christ, and we all love you because you want to live a good life and to humble yourself. If you cannot go to Matushka [to say your thoughts], do not go — I will not constrain you. And so, D., I greet you [with the feast]. And since you give yourself over to me with all your soul, I, too, will try according to my strength to do for you that which is for your good. And I will say a little word to you which perhaps you have not heard as yet.

---

1. From the Paschal Canon.
2. Cf. *The Ascetical Homilies of St. Isaac the Syrian*, Homily 16, p.90.

Do you see, Pascha is here. A holy and bright day. But this Pascha is a little one: a great Pascha will come, the great Eighth Day, of which there will never be an end unto the ages of ages.

And there, there will be gladness unspeakable and ineffable. All the virgins, the brides of Christ, who have preserved themselves in virginity here according to their strength, will there enter with the Lamb, Jesus, into His heavenly bridal hall. And the celebration of that Pascha will begin — not like this Pascha, but without end. And it will all become more and more joyous. And there will be such dancing there, and the brides of Christ will be so comely that it will be hard to distinguish them from our Lord Jesus Christ Himself. Read in the Evangelist John the Theologian, chapter 17, verses 9, 10, 11.[1] Read this passage with attentiveness and fear, and understand what glory awaits us there. And struggle! As for your temptations of the present time, they will all disappear. Only be patient. If you will be patient and struggle according to your strength, I assure you that we will celebrate the eternal Pascha together.

And you, D., do you remember what I enjoined you — do you say the Jesus Prayer?

94. YOU SIN ON ACCOUNT OF VAINGLORY

What a pity, D., that you, too, have entirely taken after me: you keep sinning and are in no hurry to correct yourself. Exactly like me, the sinner. Let us humble ourselves and ask help from God. He is able to succor them that are tempted, for He Himself also was tempted (Cf. Heb. 2:18). As for you, you've slipped so far that you even ate your fill of herring on a Wednesday! See how far things have gone! And it is vainglory that keeps consuming you! You rightly say that the labor of a vainglorious person will count as nothing. But that is when he does not repent. However, if you judge yourself, God will forgive you. As regards writing to me, write, and do not listen to the insidious thought, or you will go off. As regards stillness, it is not yet profitable for you.

---

1. *I pray for them: I pray not for the world, but for them which Thou hast given Me; for they are Thine. And all Mine are Thine, and Thine are Mine; and I am glorified in them. And now I am no more in the world, but these are in the world, and I come to Thee. Holy Father, keep through Thine own name those whom thou hast given Me, that they may be one, as We are.*

95. AFFLICTIONS: OUR WEALTH

D., you keep writing various paranoias: first you are afraid that you will not be saved; then you are afraid lest they enlist me in the army; and now D. is all set to die, and she's got it arranged for me as well. And she just can't feel happy, and she's overwhelmed by despondency. Matushka, that is precisely what comforts me, that you have afflictions like a rich merchant has money and wares — that is, outward ones, inward ones. But you are silly and do not understand that it is not afflictions but fantastic wealth that you are scooping up with both hands. And you were getting all set to teach others yet! Humble yourself! And remember that there is no one worse than you and me. If you will think in this way, you will be saved. Do not fear any obedience, and do not disdain any. God is our helper! I greet you also with the new year, D., and I wish that you may attain not only to this year of 1878 but also to that one which will never end. In that year when our Sun, Christ, is once risen, He will continue to shine eternally with unutterable light, unimaginable joy, and sweetest light. Our gladness will be proportionate to our afflictions, depending upon how much each person has endured them in this life.

I am going to Vespers now. *All ye that in Christ have been baptized, Christ have ye put on* (Gal. 3:27). You mention how hard it was to part — but after all, it was just for a time. We will see each other again. But what will it be like to be parted from one another there? When the Lord will separate people one from another unto the ages of ages? But if you are patient now, then we will always be together with the Lord and with the angels and with all the saints. And our joy no one will take from us (Cf. John 16:22). So the Lord Himself has said.

96. THE WORST THING IN A YOUNG NUN IS OBSTINACY AND DISOBEDIENCE

I received your letters. May God forgive you everything you have confessed. Only correct yourself. Know that the worst thing in a little girl is stubbornness and disobedience; soon everyone will be sick of you. And so you should set about mastering your bad temper with all your strength. It is a symptom of pride. . . As for your not having a mother, and no one coming to see you — you should rejoice. The Mother of God herself will watch over you. For it is said, *My father and my mother have forsaken me, but the Lord hath taken me to Himself* (Ps. 26:12)! It is difficult for a monastic to live with relatives. That you are living in a proper monastic manner is evident from the fact that you have trials,[1] and according to your strength, you endure them. Do not be discouraged. The Lord will save you. Nuns should always carry prayer ropes so as not to forget the Jesus Prayer. That is the very reason why the prayer ropes are given them. . .

97. CONCERNING SORROWS, AND CONCERNING THE JESUS PRAYER

I had scarcely read your letter, D., when I set about answering you. What kind of woes these are that are distressing you, I do not see from your letter. The only thing I can see is that life weighs heavily upon you. Because in the first place, they won't let you sleep all the time, and in the second place, you do not have a rowdy husband — who would beat you up and knock the nonsense out of your head — and ever so many other woes you have, one bigger than the next.

So D. thinks she is writing me a letter for the last time. But I hope to write to D. again another time, for I think she is an intelligent girl and will think better of it and set about her work. And she will come to love [spiritual] reading. And start praying to God. And she will write to me, and I will answer her. And so I remain confident concerning you.

In answer to your perplexities: the Jesus Prayer not only does not hinder but even helps one listen to the reading and the chanting, and helps regular church prayer and prayer in one's cell, and it sweetens, it greatly sweetens the heart, and it makes the spirit peaceful, and it illumines the mind. But you think incorrectly, for you are an inexperienced little girl and self-willed too. Try to humble yourself, and the prayer will soon take. Only do not be in a hurry — await God's help. As for the others talking about you, do not worry about that. You came to the convent in order to please God, and not people. And He will save you — of that I assure you — only have patience.

---

1. "Abba Poemen used to say, 'The certain sign that a monk is a monk is made known by trials (or temptations).' " *The Paradise of the Holy Fathers*, Vol. II, p.44.

IX. LETTERS TO E.K.

98. NAMEDAY WISHES

Reverend [Sister] E., I congratulate you on your nameday. I wish for you that you may ever remember that hour in which the Saint,[1] being found between Heaven and earth, gazed in terror at the fearful dragon who was ready to swallow her in an instant. Now this matter is in our hands: we can arm ourselves with power from on high so as to have no fear of him. Let us begin to humble ourselves, and our power over this dragon will be assured. The matter of our salvation depends upon our will.

99. IN REVILING ELDERSHIP, YOU ARE FOUND ON THE PATH OF DESTRUCTION

Sister E., your letter of January 11 made me most unhappy. I am sincerely sorry for you: you have slipped so far that soon you won't even be happy of life. As they say, neither a candle for God, nor a fancy bread[2] for the world. That which the holy Fathers extol, the path by which they themselves walked and which in their love they have bequeathed to us to make our way easier — this you revile: I am speaking of the path of eldership and disclosure of thoughts. Where do you think you are going? Do you really hope to escape the gates of death? Yea, you will not escape them! Take pity on yourself, sister!

From a loving heart I say to you: turn back. It is not too late: *forsake foolishness* (Prov. 9:6); set about your work at least a little, according to your strength. And the Lord is mighty to raise you up again, and you will be dear to Him and to people.

---

1. Probably St. Eudokia.
2. Kalach, in Russian.

X. LETTERS TO P.O.

100. YOU ARE OVERCOME BY PRIDE

P.O. has been overcome by pride: it seems that she does not wish to have recourse even to the Lord Who said, *Learn of Me, for I am meek and lowly in heart* (Matt. 11:29). The Lord humbled Himself — but P.O. cannot humble herself!

Humble yourself, sister, and you will be saved. Do not insist on your own way. Do not look at men, or you will suffer for it. As for your mother, leave her to God. He Himself will care for her.

101. YOU CANNOT REMAIN WITHOUT STRUGGLE AGAINST THE PASSIONS

I received your letter, P. You write that you are overcome by passions: a chaste girl can by no means remain without struggle against the passions. But we must lessen this warfare by eating and sleeping less, by not criticizing others, by not forgetting God, and by having the remembrance of death; and most important of all, by humbling ourselves — without this the warfare against the passions is difficult. But it is always possible for a repenting sinner to be saved, on account of God's unspeakable mercy.

102. WHAT YOUR BAD DREAM SHOWS

Peace to you, Sister P. Save yourself! Your bad dream shows that you do not guard your senses, and the Devil catches you in his snares. . . Fulfill your obedience with the fear of God; with regard to any virtue you have not attained, reproach yourself and entreat God for it. But do not become disturbed.

103. CONSTRAIN YOURSELF, AND IT IS ENOUGH

Do not despair, and try to please N.E. As for loving her — God will give you the feeling. Constrain yourself, and it is enough. That you are choked at night is for enmity or for condemning others. Correct yourself, and it will pass.

XI. LETTERS TO I.P.

104. IT IS GOOD WHEN THEY SCOLD YOU

You grieve because they scold you, whereas I rejoice for you. If only you knew how this aids in our salvation, especially in the case of those who are passionate. . . It is exceedingly good to imitate the Lord. . .

105. IT IS SAVING TO DISCLOSE YOUR THOUGHTS

Sister I., I seem to remember you are a candle-bearer and a chanter and such a good novice — but you do not know that the easiest and most saving thing of all is to disclose your thoughts. So go [to Matushka], and say everything.

You are consumed by vainglory, but you do not even notice this. In order to be rid of this temptation, humble yourself, reproach yourself. . . Be humbled also by the fact that you are being taught. Others, even though they are better than you, humble themselves, and the Lord will reward them with eternal good things. That is how you must think.

106. HE WHO SERVES OTHERS IS LIKENED TO CHRIST

It is sinful for you not to love a little girl like L.! The Devil keeps stirring you up: "Why," she says, "should I serve her!" But what you do not understand is what a great work you perform in doing so! You are likened to the Son of God, Jesus Christ, Who said of Himself, I came not to be ministered unto, but to minister (Cf. Matt. 20:28). And for this you will receive a great reward.

XII. LETTERS TO N.S.

107. CONSOLATION IN PERPLEXITIES

November 16, 1876

Sister in the Lord N., You see, I have only just received your letter in November, which must have been sent in September. I was in Peter,[1] and I was ill there. Otherwise, I would have answered you long ago. But now I have accumulated a lot of letters, and if I write to you, I will write briefly. It is my turn to serve, and in between, while everyone is resting, instead of sleeping I have hastened to speak with you. You write that when you visited Batiushka Amvrosy, you became scared and couldn't say what you wanted to. I can easily believe you. But do not be downcast; it may be that the Lord will bring you here again to visit sometime. If there is something on your conscience, you may write immediately either to Batiushka Amvrosy or to me. With regard to the unpleasantness arising from your obedience, that is, weighing out too little or too much for candle sales, that happens everywhere. And there is nowhere you can go to escape troubles. But endure patiently, and you will be saved. When you do not go to church because of your obedience, do not be troubled. They will pray for you in church. That you have entered the convent is good, and always thank God for this. Of course, the Devil will not cease bothering you with the thought that it is better to live in the world. But we must listen to God, to the angels, and not to the Devil.

108. HOW WE MUST GLORIFY CHRIST

December 24, 1883

Christ is born, give ye glory! You[2] also will doubtless be glorifying Him. Glorify Him not by anger, not by grumbling, not by criticizing your superiors and your subordinates — but by humility, by love for the sisters, by unceasing prayerful calling upon Jesus — and then you will come to know the glory of Christ and the gifts of our sweetest Jesus. Endure patiently, and you will be saved!

---

1. I.e., St. Petersburg.
2. This sentence is in the plural.

109. WISHES FOR ONE WHO HAS
RECEIVED THE ANGELIC SCHEMA

May 20, 1892

Sister in the Lord, Mother N., I congratulate you with the angelic schema. From my heart I desire for you that you may also live in an angelic, pure, holy manner, in humility, obedience, and unceasing prayer, in forbearance and love for your neighbor.

You may tell your spiritual mother all your sinful thoughts which particularly trouble and disturb you. When you are on duty, you may omit the reading of the Psalter at midnight.

You ask me whether the rule of prayer ropes and the Psalter are omitted on the eves of feasts, and whether to rise at midnight? When there is a vigil service, all of this is omitted; the church service is sufficient.

110. YOUR DEPRESSION IS FROM
AN INCOMPLETE CONFESSION

Your pains and your depression are very likely a result of your not having confessed completely. When we see each other, make a thorough confession. Besides, your very heart is decayed: one look at a man, and it will collapse!

Why, silly, can there possibly be anyone more comely, not only on earth but even in Heaven, than your heavenly Bridegroom, for Whose sake you have left your parents and homeland and consigned yourself to labors and afflictions? This shows that you think of Him little and call upon Him infrequently for aid. Say the Jesus Prayer more often, and your heart will be gladdened. . . Only, make an effort to scrape the decay out of your heart, that is, do not be drawn away by unchaste thoughts. One cannot remain without carrying an obedience. Besides, your obedience is particularly beneficial for you because by labors and cares, it preserves you from carnal thoughts.

111. DO NOT BE ASHAMED TO DISCLOSE YOUR THOUGHTS

Sister N. is ashamed even to write to me concerning her thoughts. Just see what a saint she is! The person who does not consider himself a saint, on the other hand, says honestly that he has done this or that.

Your fear is all for nothing and harmful. A repentant sinner is more pleasing to the Lord than an unrepentant righteous man. During the festal season, the cell rule is omitted until Theophany itself.

XIII. LETTERS TO T.G.

112. ON NOT CONDEMNING OTHERS, AND ON BLASPHEMOUS THOUGHTS

November 17, 1876

Sister in the Lord T., You made me very happy by your wise request: you ask that you may not condemn others. Truly there is no easier virtue to be saved by. No labors, no fasting, no sacrifices, no offerings. It is simple: *judge not, and ye shall not be judged* (Luke 6:37). I entreat the Lord that He may grant you this virtue (although I myself do not possess it).

Now, when blasphemous thoughts disturb you, don't even fight them, but simply disdain them, that is, ignore them: they are not our thoughts but the Devil's, and so we will not answer for them. We monastics love God, for it is for the Lord's sake that we have left the world. As for blasphemies, the Devil mixes them in and not we. Read one kathisma from the Psalter, or you may read two.

You fear death — how dense you are! You fear something nonexistent. Can it be that you don't understand and know what the entire world knows — "Christ is risen from the dead, by death hath He trampled down death, and on those in the graves hath He bestowed life!"[1] Death has been put to death by Jesus Christ, and now that it is dead, there is no reason to fear it!

---

1. Troparion of Pascha.

113. DO NOT DESPAIR OF CORRECTING YOURSELF
November 1, 1879

Reverend novice of God T., Peace to you and God's blessing! *O thou of little faith, wherefore didst thou doubt* (Matt. 14:31) God's power, instead of being convinced of it upon seeing your own powerlessness? Jonas did not lose hope at the bottom of the sea, swallowed up by a sea monster; instead, he prayed. But you, fainthearted one, enjoying the sunshine and not deprived even of spiritual sunshine, that is, of the Holy Liturgy and the church services, and moreover living amid martyrs, that is, chosen brides of Christ — you belch forth blasphemies of despair, unbelief, suspicion, and other loathsome sins? Giving way to grumbling, you've even lost your mind: you say that you've lost hope of correcting yourself — foolish words! This kid is ready to kill herself because she can't correct herself! Well, what you can do is repent! Why should we try to intrude among those who have corrected themselves, that is, among the perfect! It will be a mercy of God if we make it into the flock of the saved (that is, of the repentant).

So humble yourself! Because you smell of pride! "The superiors look down on me, all the sisters look down on me!" But do you have anything for which they should revere you? You don't? Well, then humble yourself! And you will be saved!

114. WHAT TO DO WHEN YOU ARE OVERWHELMED BY CARNAL THOUGHTS

Sister T., you write that you are warred against by passions! They have been warring against me also from my youth, but let us cry out, "Do Thou Thyself defend and save me, O my Saviour!"[1] Have patience, and it will pass! And have patience with your sister! And when you lie down on your bed, sign yourself with the sign of the Cross, and picture to yourself how they will place you in the grave for eternal rest. And meanwhile, labor. When you are strongly overwhelmed by thoughts, get up and make several prostrations to the holy Martyr Thomais, to St. Moses the Hungarian.[2] And right now chant for Pascha, "O Christ Who by Thy passion didst darken the sun, and Who by the light of Thy Resurrection didst make all things radiant, accept our hymn!"[3] And also, "We

---

1. From the Hymns of Ascent, Fourth Tone.
2. Both of these saints suffered for their chastity.
3. From the Aposticha of the Resurrection, Third Tone.

celebrate the death of death, the destruction of Hades, the beginning of a new and everlasting life!"[1]

115. RULES FOR YOUR LIFE

Peace to you, T.! We must be patient in afflictions. And if we do not succeed in mastering ourselves, we must condemn ourselves and repent. It is very beneficial to say your thoughts. Try to keep to this path. . . An obedience is generally difficult to fulfill — but your needlework is a high-class one. Many would like to have just such work but do not. You cannot destroy the passions on your own, but ask God, and He will destroy them, if this is profitable for you. Eat moderately and give thanks to God. It is good to sit in one's cell. . . Try to endure grief from all. . . Then you may be certain that you will not perish. When they read, especially in church, listen, even if it is without fervor. In time you will come to love everything, including the monastic life.

116. MURMURING AND ANGER ARE THE VERY WORST PASSIONS. COMPARE YOUR POVERTY WITH THAT OF THE PEASANTS

Sister in the Lord T., You complain that passions war against you: murmuring and anger! Well, what are we to do?. . . Where can we run away to from ourselves? Have patience, T., and the Lord will help you. Only know that these passions, that is, murmuring and anger, are purely of the Devil. St. Isaac the Syrian says that God shows mercy to the sinner when he repents: but a murmurer He will not forgive without chastising him.[2] And so do your utmost to humble yourself. And if out of human weakness you err, quickly condemn yourself and ask forgiveness from the Lord. With regard to some people being strict with you, do not let it

---

1. From the Paschal Canon.
2. "Repentance is the door of mercy, opened to those who seek it. By way of this door we enter into the mercy of God, and apart from this entrance we shall not find mercy." "A murmuring disposition always active in the heart is a guide that leads trials to the soul. God bears with all the weaknesses of men, but He will not suffer to leave without chastisement a man who murmurs continually." *The Ascetical Homilies of St. Isaac the Syrian*, Homily 46, p.223; and Homily 48, p.229.

bother you. Strictness has saved many, whereas indulgence has brought many to ruin. And St. John Chrysostom says that the majority of those who are saved, are saved by the fear of Gehenna. With regard to your poverty I will say this: recently a poor novice visited us, and like you, she had grumbled about her poverty — but when on her way she stopped at a peasant hut and everywhere saw snow, cold, hunger, a pile of little children in rags — she was ready to call herself blessed. Our poverty is not so unbearable. Moreover, for us there will be such a sublime reward, if we endure patiently. But if you do not know how to be patient, let patience itself teach you. Should you become fainthearted, once again take up this saving weapon. And thus in time you will become skilled: for just as with any art, one does not learn any virtue all at once. But after much time and putting in many labors — that is when the knowledge will come to you.

117. IN THIS WORLD THERE IS NO CONSTANCY
You write that now that you have begun to attend to yourself, you are better. That is always the way it is. Only know that in this world nothing is constant. Look outside: in the morning it rained, at noon it is clear, and toward evening again it is cold. Now wind, now calm; now storm, now heat: so it is also in our life; always be ready to follow God's will, whether we like it or not.

Serve the sick sister; the Lord will reward you a hundredfold. You become cowardly during the chanting out of vainglory. You have lots of it. Remember St. Abba Dorotheos' saying — engrave it on your mind:[1] "Your salvation lies in your neighbor."

118. WHEN THE PASSIONS WILL LEAVE US
Sister T.G. has reached an advanced age — she is going on 26. And still the passions haven't left her. Amazing — such venerable old age — and still the passions are there. It seems you have heard, but not understood, that *wisdom is the grey hair unto men, and an unspotted life is old age* (Wis. 4:9). Sometimes the Lord bestows passionlessness early, especially upon the humble; otherwise, a person dies while still in the conflict [against the passions]. But that does not mean that this person is lost. Rather, it has been said by someone that such a one will be numbered with the martyrs. You wish to know at what age the passions will leave you? Long ago it has been said, It is not for you to know the times or the seasons, which God hath put in His own power (Cf. Acts 1:7).

---

1. Lit., "on your nose."

XIV. LETTERS TO E.K.

119. ON THE FEAR OF DEATH

April 8, 1877

Good girl, L., for greeting me for the feast and informing me about yourself. Otherwise, I know nothing about how she is doing over there. True, you aren't getting along very happily, but still this is better than knowing nothing at all. Now at least I know you are a coward, an awful coward! A fifteen year old girl, afraid of death! Why, you have completely lost your mind! What then are we old folks to do? All that is left for us to do is simply to wail, to wail as loud as we can! Silly — why, during these days of Holy Pascha we chant, "We celebrate the death of death, the destruction of Hades, the beginning of a new and everlasting life. And with leaps of joy we praise the Cause thereof!"[1]

But — during such days as these yet — you've taken it into your mind to cry out of fear of death! Why, how completely out of place! Why, you are a Christian! And a monastic yet! This shows that you do not understand yourself one bit, or the Paschal celebration either! Why, you have been chosen by God for the angelic conversation out of many thousands of lay people who putter around in life's cares and pleasures. But by God's mercy and by a calling from on high, you have refused them and betrothed yourself to Christ, the heavenly Bridegroom, and become His bride! So is He about to forsake you? Silly!

Only do not you forsake Him; He will not forsake you. He Himself has said: I am with you (and it follows, with you in particular) unto the end of the world (Cf. Matt. 28:20)! Even if a mother should forget her child, I will not forget thee (Is. 49:15).

Do not be despondent — you're so scared, you've lost your wits! Let us purify our senses and we shall behold Christ, radiant with the unapproachable light of the Resurrection. The godly-wise women followed after Thee (Christ) in haste with sweet-smelling myrrh. . .[2] And you too, little nun, are found among their number, that is, among the myrrh-bearing women. For you, too, have left home, father and family and hastened

---

1. From the Paschal Canon.
2. Ibid.

after our beloved Jesus. And behold, now you serve Him, the King of kings: you serve Him, for you patiently endure afflictions — illnesses; you try not to give in to the passions. And much more. Silly, you do not understand how fortunate you are! However, I have faith that God will not remember all the sins of your youth and ignorance (Cf. Ps. 24:7) which you have confessed. . . Do not murmur about illness, but give thanks to God: *for whom the Lord loveth, He chasteneth* (Heb. 12:6).

When carnal thoughts attack you, pray to the holy Martyr Thomais. And say the Jesus Prayer harder.

120. ON THE ETERNAL YEAR OF GOD'S GLORY
December 24, 1877

I just this minute read your letter. I sincerely thank you for your greeting, and I greet you with this great feast of the Nativity of Christ and the new year. And I wish you peace in this year, health, and salvation. But most of all, I wish that you may enter into that year where there are no winters, where the sun never sets — and the Sun of that year is Jesus, eternally shining with the glory of His Father — where there will be no sorrows, no illnesses, no darkness, not even shadow: but all will be light, joy, peace which passeth all understanding, and unspeakable gladness. And in that year the gates of the heavenly Jerusalem will be opened, never to close (Cf. Is. 60:11).

But the more afflictions a person bears here, the easier it will be for him to enter into that eternal reign. For a novice who endures voluntary or involuntary afflictions patiently is a bride of Christ, and her Bridegroom is there preparing for her a royal throne and honors together with the Mother of God, as we read, *At Thy right hand stood the queen, arrayed in a vesture of inwoven gold, adorned in varied colors. The virgins that follow after her shall be brought unto the King, they shall be brought with gladness and rejoicing. They shall be brought into the temple of the King* (Ps. 44:8,13,14). But who are these virgins? They are you people, young novices who are patiently enduring afflictions for the Lord's sake. I know that you murmur and fret, but still you stay. And our merciful heavenly Father will receive even this as a gift offered to Him. Do not lose heart, L. The lot of monastics is awfully high — that is why it is difficult here.

121. MISTAKES ARE INEVITABLE; LET US HUMBLE OURSELVES

February 17, 1878

L., you aren't making any sense! You were afraid to write to me because you have not corrected yourself! Why, I myself have not corrected myself one bit; well, so what are we to do?. . . Let us humble ourselves! And thus we shall be saved! No, you will not be lost. Only, you will suffer here, as already you are suffering, because of your stubbornness and self-love. But with God's help everything will fall into place. After all, we have come to learn the spiritual life — so is it surprising if we make mistakes? Let us try to correct ourselves! It is God Himself Who will correct us!

122. A NUN SHOULD PUT TOGETHER A SPIRITUAL DOWRY FOR CHRIST

April 20, 1884

Christ is risen!. . . You are not sure what to do when you leave the workroom? A monastic, and she doesn't know what to do except needlework!. . . Some novice! Why, you are betrothed to Christ! Well, so gather a dowry for Him: adorn yourself to the best of your ability.

You will ask, how? This question St. John Chrysostom answered long ago, before you and I were even born. Read his little book on virginity. There it is explained in much detail how a bride should adorn herself and what kind of dowry her Bridegroom requires. Only nothing is said in there about needlework. Read it. L., hasten to acquaint yourself with the spiritual life. Make good use of your free time, read the books of the Fathers, but most of all learn the Jesus Prayer. Begin even if only with ten a day. And add them on, hundred by hundred. These prayer ropes, of course, are without prostrations. Without Jesus you will never cleanse your heart.

XV. LETTERS TO M. Kh.

123. *A NUN WHO IS BETROTHED TO CHRIST MUST BE FAITHFUL TO HIM*

March 19, 1881

It is not forbidden to marry, and it is not a sin if the maiden is not betrothed to a bridegroom — but from the moment the contract is concluded, it is deemed a disgrace to cast aside the promise which has been made and to break the agreement. You and I are brides now, betrothed to the Lord Jesus, and we have made a vow to preserve our virginity. And if we break it, we become guilty, as betrayers and adulterers. Now in general, while you are still young and inexperienced, and while your blood is feisty and the Devil isn't letting an opportunity slip by but stirs you up and flatters you and tricks you by the supposedly great pleasurableness of lust, everything out there seems wonderful to you. But it is not really so. Especially when the lust passes away and age gets it out of your system — then you will yourself be amazed at how everything could change so. Try to be at peace as far as possible and not to condemn others. . . May the Lord forgive you all the sins you have committed, and may He bless you!

124. *THE YOUNG SHOULD PRACTICE ORAL PRAYER*

October 27, 1883

I spoke to Batiushka about your prayer which begins in church and comes into your heart. He answered that this is not for the young ones. You should immediately say it with your lips. Save yourself! Humble yourself!

125. *THE IDEA OF TRAVELLING TO JERUSALEM IS A TEMPTATION*

March 28, 1884

I just this minute received your letter. I am very sorry that I have not written in a long time, and I even thought about it last night: but if only you knew what Great Lent means to me, you would pity me. You live and break down in one head, whereas I have to soothe hundreds of heads, your own little head included. Meanwhile, the Fast is appointed for me also.

I myself used to want terribly to go to Jerusalem — but there is a saying: patience is a remedy for desire.[1]

Only, in your case this is obviously a temptation. Knowing your weakness, the Devil will hook you. And you will hang there like a little fishy on a line.

126. HOW TO BE FREED FROM CARNAL THOUGHTS

You ask me to tell you a way to be freed from carnal thoughts? Of course, in the manner the holy Fathers teach: in the first place, humble yourself; in the second place, look neither at deacons, nor at young boys; and the third thing is the most important one — the third thing is to endure patiently. The crown of virginity is the highest Christian virtue; it is the beauty and crown of the Church. All virgins are called brides of Christ by the Holy Church. St. Dimitry of Rostov teaches, "Take away an angel's wings, and he will be a virgin. And give a virgin wings, and she will be an angel."[2] But you, runny-nosed kid, do not grasp this. . . Peace to you and the blessing of the Lord!

I repeat to you once more that despondency is inevitable for you because you do not bear any afflictions voluntarily, and you look at the deacon, and you like young boys. But nothing defiled will enter the Kingdom of Heaven, and so the merciful Lord is cleansing you by means of despondency and revilings.

Do not meddle in other people's affairs — you will lose your peace!

127. HUMILITY IS ATTAINED THROUGH PATIENCE
December 9, 1880

I received your latest letter in which you marvel at someone else's humility, but do not wish to show any for your part. However, even this is good, that you love humility and, it follows, you desire it. But being inexperienced, you do not know how to find it. Would you like me to teach you? Well, would you? Crossing myself, I turn to you and tell you a secret: the very best means of finding humility. Here it is: to patiently endure every pain which pricks your proud heart. And day and night to

---

1. This rhymes in Russian — "na khoténye yest terpénye."
2. St. Dimitry of Rostov, *Homily on the Laudation of the Mother of God*

await mercy from the all-merciful Saviour. One who thus waits will unfailingly receive. Of this I can assure you on my word of honor — if you can trust my honor, that is. Try it and you will see. The point is, you do not understand that precisely this pain, precisely this sharp, bitter sting pricking the sensitivity of your heart is in fact the real wellspring of God's mercies and of humility. It is in these pains that the mercy of God is hidden.[1] Take away these ailments from you, take away your exhaustion, take away insults, reproaches, shortcomings from you — and you will be left completely naked! Then goodbye royal purple (the mantia) and royal crown, and pearls, and precious stones, and trees of Paradise, and angels, and God Himself with His Most Pure Mother — all of this will fly away from you. Whereas right now it is all there. Only, you do not see it as yet. But in time you will see, and you will be greatly amazed.

128. HOW TO SPEND NATIVITY

December 24, 1881

I greet you with the feast of the Nativity of Christ! May God grant you to celebrate these holy days and evenings wisely — not in the way the corrupt world celebrates, where on these holy evenings all kinds of abominations take place: songs, dances, and piping — and they even disfigure the human face! But you and I, let us live in a holy manner, even if it be with pain, but in a pure, holy way. So what is going on right now in Stenin? In Kozelsk? Drunkenness! Carousing! Dancing! Swearing! Fights! Shamelessness! Foul acts! Disfigured faces! Songs! and so on — simply hell on earth! But our work is purely angelic. We sit in our little cell, we sigh, we weep, and we bring to mind, what is it that happened during these days? A newly born infant — God, but also perfect man, with all the infirmities of our mortal body — first sees the light of day in a cave for animals. It is winter, December 25, damp; the tender, child's limbs of the newborn Infant are numb with cold, but there is nowhere to take shelter; the town is far away. No clothing, no warm dwelling in sight. . . And our cell is not nice! Our neighbors are not nice! Were the neighbors of the Lord — the asses and the oxen — any better? What are we going to say when the Son of man, Jesus Christ, appears and says all this to us, and shows us His wounds and His side which was pierced by the spear?

---

1. "The mercy of God is hidden in sufferings." St. Mark the Ascetic, "On Those who Think that They are Made Righteous by Works," #139, *The Philokalia, Vol. I,* p.136.

For whose sake, He will say, did I come upon earth? For whose sake did I suffer?

You say that I do not understand your sufferings. You are blinded by self-love: I do understand them very well. But at the same time I have faith in the Lord, Who said to His beloved ones, In the world ye shall have tribulation. And the world shall rejoice, but ye shall weep. But your sorrow shall be turned into joy, and your joy no man taketh from you. . . (Cf. John 16:20,22,33).

129. IT IS GOOD THAT YOU KNOW HOW TO REPENT

April 29, 1882

Amen I say unto you, you are not behaving well. That is, exactly and precisely like me from my youth. Of course, my sins are serious, and I didn't know how to repent, whereas even though you become irritated, you do repent. But I didn't even know how to repent. And therefore, bad as you are being, still you were and you continue to be better than me. And this for me is a consolation. Of course, I am not about to praise you for being so vicious. But I will tell you in confidence that a vicious person does not repent and does not bemoan himself — whereas you are pained, and such pain is a good sign — a sign that healing is possible. Only have patience.

Be thou manful, and let thy heart be strengthened. And wait on the Lord (Ps. 26:16)!

130. CONSOLATION IN PRAYER

February 1, 1884

Your consolation in prayer is nothing new. I have told you more than once, and maybe a hundred times: labor, wait patiently, and God Himself will give you consolation. No: it's let M. go home, and to S., and to Jerusalem. But I say: persevere in prayer, and then not Rome only and Jerusalem, but the Crucified One Himself with His Most Pure Mother will come to us. Here is the explanation [of the consolation you have received in prayer]: it is precisely by this means that the Lord draws to Himself the obstinate and the fainthearted. Otherwise, they would immediately murmur against God, and against their spiritual father, and against everyone, saying that they are lost. Whereas now you can see for yourself that it is not in vain that you have labored, and that I was not fooling you. This is the first installment. The second will follow later. This consolation has given you assurance that God exists and that our reward exists. Later it will leave you, and the Lord will observe you to see whether you are a faithful handmaid of His — or a sly, pleasure-loving, mercenary handmaid, who loves her Lord only when He gives her consolation. That is when you must demonstrate the genuine love of an upright bride of His. But this also will pass. And again a ray of consolation will sparkle through. And that is how the Lord trains His beloved ones. But woe to you if you exalt yourself as though you were rich, whereas you are a beggar!. . . The Devil sees what you are doing and whence you receive everything, and so he tries to separate you from your Shepherd, as a young and inexperienced sheep. Persevere! Cats and mice have not eaten anyone up yet. Let them nibble at the floor; just guard your bread, don't let them nibble on it. Tell me that sin [you refer to]. I will tell no one and I won't scold you. If you can't tell me, tell Batiushka. But say it you must. Peace to you and salvation. Above all, humble yourself. The moment you lose humility and self-reproach — forget it.

131. ATTEND TO YOURSELF

October 13, 1887

God will forgive you, Sister M.! I, the sinner, also forgive and absolve you.

Only, remember and do not forget that you have just barely torn yourself from the hands of the demons — or else you will not tear yourself away. Attend to yourself. It is time to work on yourself, to curb your tongue and your temper.

132. AFFLICTIONS ARE A DOWRY FOR CHRIST, OUR BRIDEGROOM

Peace to you, M. Save yourself! How are you coughing along over there? How are you bearing afflictions for the Lord's sake? For it is the Lord Who is the true, changeless, most beloved Bridegroom of young nuns — and afflictions are a dowry for our precious Bridegroom. If anyone loves Jesus, he tries with all his might to accumulate as big a dowry as possible; and the more he loves Him — the most pure, most gentle, sweetest Jesus — the more he rejoices if they truck in dowry to a good bride by the cartload — that is, afflictions and illnesses. And the Lord Jesus loves such as these. And how greatly He loves them! May the Lord keep you! May He strengthen you in patience. May He give you spiritual understanding! And I always remember you and pray: O Lord Jesus Christ, preserve Thy bride Masha in purity and holiness.

133. ASK GOD FOR WHATEVER
IS PROFITABLE FOR YOU

How I grieved, I really grieved today, that the dog ate M.'s fish! But if someone carried it off — may it be to his health. Perhaps he never feasted on such a fish in his life. As for you, the Lord will send you some. And with regard to your being delivered from afflictions and my praying for this, I will pray thus: O Lord, Thou lovest Masha more than I do, and Thou canst help her better than I, and Thou knowest better than I what is profitable for her. So do for her what is best — only save her!

134. PRAY MORE

Reverend novice of God M., No, I have not forgotten you, I remember you constantly, but circumstances do not permit me to visit you. . .[1] Pray more! Pray walking, and pray lying down. As for people laughing at you, that is beneficial and saving. Give thanks to God for all things!

135. DO NOT STRIVE BEYOND YOUR STRENGTH
TO ATTEND CHURCH, BUT PRAY AT HOME

M., why can't you remember what I told you? I have told you many times not to force yourself to attend church beyond your strength — just lie under your blanket and repeat: Lord Jesus Christ, Son of God, have mercy on me, a sinner. Call also upon the Mother of God, who greatly loves young nuns! How can you possibly put yourself on a level with those who are healthy? Better to humble yourself. That will be both easier for you and more profitable!. . . As for impure thoughts coming to you — do not be disturbed. They even come to old women. But since these know that God does not punish us for thoughts of which we repent, they do not fear them.

---

1. This word is in the plural.

136. DO NOT SEEK HONORS, AND DO NOT ENVY OTHERS

I greet you, M., with the feast of the Mother of God of the Sign. What am I to do with my proud heart? The moment I am not given what I want, off it goes. Here you are so kind, you respect me and you love me — but others do not love me and do not respect me. And still I get grieved on this account. Why, I am an old man already, I've gotten gray — and still I love honor. Well honestly, Masha! And you too, reverend Mother, you grieve — they don't render you honor! What to do? Let us be patient. Mayhaps the hour will come, and the Lord will lead us out into the light as in the noonday. True, I deserve this, being an old man — I should have learned humility long ago — but your young reverence I pity more than myself. Why, you won't even be able to understand either the benefit that comes from afflictions or the wiles of the enemy. And I? What about me? Shame on me! Well, there is no way out of it: let us go about learning humility. Of course, I am a bit ashamed to be on a level with you — I who am an old fellow — but what to do! At least, more power to the little girl if she outdoes the old man. So — we will begin on this feast. The Mother of God of the Sign will be our surety! Now look, M., here is how it is: your feeling of being grieved is simply petty. You became jealous because a novice was clothed, an old woman at that — whereas you yourself have a mantia under your hat.[1] A mantia yet! Why, if this sad little old woman were to suddenly find out that there is a little girl who very, very early on was adorned with the mantia... and that this girl is jealous of her, the little old woman, because they have consoled one who is old with the rank of a novice — however, this old woman had been asking to enter the convent for many years but, unlike you, they kept turning her away (and for five years or so she suffered, wandering around out there) even though she did have better means than yours (why, you have none at all) — and here she just barely made it into the convent and they clothed her, and already someone is jealous!...Reconsider, M.! Humble yourself! O woe is me! I myself do not humble myself! Well, you — at least you, make me happy!

137. THE TRUE CLOTHING OF A MONASTIC

They say that they wish to clothe you. I am glad. Only remember that the garment of muhoyár[2] covers only the parts of the body and the

---

1. Lit., "under a bushel."
2. See footnote, Letter #54.

bones, whereas the true clothing is the works of the monastic: humility, meekness, patient endurance of illnesses and sorrows — especially tales and slanders.[1] That is the outward aspect of the clothing. The reverse side of this clothing is joy, peace, mercy, love, etc., but most of all, the ceaseless turning of the heart to Jesus, so that day and night the monastic beholds the Lord Jesus and exults in Him, and is comforted and gladdened and grows continually and blossoms forth. Save yourself, sister!

138. SHOW CONDESCENSION FOR THOSE WHO ARE WEAK

November 22, 1882

I received another letter from you, M. Still you keep getting angry. But this further aggravates your illness. I spoke with Batiushka regarding the disorder at trapeza, and his answer was that it is inexpedient to start a campaign against it. Just tell Matushka, he says, and she'll raise up a storm — let's wait on it for now. And you, learn to show condescension for those who are weak. After all, you would like to live in a better way, but in practice you can't hack it. After all, it seems like nothing could be easier than to chase away this fog of thoughts: but no — they just keep coming at you. So it is with these poor sisters. You write that in the world they have better table manners — why, out there they outstrip us poor monastics in many areas — but the moment these same strugglers show up in a monastery, you would never recognize them. Here they will suddenly develop an appetite, and sleepiness, and malice, and all kinds of things, as St. John of the Ladder writes in his third discourse.[2] After all, no need to look far — let's take me and you, M., weren't we awfully nice at first? So do not be amazed either at yourself or at anyone else. Until

---

1. Cf. Instructions of St. Seraphim of Sarov quoted in (for example) *At the Relics of St. Seraphim of Sarov,* Bishop Evdokim, (Holy Trinity — St. Sergius Lavra, 1908) p.54

2. *The Ladder of Divine Ascent,* 2:6: "It is worth investigating why those who live in the world and spend their life in vigils, fasts, labors and hardships, when they withdraw from the world and begin the monastic life, as if at some trial or on the practicing ground, no longer continue the discipline of their former spurious and sham asceticism. I have seen how in the world they planted many different plants of the virtues, which were watered by vainglory as by an underground sewage pipe, and were hoed by ostentation, and for manure were heaped with praise. But when transplanted to a desert soil, inaccessible to people of the world and so not manured with the foul-smelling water of vanity, they withered at once. For water-loving plants are not such as to produce fruit in hard and arid training fields."

God manifests His aid, we shall not be able to do anything by ourselves.

You may eat fish on account of infirmity, only please, stop getting irritated. And do not hold on to your thoughts for a long time. You write that a nun shouldn't have them: why, who are they to intrude upon if not a young nun: they have little to gain from old ones who have already been tried. But the demons torment young ones both with depression and with other passions. That is how the young ones become practiced: an untried man is unpracticed.[1]

139. WITH GOD NO ONE IS DEAD — ALL ARE ALIVE
December 22, 1882

Peace to you and blessing from our Lord and Saviour Jesus Christ Who is born, Matushka M., if you are alive. And if you have died, eternal memory to you and rest with the saints where there is joy and sweetness unspeakable, unimaginable! I think you must be there by now, because in your little letter you several times said, "I'm dying, I'm dying"; "I'm finally dying"; "I'm really and truly dying." And so I surmise that you are now there, dancing with the angels and glorifying the One Who is born. But if, beyond all expectation, you haven't quite died as yet, I greet you with the all-joyous Nativity of our Saviour and Redeemer from eternal death and tribulations and pains and Hades and everything unpleasant. And since with the Lord no one is dead, but all are alive to Him (Cf. Luke 20:38), this means that whether you are dead or alive, either way we are celebrating together our Saviour Jesus Christ Who is born, for today Heaven and earth make glad together. And let's you and I chant to the melody of "Angelic Powers":

Let the mountains drop forth their sweetness; for lo, God doth come forth from Heaven. Be ye vanquished, O ye nations; rejoice, O prophets; O ye patriarchs, leap for joy; clap your hands, all of mankind; for Christ, the great and mighty Ruler, is born. The King of Heaven is come on the earth.[2]

What joy for the Orthodox, both for Heaven and earth! Therefore, wherever you may be, I greet you, and I wish that you may rejoice together with the heavenly powers. Christ is born, give ye glory!

---

1. St. Barsanuphius, Answer #255.
2. Cf. Stichera of the Praises, December 20.

140. AFFLICTIONS: THE BEGINNING OF GLORY

April 14, 1883

Christ is risen, reverend [Mother] M.! Shine, shine, O new Jerusalem! For the glory of the Lord hath arisen upon thee.[1] But whence did the new Jerusalem acquire its new glory? From the Lord's sufferings. He adorned this new city with His sweat of Gethsemane, with His blood of Golgotha. And it turned out a wondrous Sion! Therefore, the Holy Church now invites all the faithful to come forth to meet the Bridegroom. "Bearing lights, let us go forth to meet Christ, Who cometh forth from the grave like a bridegroom, and let us celebrate the Pascha of God."[2] Before, the grave had been terrible — but after Christ lay in the grave, it became a royal palace; before, tribulations and pains had been terrible and comfortless — but after He Who is eternal Love drank to the full the cup of sorrows and even the bitter cup of death, then pains and tribulations flashed forth brighter than sapphire and gold, brighter than the stars of Heaven, brighter than the moon and the sun: because the God of gods Himself, the King of kings, was adorned with them. And he who wears these wounds as adornments, he it is who truly resembles Jesus Christ.

Rejoice, O Mary!

141. IN THE WORLD THERE ARE NO FEWER SORROWS THAN IN THE CONVENT

I hear that you are still coughing along — and getting around and even walking all the way to church. Only your cells don't satisfy you. Nonstop noise and vexations. And so I think I would go back to the world, because it is nice there. There everyone greatly loves the sick and they take care of them; and in general, in the world there is love of neighbor, peace, joy, sufficiency of everything — simply bliss. Right, M.? You baby chick! You are simply a baby chick — you don't even measure up to a brainless hen!

Who has told you that in the world people are better and afflictions fewer? After all, you were younger, healthy, not very discerning: you liked everything — but now do you really suppose that life in the world is that rosy? No, M., you think like a child. And the Devil takes advantage of your silly mind and deludes you with imaginary delights where they do not exist. The holy hierarch Dimitry, who is wiser and more

---

1. From the Paschal Canon.
2. Ibid.

experienced than you, and moreover a saint, and moreover a great teacher of the Russian Church — what does he say about the world's pleasures and alluring promises? He says, "The world promises gold, but delivers mud!"[1] That's your world for you! Just go and trust it! Why, for someone who is sick, it is wearisome and unbearable even in a royal palace. But here, at least, there is a great hope beyond any price that the Lord will recompense us for all our pains, for every sore, for every affliction, for every sigh! Do you believe me? So be at peace! Be reasonable! Be grateful to God! Why, if with your bird brain[2] you could see only a thousandth part of those blessings which are laid up by the merciful Lord for nuns, for His beloved brides, in recompense for pains and afflictions — then you would be greatly amazed, and you would even give your whole self to be burned in the fire! Save yourself!

XVI. LETTER TO M.G.

142. ABOUT THE SHAMORDINO ORPHANAGE
February 24, 1891

How are you, M. Your photograph made me very happy. I kept running around with it and just couldn't fix up a spot to put it. Well, I've found one now. I put it on my desk, and as I write I look at it, and it looks at me. And this cheers me up. How you and I used to walk in the forest. And now if only you could see: there are even more buds, and there will probably be a big crop of apples from them. And here and there you can already see signs of sweet juice oozing out.

Let me tell you some more news. In my building at Shamordino I have an awful lot of little girls downstairs. You saw them all at the orphanage, but now the orphanage has burned down, and I felt very sorry for them. And so I gave them the entire downstairs with the bath and the little fireplace. I took the littlest ones, around your height, some a bit smaller, some a bit bigger.

They bathe down there in the bath. They are happy there. And the church is close. The church is right across the street from my building. The older girls, around 30 of them, they moved down the hill, into the

---

1. This rhymes in Russian — "Mir obeshcháyet zláto, a dayét bláto."
2. Lit., "with your chicken brain."

empty laundry building. If you come, you will be a very short walk from the little ones. Your granddaughter now lives upstairs, above the little ones. She is often ill; pray for her. Pray for me also. Because I have been doing quite poorly. Peace to you, M.!

XVII. GENERAL LETTER

143. ON GOD'S OMNIPOTENCE

October 17, 1891

Peace to you, reverend mothers and sisters! On this day the Lord saved the royal family from a terrible wreck, not allowing one person to suffer injury, while everything else was reduced to splinters. . .[1] God Who then saved the royal family is the same today! His love and His might have not diminished by one iota; and therefore today, too, He is able to save His chosen flock from slaughter. We need only not become fainthearted. After all, one's life cannot be without temptations: *who is the man that shall live and not see death* (Ps. 88:46) — temptation, that is? Temptation is valuable in that it worketh patience, and patience — experience (Cf. Rom. 5:3,4). If there were no temptations, we would remain stupid ignoramuses. So let us reproach ourselves in our troubles, and not others...

---

1. October 17 — Anniversary of the Imperial Family's miraculous escape from a nearly fatal train wreck at Borki, near Kharkov in 1888, thought to be the result of two bomb blasts. Emperor Alexander III himself was able to hold up the heavy iron roof of the car so that his wife, children, and others could get clear of the wreckage. In gratitude, a large church in honor of the Icon of Our Saviour Not Made by Hands was built at the site. Each year on that day the Divine Liturgy was served in all the churches of the Empire, followed by a special service of thanksgiving and prayer for the Imperial Family and for the strengthening of piety and order in the land.

XVIII. LETTER TO V.

144. PATIENCE LEADS ONE INTO PARADISE

March 8, 1882

Reverend Sister V., I received all your letters and read them at once. And I am very sorry for you, that you grieve, and you slacken, and you become proud, and you become angry, and you do many other unmonastic things. Now, if you repent, may God forgive you. But still you must endure patiently. Blessed are they that wait patiently, for *they shall mount up with wings as eagles*, prophesies Isaiah (Is. 40:31). Now wouldn't you like to spread mighty wings like an eagle and fly around in the skies, in the gardens of Paradise? After all, this is not a fairy tale, but an eternal truth. But if you believe and you desire these mercies from God, endure patiently. This precisely is mighty wings; thus you will be exalted and glorified in the glory of God the Father and our Lord Jesus Christ.

XIX. LETTER TO E.

145. GIVE BLOOD AND RECEIVE SPIRIT[1]

November 11, 1889

Peace to you and God's blessing, reverend sister in the Lord E.! I received your letter overflowing with grief. You ask me to help your father in his grief — to comfort him with a letter: why, he is no less educated than I! What I know, that he knows also. But what is our knowledge?

In theory he has read, and written, and taught in church from the ambo[2] that one must endure patiently, have faith in God — but when he was hit[3] by practice, he lost his head. The same goes for me when it

---

1. This saying is also quoted in these letters and elsewhere, as "Give blood, and receive the Spirit." This is a saying of Abba Longinus, and is cited by St. Peter of Damascus in *The Philokalia*.
2. The word used in the Russian is "cathedra," but in contemporary Russian this word may also mean "ambo."
3. Lit., "when he was bitten."

comes to consoling others. Practice, that is, the word of God, says, "Give blood, and receive spirit," whereas our erudition schemes: isn't there some way to capture the "spirit" without losing the blood. And it won't capture it. But eternal Wisdom seeks, prods, calls us not to an imaginary life, but to the truth. And so He sends us a blow! *Give instruction to a wise man, and he will be yet wiser* (Prov. 9:9) But "an untried man is unpracticed."[1] Therefore the Apostle also teaches, *Tribulation worketh patience; and patience, experience* (Rom. 5:3,4). But we would like somehow to get around the tribulation and the patience and to be ranked with the experienced. But this is impossible! "Give blood," is what practice tells us!. . .

Again, I cannot and I will not undertake to strengthen your father in his grief, being myself none too proficient. But I am sending a leaflet of my much-beloved Father and benefactor Batiushka Makary, my first Elder and spiritual father. There you have both practice and theory to strengthen both a mind and a broken heart.

St. Mark the Ascetic writes, "It is good to help one's neighbor by counsel and by action — but even better to do so by prayer."[2] Therefore, in peace let us pray to the Lord, *Thou, O Lord, shalt keep us and shalt preserve us from this generation* (Ps. 11:7). Do not become overinvolved in the sorrows of this world, remembering the saying of our Lord to the disciple who asked to bury his father. . .

Do convey my profound respects and best wishes to your much-afflicted father, P.D.

May He Who arose from the dead and Who resurrects, Who brings forth light out of darkness, bestow upon him wisdom and peace.

Invoking God's blessing and peace upon you, and upon all of you, I remain, with sincere best wishes, your unworthy suppliant before God, the greatly sinful Hieromonk Anatoly.

---

1. St. Barsanuphius, Answer # 255.
2. Cf. St. Mark the Ascetic, "On Those who Think that They are Made Righteous by Works," #101.

XX. LETTERS TO M.G.

146. WE HAVE COME TO THE MONASTERY TO SEEK THE KINGDOM OF GOD AND NOT BODILY HEALTH

Sister in the Lord M., I received your letter, and in accordance with your request, I asked Batiushka concerning you, whether you may go home in order to recover your health. He answered, "It isn't necessary." And I, the sinner, am of the same opinion: we have come to the monastery to seek the Kingdom of God and not bodily health. If anyone needs health, "all these things shall be added unto him" (Cf. Matt. 6:33). With regard to your mother's blessing for you to enter the convent, do not worry on this account: concerning you and me and all such children, the Lord Himself has said, *He that loveth father or mother more than Me is not worthy of Me* (Matt. 10:37). But it would not be superfluous to humble yourself before her and ask her blessing now. Batiushka blesses you to stand in church, even if you sit [sometimes], or lean. . . Do not be discouraged on account of your impatience, but rather try to learn patience. If you do learn it, there will be honor for you.

147. DO NOT BE PROUD BECAUSE YOU PRACTICE THE JESUS PRAYER. THE FRUIT OF THIS PRAYER

March 1877

I read and reread your letter, and I could not get over how this little girl seemed so intelligent and alert to me — and what nonsense she's talking! She believes thoughts which tell her that to say the Jesus Prayer is something great! How silly you are, very silly! Why, I have told you that this prayer, which requires neither books nor prostrations nor other difficult struggles, is assigned to old women, the sick, and the stony-hearted. Of course, one who loves terribly to go to church will come before everyone else and will not miss a single word in church; on coming home, he sheds abundant tears, beholding his poverty and unworthiness; of course, one would not assign the Jesus Prayer to such a person. But you are silly and a failure in everything: you know neither how to pray, nor how to humble yourself, nor how to love those who grieve you, nor how to listen to God's word, nor any such thing. And yet you wish to be saved! So what were we to do with you? And so we gave you an easy, very easy little prayer, just five words long. But even here you have managed to find something specially great to set you apart from others. In other words, in your foolishness you would like to take pride in the very thing that should humble you. Naturally, the enemy is afraid that such a good-for-nothing girl will all of a sudden be saved, and so he tries to catch you any way he can and suggests false and stupid thoughts, as if you should take pride in the very thing that should humble you.

So stop your foolishness; hasten to Jesus, and not to the Devil. Jesus died for you, which means that He loves you. Whereas the Devil did not die for you, but rather wishes to kill you. And so do not listen to him. I asked Batiushka Amvrosy about you, and he said the same thing, "Let her continue, and not pay any attention to the Devil. As for her throat and her chest aching, it is on account of unworthiness." For every prayer, but especially this old folks' prayer, is appointed only for the sick and the unprofitable — of whom I, the most unprofitable one, am the worst — and requires humility and an awareness of one's infirmity. But out of stupidity you have taken it into your head to become puffed up! How silly you are, very silly!

Well, God will forgive you! Let us begin to correct ourselves! I myself also wish to make a beginning. Bless, O Lord!

With regard to joy welling up in your heart — this happens sometimes, as I think I have already told you. Sometimes the Lord wishes to console the struggler, seeing that he is already spent, sometimes from strenuous self-constraint in this prayer. It is said that *God* — that is, Jesus — *is a consuming Fire* (Heb. 12:29) (consuming sins and infirmities)! And so when one calls upon Him often, our sweetest Jesus cannot but gladden the heart. Only one most wretched like me, one calloused, may perhaps not be able to experience joy for a long time. But true workers of prayer after several days experience joy and sweetness welling forth from the heart into their entire being. Only, it is dangerous to accept it indiscriminately: for *Satan himself is transformed into an angel of light* (II Cor. 11:14). Therefore, as you are inexperienced in the spiritual life, be careful, and beware both of accepting it and of rejecting it. Read Mark the Ascetic's second discourse, chapter 28.[1] Read also chapter 134 of this sec-

---

1. "There is an energy of grace not understood by beginners, and there is also an energy of evil which resembles the truth. It is advisable not to scrutinize these energies too closely, because one may be led astray, and not to condemn them out of hand, because they may contain some truth; but we should lay everything before God in hope, for He knows what is of value in both of them." "On Those who Think that They are Made Righteous by Works" #101.

ond discourse.[1] But if you leave off prayer, then what are we going to do with you? Endure patiently. This will all soon pass, and you will come to love it. Prayer ceases usually from idle talking, gluttony, condemning others, and above all from pride.

Now since you are particularly proud, hold particularly tightly to this prayer. But since you are a little young for it never to cease — sit by the seaside and wait for fair weather!

You also cannot as yet refute thoughts — it is enough for you if you endure patiently and call upon Jesus. But if you do not see any sins in yourself, you are found in line with the Devil: he does not see his sins either, and since he never repents or blames himself, he thinks that God shows favoritism towards man because He loves him — but it is for this reason that God loves man, because he repents and humbles himself. So repent of everything and humble yourself, and God will save you!

148. ON THE GIFT OF THE DISCERNMENT OF THOUGHTS

April 6, 1877

In answer to your letter: 1) now have you learned from experience not to trust your thoughts? Be prudent in future. 2) I believe you do not have the virtues of humility and patience, which are essential for salvation: learn them. For God is not untrue, Who has said, "Seek, and ye shall find; ask, and it shall be given you" (Cf. Matt. 7:7). But if one were to simply give you this good thing, you would not even go about seeking it, and you would fall into pride. And so, humble yourself and pray, "Lord Jesus Christ, Son of God, have mercy on me, a sinner." And let that be enough for you. God will give you all that is needful — in its proper time.

A certain silly young girl asks, "Beg for me enlightenment of heart, so that I might be able to distinguish a right thought from a harmful one." Why, what is one to answer to this? You are aiming quite high, Matushka M.! You have someone to take your questions to, and so ask! And when you receive an answer, that's that. But as it is, this girl is a little presumptuous! Ask for her the gift of discernment yet! Why, this gift

---

1. "If you wish to remember God unceasingly, do not reject as undeserved what happens to you, but patiently accept it as your due. For patient acceptance of whatever happens kindles the remembrance of God, whereas refusal to accept weakens the spiritual purpose of the heart and so makes it forgetful." Ibid., #134.

is higher than all the Christian virtues! But give it to her! Look where she is climbing to! Now you have read the Patericon,[1] haven't you? In ancient Egypt not all of even the great Fathers possessed this gift. Just look what kind of Fathers: Makarios the Great in his old age went to Anthony to ask him [concerning his thoughts]. Pimen the Great went with his thoughts to Joseph of Panephysis; Pambo, Ammon, and many, many great saints did not dare to presume to such a virtue! But M.G-va wants it! A bit proud she is. . .

If you wish to have a conception of discernment, ask Matushka for the part of the Philokalia which has the discourse of Cassian to the Abbot Leontios[2] — that is, the last part of the Philokalia — and read it.

You ask that I not forsake you. Remember what the Lord said, "If a man keep My word, I and My Father will come unto him, and make Our abode with him" (Cf. John 14:23). And let that be enough for you.

You ask me to teach you "perfect kindness." Better go ask the Lord. He Himself invites those who desire it, *Come unto Me, all ye that labor and are heavy laden. Learn of Me, for I am meek and lowly* (Matt. 11:28,29). Cry out often, "Lord Jesus Christ, Son of God, have mercy on me, a sinner." And He Himself will teach you! Batiushka Father Amvrosy sends you his blessing. And I likewise.

149. AFFLICTIONS TEACH ONE PRAYER. THE EFFECT OF THE JESUS PRAYER

February 16, 1878

Batiushka Father Amvrosy sends you his blessing. And I, the sinner, pray for you, that the Lord may deem you worthy to reign with the saints in His eternal glory. As regards Matushka and the treasurer scolding you, I am very, very grateful to them for this. And not for nothing. Because nothing in the world so aids prayer as the patient endurance of tribulations, and love for one's neighbors. So if you did not have any tribulations, we would need to entreat the merciful Lord to send you some. Read the eighth point in the Instructions of Father Seraphim (of Sarov).[3] As for what is going on in your heart, do not worry about it. The

1. Patericon — A collection of Lives of monastic Fathers.
2. See St. John Cassian, "On the Holy Fathers of Sketis and on Discrimination," *The Philokalia*, Vol. I
3. In some Russian editions of St. Seraphim's Instructions, the eighth point is the one "On Prayer," emphasizing the Jesus Prayer.

name of Jesus bothers the enemy of our souls, who would have liked to make his dwelling in our heart, and so he goes to great lengths; but you do what you have been enjoined to do. Remember that Jesus, upon Whom you are calling, is mightier than the enemy. You absolutely must look up the book Seven Discourses of Mark the Ascetic and read it constantly. Glue yourself to it. Peace to you!

Consider yourself worse than everyone else in the world — and you will feel happier.

150. PRECAUTIONS IN SAYING THE JESUS PRAYER

April 16, 1886

Truly Christ is risen!. . . I received your letter and I am hastening to set your mind at rest. In the first place, you did not listen to me. I warned you not once but many times: when the prayer takes hold, by no means direct your attention downward. Otherwise you will be tormented by the passion of fornication. And this is not deception[1] but something pertaining to nature, resulting from incorrect mental activity. Now, if you were to take this sweetness for grace, then that would be deception. But as things stand, the situation can be corrected. The more so as you yourself recognize the muddle. Begin your correction with this: do not direct your attention downward, but keep your mind in the midst of your heart. But if it has already gotten into the habit of climbing downward, stop for a time and take up your reading. It would be good for you to obtain the book of Paissy Velichkovsky. You need to read it. Keep to this rule, and you will not be lost. But do not leave off saying the prayer. Such aberrations happen with many. Peace to you and salvation.

151. WITH INSTRUCTION IN MENTAL PRAYER, EXPERIENCE IS NECESSARY

January 26, 1887

Peace to you and God's blessing, suffering sister, Mother M. I received your letter. I see your sorrow and your pain. You complain that I have forsaken you. That is not true: I remembered you always, and I still remember you, and I heartily sympathize with you, only I did not want to constrain you when you expressed your desire to change to another father.

If I were to give you an answer, I would need either to permit you to do so or to forbid you. But if I were to forbid you, you would probably ascribe this to self-esteem on my part, whereas to permit you to do this

---

1. Prelest, in Russian.

would mean taking upon my soul the responsibility if your new teacher were to lead you by a different path. But for you that would be doubly dangerous, because you are going by the path of mental prayer. If he himself does not even know this way, then where is he going to lead you to? In my experience, those with learning, even with much learning from books, in practice have not understood this spiritual activity one bit.[1] Because this way comes to one not by books but by blood. "Give blood, and receive spirit."[2] But now I see that your wish to change to another was a whim, and so I am addressing you as of old. May God forgive all your sins! Say the Jesus Prayer according to your strength. And when you weaken, have just the remembrance of God's presence. Do not grieve that the prayer is not uninterrupted — it is too early for that. Instead, thank God for what you do have. Save yourself, and may the Lord save you.

152. ON THE JESUS PRAYER OF THE LIPS AND OF THE HEART
(LETTER OF THE ELDER AMVROSY)[3]

April 24, 1887

Sister in the Lord and my spiritual child M., I received your letter of April 4. You write that your Elders have entirely forsaken you. They haven't at all forsaken you, only lack of time does not permit us to write to you often. You write that during the time of prayer you have movements of the flesh and polluted, blasphemous thoughts. Probably during the time of prayer you keep the inner attention of your mind very low. The heart of a person is located under the left nipple; if a person who is praying keeps the attention of his mind lower than this, then there occur movements of the flesh.

Practice oral prayer more, and you will be freed from such movements. No one has ever fallen into deception from oral prayer, but it is dangerous to practice mental prayer of the heart without guidance. Such prayer requires guidance, angerlessness, silence, and humble self-

---

1. Lit., "one hair."
2. See footnote, Letter #145.
3. Alongside Father Anatoly's letters there were found several letters of Hieroschemamonk Father Amvrosy to the same person and on the same subject. Since these letters are both interesting in themselves, and also supplement and clarify Father Anatoly's letters, we have deemed it essential to include them here also along with the letters of Father Anatoly. By reading and comparing them, one may see what a spiritual closeness existed between the two Elders. (This footnote is from the Russian text.)

reproach in all adverse circumstances. Therefore, it is always safer to practice oral prayer, since we are poor in patience, humility, and angerlessness, which is why we must pray especially at times of disturbance both for ourselves and for those who have grieved us, "Lord Jesus Christ, Son of God, have mercy on us sinners."

There is no time to write more. Hold to humility and self-reproach, and the Lord will help you. You ask to come: even if you do come, you won't get to me quickly because I have gotten old and weak, and I am greatly burdened with many visitors. Peace to you and God's blessing!

Greatly sinful Hieromonk Amvrosy

P.S. — Write to Father Anatoly and ask him to answer.

153. MORE ON THE JESUS PRAYER

October 30, 1889

Peace to you and God's blessing, reverend Mother M.! I received your letter. There is no indication when it was sent. Now, I asked you to indicate the date, the year, etc. And I threatened you that I would stop writing. All to no avail! Which is why you are permitted to experience trials.

On receiving your letter, I put it aside in order to give special attention to it later. But it disappeared. The cell attendants and I went through everything, shook everything out — no letter. Only just now we found it by accident. After reading your letter (of unknown date), I went immediately to Batiushka Amvrosy. And we went through it together. We found nothing incorrect in your prayer. Only one should not accept such things as fragrance. St. Symeon the New Theologian writes about this in his second method of prayer.[1] One should not insistently search out the place of the heart: when the prayer develops, it will find it of itself. Our endeavor

---

1. Actually, this is mentioned in his discussion of the first method of prayer. See *Writings from the Philokalia on Prayer of the Heart*, trans. E. Kadloubovsky and G.E.H. Palmer, (London: Faber & Faber, 1951), p.153.

is to enclose the mind in the words, "Lord Jesus Christ, Son of God, have mercy on me." The holy hierarch Dimitry teaches, "Where the mind is, there the heart is also."

With regard to your prayer being interrupted — there is no way it can be otherwise. If it were to remain constant, the holy Fathers teach, "then fear. That is the way of wolves."[1] But how to describe our situation? What do we observe in the atmosphere? Alternating rain and sun, snow and wind, heat and cold. Thus it is also with our condition: our state cannot and should not remain the same. Now when mental prayer ceases, take up oral prayer or reading. And when even this won't go forward, take up handiwork.

To change your guide in mid-course is dangerous. Of course, to change to Batiushka Father Amvrosy would make absolutely no difference, but that is because our teaching is one and the same, and we had one and the same teacher. But not everyone is like this. There is a proverb, "Every fine fellow takes after his own model."[2] To Batiushka Amvrosy you may always write without the least hesitation. But beware of consulting those whom you do not know — especially in your halfway-there condition. God will bless you to continue the work you have begun, without the least fear or hesitation. God is our helper. Those who are self-directed, it is true, ought to fear. But he who acknowledges his infirmity and inquires of others has good hopes. Only always reproach yourself and humble yourself. Peace to you and salvation. Your unworthy suppliant before God, the greatly sinful Hieromonk Anatoly.

154. MORE ON THE JESUS PRAYER, AND ON VISIONS (LETTER OF THE ELDER AMVROSY)

November 7, 1889

Sister in the Lord and my spiritual child, Mother M., Peace to you and God's blessing and all establishment in the truth. *Be strong in the Lord, and in the power of His might* (Eph. 6:10). I received your letter. You bring forward a complaint against Father Anatoly, that he does not

---

1. "One moment there is cold, and soon after, burning heat, and then perhaps hail, and after a little, fair weather. This is the manner in which we are trained. . . In a time of joy let us expect affliction, and in a time of affliction let us expect help. In this manner our path is made smooth. But the man who deviates from it will be prey for wolves." — From the *First Syriac Epistle of St. Makarios of Alexandria*, quoted in *The Ascetical Homilies of St. Isaac the Syrian*, p.455.
2. This rhymes in the Russian — "Kázhdi molodéts na svóy obrazéts."

answer you. Father Anatoly came to me not long ago and said regretfully that it had taken him a long time to answer your important letter due to many things to do, and due to forgetfulness. And he added that he had just sent you a registered letter, which you have probably already received by now.

The enemy disturbs you with various perplexities. The holy Fathers advise us not to fear when we call upon the name of God, the more so as you have begun this work not in a self-directed manner but with a blessing. With regard to what you do not understand, leave it without special significance, neither rejecting it nor accepting it, as St. Mark the Ascetic advises those who are children spiritually — as, for example, that you beheld Christ crucified within your heart, and our Saviour imprisoned, wearing a red garment, and some kind of incomprehensible light. This and all similar things leave to the will of God, saying to yourself, "God alone knows what is beneficial and saving."

Read in the Philokalia all the passages on deception, and beware of the indicated signs of deception. Leave everything else to the will of God.

You write that as you say the prayer, you look at your heart. The holy Fathers advise us during the time of prayer to look within the heart, not from the top, or from the side; and especially if the mind's attention descends below the heart, carnal passion is aroused.

You write that on the feast of St. John the Theologian you left the church because of exhaustion and went to your cell, and as you lay on your bed, you saw the enemy in all his hideousness, running. In future, if you become exhausted in church, sit or lie down, but do not leave. Know in general, as you yourself have also read in the books of the Fathers, that there is nothing that antagonizes the enemy so much as the Jesus Prayer. Therefore, as you have begun to practice the Jesus Prayer, do not leave off, but continue, trusting in God's help and mercy. The Lord and the Heavenly Queen are mighty to keep us from evils and calamities inflicted by our spiritual enemies.

You write that some of the sisters there turn to Athonite elders for guidance. But you do not know them, nor they you. Therefore, such relations with them cannot be opportune. Invoking upon you peace and God's blessing, I remain, with sincere best wishes, the greatly sinful Hieromonk Amvrosy.

P.S. — It also says in your letter that for about three days you had strong disturbance and rebellion of the flesh. Probably you condemned someone, or it was permitted as a trial unto humility.

155. MORE CONCERNING OCCURRENCES WHILE SAYING THE JESUS PRAYER

July 18, 1890

Peace to you and the blessing of the Lord! I received your letter and read it carefully. I found nothing remarkable in it with regard to your practice of prayer. Read also chapter 43 of Callistus and Ignatius; there all eventualities are described.[1] With regard to the prayer having stopped, of course there is a reason for this: either conceit or condemnation of others. Above all, we must be humble. . .

With regard to apparitions of light — yellow or white or whatever — do not accept them, as you have been told: that is, neither exile them nor become enthralled by them. Read about this in Mark the Ascetic's centuries,[2] and be at peace.

156. ON TEMPTATIONS DURING THE TIME OF PRAYER

August 11, 1892

Sister in the Lord and my spiritual child, Mother M., I received your

---

1. This chapter, "Of the alterations and changes which occur in every man and about the high rank of humility," begins "We wish you to know also that even those who have reached perfection through self-purification and enlightenment, as far as this is possible (for in our imperfect age there is no perfect perfection but only partial perfection) — even those do not always remain unchanged. Owing to natural weakness or through self-aggrandizement which at times steals in, such men occasionally suffer a change and are robbed of their gains as a test, but later are again granted the most powerful intercessions. For stability and unchangeableness is a property of the future life; in the present life, there may be a time of purity, peace and Divine comfort, and times when impure agitation and sorrow become mixed with them. This happens according to the life and progress of each man, and according to the Lord's own inscrutable ways, so that we may realize our weakness (for blessed is he who is aware of his weakness, as someone says); and, according to St. Paul, we *should not trust in ourselves, but in God which raiseth the dead* (II Cor. 1:9)." The chapter concludes with extensive quotes from St. Isaac the Syrian. See *Writings from the Philokalia on Prayer of the Heart*, pp. 216-218.

2. See Footnote , Letter #147.

letter of August 5. . . As you perform prayer, sometimes you have sleepiness, lethargy, weariness, and lukewarmness toward everything for several days at a time or even a week. It is very possible that prior to this you were plundered by a secret adversary — vainglory, pride, or condemnation of others, or anger, or some other thing. Thus our spiritual enemy tyrannizes over our nature so that we would waste our days in idleness and slothfulness instead of preparing for eternity. "The slumber of my slothfulness," it is written, "prepares eternal torment."[1] Sometimes it providentially happens even with great strugglers that grace as it were withdraws for a time so that a man would recognize more fully the infirmity of his nature and have recourse the more to God, asking His assistance and protection. For great strugglers striving and laboring in prayer, this is the most auspicious time to lay hold of great crowns, since the Kingdom of God suffereth violence, and the violent take it by force (Cf. Matt. 11:12). But even if we are vanquished by our weakness, let us not be despondent on this account but rather, humble ourselves and struggle with God's help. The strength of God is made perfect in weakness (Cf. II Cor. 12:9). Mourning according to God is most profitable, and *they that sow with tears*, it is said, *shall reap with rejoicing, bearing the sheaves* (Ps. 125:6,8) of good intentions and works. Of course, it is good to choose a suitable place in the church so as to conceal this gift of God from others. Both lying down and arising it is good to have mourning according to God. The holy Prophet-King David even while on the royal throne had time and had the custom of watering his couch with his tears (See Ps. 6:5). And for us sinners it is even more fitting to do so. Help us, O Lord!. .

Pray for the one who hates you; the Lord is mighty to reconcile her with you. By her hatred she harms herself spiritually, being incited by the enemy — whereas she benefacts you, for *blessed are ye, when men shall revile you*. . . (Matt. 5:11).

157. TAKE CARE FOR YOUR SALVATION WITHOUT BEING HINDERED BY WHAT OTHERS WILL SAY

September 20, 1892

Sister in the Lord, Mother M., I received your letter. I am not resigning from myself writing you letters. But what am I to do? Out of neces-

---

1. Cf. Sessional Hymn of Compunction, Tuesday, Plagal of First Tone.

sity sometimes I will have to entrust someone else with it, like this time, on account of my weakness and illness.

May the Lord help you to peacefully endure the afflictions which are befalling you. Such is the path of the friends of God: to pass the days of this fleeting life in constriction and tribulations, in order to inherit eternal blessedness with all the saints. *Many are the tribulations of the righteous* (Ps. 33:19), *many are the scourges of the sinner,* says the Psalmist, *but mercy shall encircle him that hopeth in the Lord* (Ps. 31:10). *In your patience possess ye your souls* (Luke 21:19), and it is only he that shall endure unto the end, who shall be saved (Cf. Matt. 24:13). As you have been writing simply and straightforwardly,[1] so continue to write. Do not listen to the demon of vainglory concerning what others might think of you; let each attend to himself. The enemy of man's salvation never spares but wounds people in various ways. It is enough for each to attend to his own salvation and see to the healing of his wounds, without analyzing the political situation.[2] You can see from your own experience what manner of warfare and how great an army is raised up against our infirmity. Except the Lord guard the city, in vain do they labor that build it (Cf. Ps. 126: 1, 2). But God is our *helper and protector*(Ex. 15: 2; First Ode). So let us *not be afraid for the terror by night, nor for the arrow that flieth by day* (Ps. 90: 5). *Let Israel hope in the Lord, and He shall redeem him out of all his iniquities. . . (Ps. 129: 5, 6).

A postscript in Father Anatoly's own hand —

. . . You write of unspeakable spiritual joy after Communion of the Holy Mysteries of Christ. The all-good Lord knows how to comfort His servants who often faint beneath the burden of tribulations, so that in future also they would not become despondent and fainthearted but trust in God's mercy. . .

Do not use cleverness in prayer, but go about it more simply. The Lord said, "Except ye become as little children, ye cannot enter into the Kingdom of God" (Cf. Matt. 18:3).

Do not let it disturb you that I do not always write personally. Father V. has written for Father Amvrosy for many years. He has experience. However, I will of course write the more important ones. . .

---

1. Lit., "unpolitically."
2. I.e., without worrying about what others might think.

158. YOU WILL NOT PERISH ON ACCOUNT OF THOUGHTS WITH WHICH YOU DO NOT SYMPATHIZE

You will not perish on account of thoughts with which you do not sympathize and from which you at least try to be freed. Only repent, and humble yourself. And God will forgive you. With regard to the enemy depicting for you life in the world, and marriage — that is his wont. Both in olden times and in our own, fornication and the supposed ease of life in the world are the very first weapons of the Devil against monastics. However, if you are enticed by these things but later repent, God will not account it to you as a sin. You may take in your sister for now for a visit. But take care lest she ruin your manner of life, which is feeble enough as it is.

To ask elders for advice and then not fulfill it out of reliance on one's own cleverness is sinful — but not to fulfill it out of weakness is pardonable. And to reproach oneself for not having fulfilled it is saving. The Lord hears everyone's prayers. It is only those of the proud that He does not accept. But He always accepts the prayers of the humble and of those who reproach themselves. The Lord is helping you, only you do not see this. He cannot forsake you, because He loves you.

159. CARNAL THOUGHTS ARE A SURE SIGN OF DECEPTION IN PRAYER

Peace to you, Sister M.! Do not let your prayer descend downward. Keep it at the top of your heart. Otherwise, you will have grief. If you begin to have warmth lower down [in your heart], try to move it upward or at least into the middle of your heart — otherwise, better stop. Carnal thoughts are a sure sign of deception. Now if you have warmth in the loins, that is, the small of the back, that is all right, so continue — but again, only so long as carnal thoughts do not appear. If they do, stop. And that is how you should pray.

160. YOU ARE SAVING YOURSELF QUITE INEPTLY

Matushka, you seem to be saving yourself quite ineptly! Be more humble. . . Do not be overzealous about prayer. Remember what the holy

Fathers have said: "Your salvation lies in your neighbor."[1] Read the seven discourses of St. Makarios of Egypt. Especially chapter 14 of the first discourse.

161. THE JESUS PRAYER CANNOT BE STRONG WITHOUT STRONG AFFLICTIONS

Again you enumerate your troubles, M. They are still the same and in them I find nothing particularly terrible or dreadful or hopeless.

You have simply lost your wits, and all kinds of awful things are befalling you — despair, despondency. . . Now, I have told you that the Jesus Prayer cannot be strong without strong afflictions. But you don't even want to hear about this — you don't want either Jesus or Paradise or anyone in the world: all you want is to run away from your troubles... Once more I repeat God's word to you, and not for the first time or for the second, *We must through much tribulation enter into the Kingdom of God* (Acts 14:22). "The mercy of God is hidden in sufferings."[2]

"Blessed are ye, when men shall revile and persecute you, and say all manner of evil for My sake. Rejoice and be glad, for your reward is great in the Heavens" (Cf. Matt. 5:11,12).

But M. wants neither reward, nor Heaven, nor God, nothing — just to run away to T. from her troubles. Well, you will run away from God, too. Why, you are a nun yet: you have come to the convent for the sake of God, to patiently endure everything for the Lord's sake — for the sake of our Bridegroom Jesus, Who laid down His life for us, Who died a dishonorable death upon the Cross. Therefore, He is preparing His glory for you by means of tribulations and revilings. And you will be with Him unto the ages — I both assured you of this, and I continue to assure you of it by a true word. Not by my own sinful word but by His word, that of the Lord Jesus: *Where I am, there shall also My servant be* (John 12:26). "If we suffer with Him, we shall also be glorified with Him" (Cf. Rom 8:17; II Tim. 2:12).

---

1. See Letter #117.
2. St. Mark the Ascetic, "On Those Who Think That They are Made Righteous by Works," #139.

162. PATIENTLY ENDURE AFFLICTIONS AND SCORN IN ORDER
FOR THE PRAYER TO BE STRENGTHENED

At last M. has managed to make me happy by drying her bitter tears! Why, I wrote to you that you find things difficult not because your troubles are unbearable, but because you yourself are half-baked. See, you were patient, the storm of temptation passed — and your troubles are the same, your life is the same — but it is bearable, it is all right!

Know that if you will listen from now on, you will find so much consolation that you yourself will want tribulations — this matchless treasure — but it will be too late![1] Batiushka sends you his blessing. I told him how you are suffering; he answered that this is permitted on account of the prayer. This means if you leave off the prayer, then the tribulations will go away too. . . The prayer can only cease on account of great sins, or if someone does not repent and condemn himself. The person who repents, on the other hand, feels the need for this prayer. Only one must maintain profound humility and an awareness of one's vileness. The very best means for the prayer to become firmly established is patient endurance of afflictions and scorn. . . which means that you yourself have ruined everything!

. . . As for carnal thoughts before Communion, they are from the enemy!

163. YOU CANNOT ESCAPE YOUR CROSS

Reverend Sister M., Many are your letters which I have lying here. But much more numerous are your woes! So what am I to do with them, weak and sinful as I am myself? I have told you, just like I always tell myself, *Have patience! Have patience until the anger of the Lord shall have passed away* (Is. 26:20). After all, it is not eternally that you and I will suffer! The Lord Himself has said by the mouth of David, "According to the multitude of sorrows, Thy consolations brought gladness unto my soul" (Cf. Ps. 93:19). Now, consolations M. wouldn't mind having! As for her

---

1. See Letter #328, on the "Dread Judgment": "Of course, at that moment those who ran away from afflictions here will grieve a little. Those afflictions there crown those who were afflicted. . . Still, the common rejoicing will be so great that just looking at our neighbors we will have consolation and gladness."

sufferings — isn't there some way she can blame them all on Matushka? And maybe on her favorite Batiushka as well! If only she could be rid of those accursed illnesses! Poor M.! And I had such hopes for you!

What Matushka says to you, receive as from the Lord's mouth! And He Who is all-merciful and abundant in love will reward you for this — that is, He will Himself reward you personally. Love your neighbors and those living with you, and think well of them. If you cannot, then bemoan yourself and cry out to Jesus! Even if N— takes you into her cell, and. . . and even if the Tsar Emperor himself were to take you into his palace — still, you yourself and no one else must carry the cross appointed for you! You have been baptized (krestílas) — well, so carry your cross (krest)!

164. NOT EVERY ENERGY OF PRAYER IS COMPREHENSIBLE FOR THOSE WHO ARE INEXPERIENCED

Do pray, but do not evaluate your prayer. That is not your business. Remember the chapter of St. Mark the Ascetic, chapter 28 of his second discourse: "There is an energy of grace not understood by beginners, and there is also an energy of evil which resembles the truth. It is advisable not to scrutinize these energies too closely." What one should do is ask those who are practiced in spiritual matters. And so, you too, do not seek to find out what is sent from whom; instead, have patience in all things, and notify us. If oral prayer of itself turns into mental prayer, there is no need to stop. Only reproach yourself constantly, and do not be anxious... Do not ask God for tribulations, but patiently endure those He sends.

When they reproach you, if you can endure it, endure; if you cannot, answer quietly.

165. IN PRAYER RELY UPON THE WILL OF GOD (LETTER OF THE ELDER AMVROSY)

(This first part was written at the dictation of Father Amvrosy)... You ask me to pray that the Lord would either deliver you from your illness or cut short the days of your life, but it is the latter that you would prefer. I will say to this that it is better and more profitable to rely upon the will of God and pray thus: "O Lord, as Thou knowest and as Thou wishest, do that which is profitable for me according to Thy holy will." Have you not read what an elder replied to a brother who asked him, "Why does my soul desire death?" The elder answered, "Because you wish to avoid tribulation, and you do not know that the tribulation to come is much more grievous than the present one." And another elder said that if you understood what future rest is and future torment, then even if your cell were full of worms so that you stood in them up to your neck, you would endure this without faltering (Abba Dorotheos, 12th instruction). Therefore, let us instead surrender ourselves to the will of our all-good Lord, that He may arrange for us that which is profitable.

One should on no account despair of God's mercy, bringing to mind the examples of the harlot in the Gospel, the thief, and the publican, who repented and received forgiveness from the merciful Lord. . . (A postscript of Father Anatoly:) Batiushka himself dictated this in answer to your letter. As for me, the sinner, I wrote to you not long ago. For now I will just confirm Batiushka's words, wishing you salvation.

XXI. LETTER TO ABBESS N—

166. CONCERNING A CONFUSED NOVICE AND CONCERNING AN INCIDENT WHICH OCCURRED IN FATHER MAKARY'S TIME

Your right reverence, all-honorable and most worthily respected Matushka N—,

I read your letter with the evaluations of the two young novices. I asked Batiushka about both of them. I am writing them each a letter. Batiushka enjoins M. not to leave off saying the Jesus Prayer. As for stubborn E., he said she was to blame. He says it is her own fault: why does she accept the thoughts. These thoughts are the same as blasphemous thoughts: one should not listen to them but reject them — that is the whole secret — whereas she herself grieves and yet listens to the Devil and believes him, as if he really could do something. I told her all this and she was steadied, but now again she has begun to waver. On this subject Batiushka told me of an incident in Batiushka Makary's time. There was a Father P. living here with us... At that time he was accepting the same kind of thoughts, as bad as E. Once Batiushka Makary scolded him and threw him out. Father P., not knowing why Batiushka Makary had become angry, told everything to Batiushka Amvrosy, who himself turned to the Elder, expressing his surprise that here Father P. was battling so with his thoughts, and yet it was his fault and he had incurred Father Makary's wrath. Batiushka Makary answered, "It is because I told him to pay no attention to his thoughts and to shun them — and instead, he still keeps listening to them. . ."

. . . From my heart wishing you all peace, consolation, and joy in the risen Lord, I remain with sincere deep respect and devotion, the unworthy Hieromonk Anatoly.

XXII. LETTERS TO A.N.

167. FIGHT YOUR LITTLE PASSIONS

October 30, 1879

Peace to you, S., novice of God! Are you still well? Do you still become angry as before? And are you fighting your little passions? Fight on, fight on, be a good soldier of Christ! Do not give way to malice, and do not be captivated by carnal enticements. And if you should slip, hasten to the Physician, crying out with the Holy Church, our mother, "O God, number me with the thief, the harlot, and the publican (repentant, of course), and save me."[1] And know that a repentant sinner is dearer to God than a self-satisfied righteous man. And so beware of condemning others!

168. WHAT "LET US ARISE IN THE DEEP DAWN" MEANS

March 20, 1885

Christ is risen! I greet you, reverend Sister A., with the radiant feast of the Resurrection of Christ. "Let us arise in the deep dawn."[2] This does not mean simply to get up early and start chanting, "Let us arise. . .," but to be vigilant both day and night, that is, not to become despondent in tribulations, not to despair when we do not see our desire fulfilled, not to become puffed up in successes, and so on. It is such virgins, that is, vigilant ones, who are called "wise." And there is no one to prevent your having a brightly burning lamp, too. But if you do not wish to, well, go ahead and sleep. That is, quarrel with those who are quarrelsome, work

---

1. Cf. Sessional Hymn of Compunction, Monday, Grave Tone.
2. From the Paschal Canon.

for gain, let your mind wander during the services, stuff your stomach with food, etc. . . And, well, you will sleep right through the Kingdom of Heaven. But may this not be, and I trust in the Lord that it shall not be. But we shall behold Christ radiant and saying, "Rejoice!"[1]

169. IT IS GOOD TO SAY YOUR THOUGHTS

I praise your wise emulation of the good sisters in going to Matushka [to say your thoughts]. May God bless you in this good work.

Say what you can. . . If you do not correct yourself, reproach and condemn yourself. The Lord will receive even this as a good work. Avoid conversations, and in general, every sin; and if you slip, repent, and the Lord will help you, and you will be more practiced and more careful. Above all, never become disturbed.[2]

170. ONE MUST BE PEACEFUL

. . . Still you fight with Nastya. It has become perpetual: two bears in one sewing room. So here is what you should do: at a convenient moment, talk to Nastya about getting along peacefully. Only know that you will have to give in to her: *in honor preferring one another* (Rom. 12:10) Without love for one's neighbor, it is hard to be saved. One way or another we are going to have to tackle this virtue, or we won't be saved, period.

171. RULES FOR YOUR LIFE

I received your letter. . . And I make answer to your questions. If they read the Gospel in trapeza, you may omit it in your cell. About fulfilling the prayer rule of 100 — may God bless. About drinking tea on days you receive Communion and on feasts — you may if you wish. Do

---

1. See the Paschal Canon.
2. See *The Ascetical Homilies of St. Isaac the Syrian*, Homily 8, p. 70: "Therefore, whoever is walking upon the path of God must give thanks to Him for all things that come upon him, and revile and blame his own soul, and know that he would not have been delivered over by his Provider except for the sake of negligence, in order that his mind might be awakened, or else because he has become puffed up. But he should not be overly disturbed on this account, nor quit the arena and the fight, nor leave himself free of self-reproach, lest his evil grow twofold."

not let thoughts bother you which say that tomorrow and the day after you will still be suffering the same as now — that is the Devil's wont. What will happen is not what the Devil foretells but what God ordains. Regarding your having become all involved in a thought in church, may God forgive. Only try to collect your thoughts. That is the work of monastics. Try to say the Jesus Prayer often, especially when thoughts bother you. If you become distracted, reproach yourself. And that will be enough.

It is good that you are trying not to condemn your neighbor and not to be proud: if you will attend to yourself, in time the Lord will help you, and you will receive eternal salvation!

172. DO NOT BE AFRAID TO DISCLOSE YOUR THOUGHTS

Christ is risen! We celebrate the death of death, the destruction of Hades, the beginning of a new and everlasting life. And with leaps of joy we praise the Cause thereof,[1] that is, Jesus Christ. But you are in despair and are so afraid to disclose your infirmities to me that you are overcome by fear and choked. I myself am a sinful man, but I believe the Lord Who said, "I came to save sinners" (Cf. Mark 2:17). And I am a sinner, so it follows that the Lord will save me also. What is frightening is when someone sins and does not repent. But you and I, we try to repent, as much as we can. So do not be despondent. Thoughts war against very many people — it is only the humble whom they dare not touch. But we do not have humility, and therefore we suffer disgrace. You cannot repulse these thoughts as yet; instead, have recourse quickly to Jesus, i.e., say the Jesus Prayer.

---

1. From the Paschal Canon.

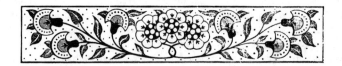

XXIII. LETTERS TO S.Ch.

173. YOU CANNOT LEARN THE SPIRITUAL LIFE RIGHT AWAY

November 27, 1888

Peace to you and God's blessing! You grieve that you are living poorly. In that case, there is hope of correction. But it is not surprising that you are not the person you should be: you have come to learn the spiritual life. After all, no doubt you did not grasp the simple alphabet right away — and this is a lofty discipline. You cannot learn it right away. Even great saints of God — Basil the Great, Gregory the Theologian, Tikhon of Zadonsk, and many, many Fathers — none of them shone forth right off. Learn. Be patient, and await God's mercy. You have fears? That is childishness. It will pass. Read in St. John of the Ladder the step "On Cowardice." It is all right to love one's relatives, but in moderation. *He that loveth father or mother more than Me is not worthy of Me* (Matt. 10:37). Read the second and third steps in this same book. Guard your eyes. The Lord commanded, *If thine eye offend thee, pluck it out* (Matt. 18:9). You will bring warfare upon yourself if you do not learn to guard your eyes and your tongue.

Learn to be meek and silent, and you will be loved by all. Senses which are left open are like an open gate: dogs and cats run in. . . and make a mess. You cannot leave your epitimia[1] unfulfilled. Not even the Bishop can release you from it. Figure out how much you have not fulfilled, and complete it. Perform the Rule of 500[2] — but perform the epitimia first.

Ask to be excused from reading, or you will lose your eyesight. And in time also from close work, if your eyes continue to hurt. Save yourself, sister!

---

1. Epitimia — A rule given by a spiritual father to a penitent to help in correcting some sin. In Letter #173, this is a rule of prayer. In Letter #351, it is God Who chastises the sinner with an inner chastisement.

2. A cell rule of prayer of Optina Hermitage, cited in full in *The Elder Joseph of Optina*, trans. Holy Transfiguration Monastery, (Boston, 1984), p. 208.

174. FIGHT COURAGEOUSLY AGAINST THE DEVIL

April 2, 1889

I greet you, sister in the Lord S., with the radiant feast of the Resurrection of Christ! "It is the day of Resurrection, let us be radiant, O ye peoples! For Christ God hath brought us from death unto life, and from earth unto Heaven."[1] It is frightening that even after this there are found foolish people who do not wish to behold this grace. They do not rejoice that they have been raised from earth unto Heaven, from a sinful life to a holy one! Even the young novice S. finds reasons to despair. But who, it would seem, has more cause for thanking God than you? In your youth the Lord has brought you into the choir of His elect women; He has showed you the convent most conducive to your salvation; He did not deprive you of nearness to elders — but all this is too little for you, and you are sad. Turn to the Mother of God and say to her, "Thou, O Lady, hast brought me to thy chosen flock; do thou also pasture me. Thou wast able to save Mary of Egypt — wilt thou not be able to save me also?"

The Devil has much malice because you have escaped his claws; he wanted to make short work of you as he has of your relatives. And so now he is jealous, and ashamed in front of his demons that he has let a victim get away, and that a young girl has outwitted him. All this aggravates him, and he wars against you, thirsting to swallow you up — but he will not be able to. For the Lord Himself has said, *Greater is He that is in you, than he that is in the world* (I John 4:4). That is, Jesus, the Vanquisher of Hades and of the Devil, is greater than the prince of this world. "He that trusteth in the Lord shall be as Mount Sion, nevermore shall he be shaken" (Cf. Ps. 124:1). So forsake childish faintheartedness: this is a serious matter — your soul, and the endless Kingdom which your enemy, the Devil, lost. All the heavenly powers are watching you struggle against the prince of this world and entreating the Almighty to help you. Yea, He will help you, only do not be despondent! The Lord is near! "We celebrate the death of death, the destruction of Hades, the beginning of a new and everlasting life. And with leaps of joy we praise the Cause thereof, the only blest God of our Fathers."[2] Peace to you! *Be thou manful, and let thy heart be strengthened* (Ps. 26:16)!

---

1. From the Paschal Canon
2. Ibid.

XXIV. LETTERS TO A.S.

175. AN ENCOURAGEMENT IN THE DECISION TO ENTER A CONVENT

August 27, 1881

Peace to you and the blessing of the Lord, A.! You write that your mama and grandpa are glad about your desire to join the choir of the holy and wise virgins. I, too, rejoice and am comforted by your desire. And how can we not rejoice over you when even the angels in the Heavens rejoice over such a work? *Blessed is he whom Thou hast chosen and taken to Thyself* (Ps. 64:4), O Lord! Especially in youth! As for the speeches of those who love the world — forget about them. Concerning them, the Lord Who is eternal Love incarnate said, *Let the dead bury their dead* (Matt. 8:22). It is not given to them to know the mysteries of the Kingdom; their joys and delights are from the earth and will depart with them into the earth. But you, young and feeble though you may be, because of the heavenly Father's love for you and without yourself realizing it, have come to know and to love the angelic life, the God-like life — and there awaits you the lot of the saints and eternal gladness! Do not be downcast on account of your weakness and inexperience; Paul himself, who was firmer than a rock, teaches, *My strength is made perfect in weakness* (II Cor. 12:9). So will you ever dare to imagine, little girl, that of yourself you can do anything? God is our helper! If He did not forsake you while you were living in the world but taught you to seek out eternal truths, (which the wise men of this world cannot even understand) — then is He going to forsake you now as you consecrate your entire life to Him? You need never worry about that. God loves you much more than you imagine. And here is the best sign of this: you are sad when the topic of conversation is worldly but rejoice when the conversation is about spiritual things. Where did you learn this? God placed the spark in your heart. So be careful — do not quench it! Your fearfulness is natural. It happens even with those who have lived in the monastery for a long time. A man who is untried is unpracticed.[1] Your mother is having you wait a year to

---

1. See footnote, Letter #85.

test your aptitude for monasticism — but how can you be making trial of it without even seeing the convent? Wouldn't it be better to spend this trial year profitably in the convent? . . . Save yourself, A.! *The Lord bless thee out of Sion, and mayest thou see the good things of Jerusalem* (Ps. 127:6)!

176. YOU WILL NOT LEARN MONASTICISM WITHOUT LIVING IN A MONASTERY

September 7, 1881

I received your letter, A. And your second one, too. About 50 years ago I was studying Greek anecdotes in my reader. There was one story there about how a certain scholastic very nearly drowned while bathing. After that, he wouldn't go near any water until he learned to swim. In the same way you want to learn how to swim on dry land — that is, to learn monasticism at home, in town. Plenty of opportunities for it — especially at the time of the fair. Better try monasticism in a monastery. In any case, it is better to live for a while in a holy convent, even if it is just as you are, as a guest. Our forefathers, even people of the upper class, used to do this in olden times. With the [Roman] Catholics, noble maidens would be brought up in convents even in preparation for married life. I would add more, only I am very pressed for time. Tomorrow we have the memorial of our great Elder, Father Makary. And you people will be free to walk about the skete all day. This is once a year.[1]

Save yourself, A.!

177. DO NOT BE ASHAMED TO SAY YOUR THOUGHTS. ADVICE FOR A BEGINNER

October 23, 1881

I read your confession in your letter of October 19. And I am answering as best I can. You are ashamed to say your thoughts. But the Holy Scriptures teach, *It is good to confess unto the Lord* (Ps. 91:1).[2]

---

1. Women were permitted to enter the skete proper once a year until 1899, when this custom was abolished at the request of the Elder Joseph, in obedience to the will of the Mother of God and the reposed Elder Amvrosy. See, *The Elder Joseph of Optina*, p. 208.

2. Psalm 91:1. In the context of this psalm, the word "confess" actually signifies "give praise," although this latter meaning tends to be lost on the modern Russian speaker.

Therefore, this is from the Devil, who fears our good, our spiritual profit.

You are afraid that they will throw you out of the monastery, that you are sinful; in that case I should be thrown out too, for I am chief among sinners (Cf. I Tim. 1:15). The men in L— think it is a pity that you went off to a convent! Naturally! Haven't you read Step 3 of the *Ladder*!. . . [1]When a monastic is envied, she should humble herself all the more. You do not have to perform your rule all at once!. . . There is no need to be scared of Matushka. You should love her, though with an element of fear. You should bow to all the nuns. Your awkwardness will go away of itself. Not everyone can weep, only those to whom God gives tears. But God rarely gives tears to beginners, or they would become proud and be worse than those who do not weep. So not to enter a monastery because one does not have tears is simply unreasonable. For some people it is better if they do not have tears. It is true that more is demanded of monastics — but neither are lay people the more holy just because of what is not demanded of them. Moreover, the commandments of the Gospel were written for lay people as well as monastics. That which is bad, is bad everywhere, and that which is good, is good everywhere — both in the world and in the monastery.

Condemn no one. But one cannot attain to this quickly. The best thing for us to do is to reproach ourselves quickly when we do condemn someone. Try to fulfill the appointed rule, but with humility. Without this, it is difficult and dangerous.

It is all right to be sick — but only when God sends it.

That the Devil frightens you and forbids you to disclose your infirmities and your thoughts to me is nothing new.

I showed you chapter 43 of Theodore of Edessa.[2] The demons gnash their teeth exceedingly against those living under the guidance of spiritual fathers. But what you should do is write, trusting in God. And you will be saved.

---

1. *The Ladder of Divine Ascent*, 3:17: "Look, beware, lest you who cherish attachment to kinsmen be exposed to the all-engulfing deluge, andyou be swept away by the cataclysm of love for the world. Do not be moved by the tears of parents or friends; otherwise you will be weeping eternally. When they surround you like bees, or rather wasps, and shed tears over you, do not for one moment hesitate, but sternly fix the eye of your soul on your past actions and your death, that you may ward off one sorrow by another. . .

2. See footnote, Letter #61.

178. TRIBULATIONS ARE OUR GLORY.
THE PATH TO HOLINESS IS HUMILITY

December 7, 1881

Peace to you, A.! I congratulate you upon your first taste of monastic glory, that is, of tribulations. This is our crown. This is our boast. This is the cause of eternal delights and of exalted majesty! I can see that you don't much like it — but all the better! Otherwise tribulations too would lose their value and their glory. You became scared of a thought which whispered to you that you will be a saint — so what is so scary about that, it's even very nice. And then we would venerate you. Only know that real saints, having fulfilled all the virtues, in the depths of their hearts accounted themselves as worse than all, worse than other creatures, worse than the demons. But you and I have not even begun to perform good works. However, there is no need to be scared of it. A blasphemous thought is the work of the Devil. Just do not accept it — that is, do not linger in it and do not get involved with it. But there is nothing here to get disturbed about. We know you are not a saint as yet. We also know that you are inexperienced. Be at peace. It is enough for you to confess it!

179. CONGRATULATIONS ON BECOMING A MONASTIC

January 16, 1882

Peace and salvation to your young reverence!

If you have been clothed [as a novice], I congratulate you! *For He hath clothed me in the garment of salvation and covered me with the robe of gladness. He hath placed upon me a crown as upon a bridegroom, and adorned me with ornaments as a bride* (Is. 61:10). Only humble yourself and try to prove worthy. I got the prayer rope from Batiushka Amvrosy at the time, and I thought it had already been sent to you, but it hasn't.

Now I am sending it, and a prosphora from our skete — with the wish that you yourself may become a nice prosphora for your heavenly Bridegroom. But for this it is needful that you be baked in the fire of temptation! Save yourself!

180. ON DRINKING TEA DURING THE DAYS OF THE FAST

January 29, 1882

Save yourself, new novice! I received your letter, and I am answering briefly. During Lent you should use discretion in drinking tea, weighing the typicon against your strength and your obedience. When there is Liturgy, you should not drink tea before; when the Hours, reproach yourself as much as possible, and drink as little as possible, but probably you should permit yourself to do so.

During the first week, if you cannot take it, eat after the Liturgy, in the evening. You can and should have spiritual love for those people [you mention] — but do not forget, either, that the spirit is not far from the flesh.

181. A NAMEDAY WISH

February 3, 1882

I congratulate you on your Saint's day. I wish for you that you may emulate this angel-like doer of prayer. She even lived in the temple of God.[1] As for us, if we will live at home as though in church, that will be the same thing. Moreover, it is said in Scripture, *Ye are the temple of God, and the Spirit of God dwelleth in you. . .* (I Cor. 3:16). I thank you for your offering. . . for this, I wish that you may eat the eternal Manna, Which is Christ!

182. ON DREAMS. ON BLASPHEMOUS THOUGHTS

February 17, 1882

Reverend novice, new struggler, Save yourself! Peace to you and the blessing of the Lord. See, both in your clothing and in the afflicted monastic life you have embarked upon the path of the holy righteous Fathers and Mothers who have saved themselves. Evidently God is not forsaking you. Learn patience. I have already written to you that you should not believe dreams. The frightening dreams you are having now are from the evil one. Know this, and do not be troubled. I, too, suffered terribly from thirst. That is from not being used to fasting. Drink water

---

1. St. Anna the Prophetess (Luke 2:36, 37).

on account of your weakness, adding a little something sour. [1]The water should not be too cold, at room temperature. . . Do not be disturbed on account of blasphemous thoughts, but try to disdain them. God will not call you to account for them — they are from the Devil. Concerning this, read *Spiritual Medicine*.[2] And be at peace! In spirit I am always with you!

183. ON WRITING DOWN THOUGHTS. DO NOT BECOME PUFFED UP ON ACCOUNT OF MATUSHKA'S LOVE FOR YOU
March 8, 1882

I received your letter of the 3rd on the 7th, and I am hurrying to answer it. As regards the diary which scared you so much, Batiushka Amvrosy himself is answering you on a separate sheet — that is, in what sense to write down your thoughts. And I also talked to you about this in person. So: go about it with carefulness and discretion. What you can write, just write, as for example: "I was on my way to church, and I got to staring off into the distance, and mentally I went off to L. I slept in church and had various thoughts." As for more important things, write them after careful thought. Of course, you should not write sins you have confessed in Confession and that we know about. The everyday ones which are usual, write, but not in too much detail.

It is very unwise of you to become puffed up over Matushka's love for you. Because if her love should turn to the opposite, you will despair totally. And that is very possible. In fact it has already happened a little. Remember the verse of the Prophet David, *Trust ye not in princes, in the sons of men. . .* But in whom? *Blessed is he of whom the God of Jacob is his help, whose hope is in the Lord his God. . . The Lord shall be King unto eternity* (Ps. 145:2,5,10).

184. DEPRESSION IS FROM INNER DECAY
April 12, 1882

Christ is risen! I greet you with the present Paschal season.[3] For meet it is that the earth should be glad... For Christ our everlasting Joy

---

1. E.g., lemon.
2. The full title of this anthology compiled by St. Dimitry of Rostov is *Spiritual Medicine for Disturbance of the Thoughts, Compiled from Various Patristic Books.*
3. Lit., "Paschal fifty days", "Pentecostarion."

hath arisen.[1] However, A. is depressed — as if heedless of everything. And why? Because there is unsoundness inside. What is the remedy? To endure patiently. Look at the young birch trees: how awful it was for them in the autumn winds and the winter snowstorms — and now see how they are putting forth little buds — simply boasting they are. It is the same with us: to the extent that we endure patiently, we will also rejoice. Yesterday I was buried with Thee, O Christ, and today I arise with Thine arising. . .[2]

185. DO NOT GRIEVE BECAUSE YOUR RELATIVES HAVE FORSAKEN YOU

January 26

Peace to you and God's blessing! No need to discuss a move right now, of course, because as the Gypsies say, it is "something to do not by Nativity, but by the Great Day."[3] Hopefully, in March we will not freeze. But besides the cold you have another woe as well — your grief for your relatives — things are not going well for them. *Cast thy care upon the Lord, and He will nourish thee* (Ps. 54:25).

Yesterday I received the news that you are sick again. I am very sorry. In addition to everything else, there is your grief that your relatives have forsaken you: they have not forsaken you at all, they remember you more than you imagine — only, God is not suggesting to them that they hasten to console you. But when the time comes, they will all come around and cart in all kinds of things for you. Only then, because of this, you will be deprived of much that is more precious than the entire transitory world. But right now the Lord is testing you, what kind of a person you will turn out to be. But for Him to dispose your relatives to kindness is the work of a single moment. Remember Mordecai in the Book of Esther. How the king for many years rewarded him with nothing, although he was the kinsman of the king's wife and his most devoted servant. But all this was only for a time. . .

He that shall endure unto the end, the same shall be saved (Matt. 24:13)! They that wait patiently, it is said, *shall mount up with wings as eagles* (Is. 40:31). The holy righteous Anna, the Gospel says, endured patiently

---

1. From the Paschal Canon.
2. Ibid.
3. I. e., something that can be postponed. In the Russian, "ne k Rozhdestvu, a k Veliku Dnu." "The Great Day" sometimes means Pascha, sometimes the Day of Judgement, as in letter #328.

abiding in God's house unto deep old age (See Luke 2:37). So you, too, try to emulate her. Peace to you! Save yourself!

186. THE FAST IS A HAPPY TIME. HOW ONE WHO IS PHYSICALLY INFIRM SHOULD SPEND THE FAST

March 3, 1883

Peace to you and God's blessing! I greet you with the Fast, and I wish that you may spend this "gladsome season," as we shall chant during the second week of the Fast, in joyfulness of spirit and consolation.

In view of your illness, do not force yourself strenuously to go to church. God will not demand this of one who is ill. If you will say the Jesus Prayer at home during the time of the service, that will be more profitable for you. Fasts, prostrations, and labors are assigned to subdue the uprisings of the flesh — but they harm one who is ill, for they make him useless and unfit for anything. St. Basil the Great teaches that we should be slayers not of our flesh but of our passions — but what helps us more in this is humility and acknowledgement of our weakness. Go ahead and have tea and rolls to the glory of God! And do not let it bother you! Only humble yourself. However, do not go announcing this to others because to each his own rule is appropriate. Just as it happens with doctors: two people come, and one is prescribed a laxative, the other just the opposite. In general, do not tell anyone what your elder gives you to do. Go to Matushka [to say your thoughts] when possible, and say what you can. We will not demand the impossible from you. May the Lord help you to arrange your little cell. Only, will you really be better off there?

So: I will not obligate you to go to all the services because of your ailments, but try to be in church on the last day. As for standing, stand as much as your strength will allow. But to do so beyond your strength is even a sin. Do not be angry with your relatives. They do not understand us. If one were to put them through what we go through, they would find out how hard it is here. As for your feeling miserable — do not lose heart! In this lie all our crowns — in this very heaviness. Peace to you! Save yourself!

187. THE OPINION OF WORLDLY PEOPLE CONCERNING THE MONASTIC LIFE. ADVICE FOR A BROTHER

June 14, 1883

Peace to you, A.! I received your letter. Only, you were silent for so long, I had begun to wonder. But you are alive, thank God. I am sorry about your unsettled situation. Pray to God, to St. Nicholas and to all the saints, and beg your grandpa to fix you up. It is a pity that you are not happy. But at least you recognize the value of the monastic life. Worldly people swarm around without any consciousness of what they are doing, like worms burrowing in the dirt. All they do is look at other people's weaknesses and judge monastics as worthless — whereas they themselves have no conception of monasticism. And even concerning God and the future life, they speak alluding to books read long ago or even simply off the top of their heads.

What can I say concerning your brother? I am sincerely sorry. Tell him not to despair. He has not gone so far yet that he can't turn back. But if he doesn't do so quickly, he will be miserable and regret it a hundred times over, but it will be too late. May God bless him to go to his new position. Your young people there are somehow crazy — they will corrupt even a sensible man. It is timely and easy for him to leave. You may have a doctor examine you. . . Ask your grandpa for [money for] a new cell, that is, to build one! Save yourself! I ask the blessing of the Lord for you and for your relatives!

188. HOW WORLDLY PEOPLE VIEW MONASTICS

July 21, 1883

Peace to you, A.! I hope to see you soon. . . What a pity!. . . Not so much for you as for your grandfather. If he withholds what you need, he will lose it ten times over. St. Basil the Great severely threatens with the wrath of God those who deprive their relatives of their fair share. And so do the other holy Fathers. In the minds of lovers of the world the idea has formed that the moment a monk has been numbered with Christ's flock, he is obliged, in their opinion, to sleep on the ground, eat food fit for animals, and to endure everything, as if this chosen one of God had committed some terrible crime. Mindless ones! We see that the holy ascetics suffered affliction — but neither kings nor princes who were pious forsook them but generously sent them gold and bread. . . Save yourself!

189. DISCRETION AND MEEKNESS ARE THE BEST ADORNMENT FOR A YOUNG NUN

September 13

Peace to you and salvation! I am very sorry about the unsettled situation with your cell. Of course, it is best to let your cell attendant go home to recover. As for yourself, ask to be included in the common trapeza. But above all, I ask you to be more circumspect and not to trust just anyone. Discretion and meekness are the best adornment for a young girl.

You should not have undertaken to do everything yourself — you will soon lose your strength and have a nervous breakdown. Already you become so irritated you have pain. It would be better if you kept one or two subjects for yourself, and let others teach the rest. Besides, your absolute authority is very harmful for your soul as well. You will get used to subjecting others to yourself, and you will completely forget how to yourself be submissive. Save yourself!

190. DIRECTIONS FOR A NUN WHO IS A TEACHER

September 24, 1883

Peace to you, A. I received your letter and I am writing you "a line." I am glad you are at peace — be modest also, that is, do not exalt yourself; neglect nothing, be circumspect, discreet; know that sometimes a single word can destroy happiness, and that not for nothing is the saying popular, "A word is like a sparrow[1] — once you let go of it, you won't catch it again." But you and I couldn't even catch a sparrow, let alone a word. Save yourself! Take care of your health! Above all, do not become angry with the girls. By so doing you both upset yourself, and you will be a temptation to them. And so go about it like this: teach them, and learn yourself. And you will be clever.

---

1. The Russian printed text adds a negative, but the saying is generally as written here. If one does insert the negative ("A word is not like a sparrow"), the meaning would seem to be that words are even more elusive than sparrows

191. DO NOT EXALT YOURSELF. OBEY THOSE WITH EXPERIENCE

October 20, 1883

I received your sad letter, A. That you are a little girl and not very wise — this you have told me yourself, and I, too, had been used to picturing you that way. But now all of a sudden you have flared up, and you are upset that others have started teaching you. In other words, you are not a little girl any more but a seasoned teacher — overseasoned: you don't want to learn any more; the Russian proverb "Live a century, learn a century" does not apply to you. Is this really you, my obedient, modest pupil? The moment I remember you I immediately picture your meek and obedient appearance. But now you don't want to learn anything even from a schoolmarm! Why, she has taught daughters of princes, counts, generals. . . and she has a certificate attesting to her diligence, erudition, and excellent conduct. And we, having none of these things, have gone and found fault with her! A.! Just be as I have always pictured you, and God and kind people will all come to love you. And happiness will come out to meet you. Because look, even your favorite grandpa has begun to regard you differently. Is not God's hand in this? Meanwhile, you have taken upon yourself the monastic schema and manner of life, you have vowed to imitate Christ your Bridegroom, Who was *obedient even unto death, even the death of the Cross* (Phil. 2:8)! Thank God from your heart, thank God that He sent you help in time, and you saw your weakness. It is not too late yet. Only, do your best not to let N— see that you are unhappy with Matushka's appointment of her as your instructor. For this, people are paid with money and with gratitude — whereas you profit by her lessons for free. As for this weakness of ours, no one need know about it except you and me!

192. DO NOT BELIEVE DREAMS

September 11, 1884

Watch out, A.! The enemy is trying to catch you. Forget about your dreams — they are from the Devil, whereas you believe them. And you even find consolation in them. If you do not stop this, deception will inevitably follow. So stop. Humble yourself before God. Humble yourself before people, too, as much as you can. Judge no one. And if you slip, repent immediately: Lord, forgive me! Lord, have mercy! Lord, help me! Peace to you and God's blessing!

XXV. LETTERS TO I.

193. WHAT THE CHANTING OF NUNS SHOULD BE LIKE. THE KIND OF FLOWERS WE MUST SEEK

February 22, 1882

Peace to you and salvation, reverend novice! Thank God that you arrived safely — S. got stranded. All the roads are in bad shape, not to even mention the river crossing. They let no one on the Oka [River].

So you have started to chant "Let my prayer be set forth." But the fact that you have started to chant it is not important. The roosters out on the farm sing like anything — they will drown you right out. But you are not a rooster, and you are not a hen. You have to remember that your singing should be not like that of roosters but like that of the angels — that is, done with profound humility, fear, ardent love, and self-reproach. Such is true and God-pleasing chanting. But the vainglorious kind, designed to please not God but men, is worse than that of roosters. And this is precisely what you did not specify for me, that is, whom did you come closer to imitating, the angels — or a hen?[1] I am sending the seeds you requested, and a hollyhock. Only do not get too excited about flowers, remembering that this beauty lasts only until autumn. Seek rather those flowers I recommended to you — the immortelles[2] of Paradise, such as humility, obedience, love in the Lord, reading, prayer — especially the Jesus Prayer, as I have taught you. Seek these tirelessly, crying out ceaselessly to our sweetest Bridegroom Jesus, "Lord Jesus Christ, Son of God, have mercy on me, a sinner."

A thousand times over you will come to love it!

I am sending your L. a photograph, and the blessing of the Lord to her and to you, wishing that you may live a truly monastic life and inherit the eternal Kingdom. . . As for that money — buy what you need, and give away the rest. It is not good for young people. If you should make the trip to Optina, you can always get some from us. We will help you always and with everything, only do not disobey us: be meek and obedient. May God preserve you from pride, audaciousness, and disdain of others!

---

1. In contemporary Russian practice, as probably in this instance, the "Let my prayer be set forth" of the Presanctified Liturgy is often chanted by "select voices," e.g., a "trio" standing in the middle of the church — hence the temptation to show off one's voice, and the comparison to roosters.
2. Immortelle: an everlasting plant or flower, especially Xeranthemun annum.

194. A NAMEDAY[1] WISH. SERVING THE SICK IS A GUARD FOR ONE'S PURITY

December 30, 1883

I congratulate you on your Saint's day. . . I wish for you that you may be like your angel or, more precisely, like all the angels. For concerning the chaste and obedient maiden, St. Dimitry of Rostov writes, "Take away an angel's wings, and he will be a virgin. Give a virgin wings, and she will be an angel." Read his homily for the Laudation of the Most-holy Theotokos, that is, for the Saturday of the Fifth Week of Lent. But this is only regarding a chaste virgin. . . But if, alas, she should stumble, she repents, as the holy Fathers write, and immediately the Lord forgives her sins. And again she is an angel. So be careful. *Two-edged swords shall be in their hands* (Ps. 149:6), that is, in the hands of such wise virgins. As for what these two-edged swords might be, again this same saint explains this.[2] As for my not writing to you often, do not lament. . . I always do remember you and pray for you. Only obey. Humble yourself. Do not be rude to the venerable eldresses, and in God submit yourself to all.

We send our blessing to Mother N—. Tell her to read often the psalm, *The Lord is my shepherd, and I shall not want* (Ps. 22) and so on, and also the 26th psalm, *The Lord is my light. . .*[3] As for you, serve her. Serve her with all your heart. For her sake the Lord will not forsake you. This will safeguard you from carnal temptations. . . Not for nothing am I citing for you the quote from St. Dimitry of Rostov. Guard yourself by every means. Serving the sick is one of the most powerful weapons for guarding one's purity.

---

1. Lit., "angel's day."
2. St. Dimitry explains concerning the guarding of one's virginity against spiritual enemies, which the Elder Anatoly also mentions further on in this letter.
3. Actually, this is Psalm 26.

195. CONCERNING THE BOOK OF ST. JOHN CHRYSOSTOM, "ON VIRGINITY"

February 19, 1884

On the day of forgiveness itself[1] I am writing to you, being very pressed for time, and this is as a consolation for you, and in order to grant you forgiveness of your sins and ask the same for myself. I sent you the book, *On Virginity* by St. John Chrysostom, but apparently you have not received it. But I did not hope to comfort you by anything so much as by this book. For I am deeply moved by it myself, knowing how many of your sisters are tormented by the indefiniteness of their expectations and hopes, seeing nothing before them save afflictions, labor, weariness, uncertain recompense in the future. Whereas here there are presented, clear as day, the disadvantages of those who marry and the beauty and loftiness of virginity. Carefully read this book and give it to others to read. Without afflictions a monastic is pretty worthless.[2] But your Bridegroom ardently desires that you should shine like sapphire. So be patient. After all, you did not jump into this obedience on your own, but God sent it to you. And what comes from God cannot be bad or unprofitable. We *shall receive a hundredfold and shall inherit everlasting life* (Matt. 19:29). "It is the gladsome season of the Fast; wherefore, having abundantly taken our fill of radiant purity, sincere love, and enlightened prayer, let us cry out joyously: O all-holy Cross of Christ, blossom forth the bliss of life. . ."[3]

196. CONCERNING THE ETERNAL PASCHA, AND CONCERNING INNER DECAY

April 15, 1884

Truly Christ is risen! I thank you for your greeting, and greet you with the wish that you may celebrate the eternal Pascha, where there is both everlasting joy and unsetting, unwaning light. Concerning it, Isaiah wrote, "Thy gates shall be opened, O Jerusalem, and shall not be shut

---

1. I.e., Forgiveness (Cheesefare) Sunday, the Sunday before Great Lent.
2. Lit., "more worthless than a stewed turnip."
3. Cf. Stichera for "Lord, I have cried," Tuesday of the Second Week of Lent.

day nor night" (Cf. Is. 60:11). *Shine, shine, O Jerusalem, for thy light is come, and the glory of the Lord hath arisen upon thee. And kings shall walk in Thy light. . . and thy daughters shall be borne on men's shoulders* (Is. 60:1,3,4). *Let my soul rejoice in the Lord, for He hath clothed me in the garment of salvation and covered me with the robe of gladness, and adorned me with ornaments as a bride. . . And as a young man liveth with a virgin, so shall thy sons dwell in thee; and as a bridegroom rejoiceth over a bride, so will the Lord rejoice over thee* (Is. 61:10; 62:5). All this is prophesied concerning that Pascha. And much, much more. And as for what has not been revealed as yet — that is an immeasurable sea of light and of joys without end.

But the present Pascha is not a happy time always or for everyone. Inner corruption hinders us from celebrating as we should. And so we try to scrape out this decay little by little. And the supreme Artist sends us suitable tools for this — files, rasps, pincers, hammers, fire, water, etc.

I kept scaring the sisters from the farm with your egg. A.S. screamed bloody murder when the worm crawled out at her. And I scared a lot of other people too. But I was the very first to get scared myself. Nevertheless, as you can see, I continue [writing to you] as a consolation to you. Save yourself!

197. ON THE OPENING OF THE SHAMORDINO COMMUNITY. ON ESTABLISHING JESUS IN THE HEART

July 18, 1884

Save yourself! I received all your letters, but partly due to weakness, partly to lack of time, and a little due to illness, I have not answered a single one, although I did want to. You did well in not asking, since it would have been to no purpose. Better to wait until a more opportune time. Around the 7th there will probably also be the opening of the Shamordino community, that is, the consecration of the church. Anyway, that is what our Vladika[1] had in mind before; apparently he wishes to consecrate the church himself and to open the convent. . . I will send the photograph with the little cross when we have one. Although there is one in the shop right now, it is falsified and lobster-eyed and frightful even to look at. I don't want to send you one like that. Better let us wait. But what is better than any little cross or wearer thereof, better than any little portrait or its original — is to trace upon an impressionable young heart the sweetest Name, the radiant little prayer: Lord Jesus Christ, Son

---

1. Vladika — Lit., "Master"; used especially in addressing or referring to a bishop.

of God, have mercy on me, a sinner. Now, then you will have supreme joy, unending gladness. Then — that is, when Jesus is established in your heart — you will desire neither Rome, nor Jerusalem.[1] For the King Himself with His all-hymned Mother and all the angels and saints will themselves come to you and dwell with you. "I and My Father will come unto him, and make Our abode with him" (Cf. John 14:23).

198. DO NOT FORGET THE JESUS PRAYER

Peace to you!. . . The prayer rope does not suit you — I believe you, I am sending another more your size. . . I am sending you both an apple and a pear. And I will fulfill all your whims with love, only do not forget the most important thing, my testament to you: Lord Jesus Christ, Son of God, through the prayers of the Theotokos, have mercy on me. I know that at first this is a difficult work, but for this you will see light and joy. Whereas without this labor, the monastic life — if it continues to exist at all — is distressing and cheerless. It is true that it is difficult — but if you look closely, there is nothing very special here. Neither books, nor candles, nor time is required. Sitting, walking, eating, lying down — keep saying, Lord Jesus Christ, Son of God, have mercy on us!

199. HOW TO WALK TO OPTINA, AND CONCERNING THE JESUS PRAYER

April 27, 1884

I received your letter, and I received the previous ones in good order. You would like to visit Optina — may God bless you to put in a request. Just do not be insistent; [come] only if they let you go willingly. Now it will be difficult for you to walk, but better for your physical health and probably your spiritual health as well. Right now the air is salubrious, which is good for your ailing chest. Only, you should not walk too fast. If you do make the trip, the first thing is, your footwear should not be tight, and your feet should be well cushioned. . . You should be no less than five travelling companions, two of them elderly. And if they do not let you go, then as it is written, sit in your Jerusalem until the Lord look down [upon you] from on high (See Luke 24:49).

1. This rhymes in the Russian — "ni Ríma ni Ierusalíma."

Only in either case, sitting or walking, do not let go of the name of our sweetest Jesus, saying, "Lord Jesus Christ, Son of God, have mercy on me, a sinner." Forget about your scores with the older ones — it is unmonastic. The evil one whispers to you that you have reached the venerable age of 18, but to me it seems you are just a little kid. And the older ones would say the same.

200. BE MEEK. DO NOT PAMPER YOURSELF — SWEETS ARE DEBILITATING

December 20, 1884

I am fulfilling your request with pleasure; I am sending what you wanted. Only, you too fulfill my wish — bear in mind your weakness, your youth, your helplessness, and hold firmly, very firmly, to meekness. "Happy the mother of a meek man," says the old proverb. But a high-strung person, they say, will get himself into trouble on his own. Flippancy, audacity, and stubbornness ill befit a young girl. Try to work on yourself. I do not demand that you be a model of perfection, but I do want you to try to be one. Meekness and modesty are the best adornment for a young girl. I do not say this so that you would be unsparing with yourself, but so that you would judiciously work out your salvation. You can decline an obedience insolently, and you can do it quietly, asking that your infirmity be excused. The end result will be quite different. Above all, I fear lest you get a bad name for being obstinate! But that's the way it is! Admit it!

They say that you are a big sweet tooth! Try to eat and live more simply! Sweetness, both in spiritual things and in food, does not strengthen but debilitates. Above all, be submissive and humble, and the Lord will be with you. *Upon whom shall I look but upon him that is humble and meek and trembleth at My words* (Is. 66:2).

201. CARNAL THOUGHTS ARE FROM LACK OF HUMILITY

January 29, 1885

That the demon of fornication wars against you is not surprising — he did not even overlook Anthony the Great, let alone you and me. However, that you are vanquished and mentally give way to him — this means that God has abandoned you on account of something. Here the very handiest thing for the Devil is your self-will. And your frankness, too, is questionable. . . Before anything else and above everything else, try to acquire humility — then God's help will not be far off! Peace to you and God's blessing!

202. WISHES ON THE DAY OF PASCHA
March 16, 1885

I greet you with the joyous greeting, Christ is risen! If they have not started to chant our joyous "Christ is risen" quite yet — they soon will!

May God grant that you meet this "day of Resurrection" in joy of spirit and consolation of heart, that you may follow with your heart the entire Paschal Canon replete with lofty and comforting truths, which you will be chanting each day, and conclude it with the gladsome and hope-filled verse, "O Wisdom and Word and Power of God! Grant that we may partake of Thee fully in the unwaning day of Thy Kingdom!"[1]

203. REJOICE AT BEING UNJUSTLY CONDEMNED
July 5, 1885

Peace to you and blessing from the Lord! I received your letter and sorrowed greatly for my sake and for yours. But I believe, and you should believe also, that everything which comes not from us but from God is very good. You did not go asking to be slandered, but God permitted it. And good will come of it for you and the forgiveness of sins, of which we all are guilty. . . Know and firmly believe that dishonor is a monastic's true honor and glory. I rejoice that they blame you for something of which you are not guilty — for this, God will deliver you from other perils. When I entered the monastery, they told my relatives that I had become an inveterate drunkard — whereas I was drinking two glasses of beer a year in trapeza, on Nativity and on Pascha. Be thou manful, and let thy heart be strengthened. Wait on the Lord, and be thou manful (Cf. Ps. 26:16). Say the entire psalm, *The Lord is my light. . .* (Ps. 26) every day at least twice, and repeat it when you are in straits. As for the malicious talk, it will blow away like dust. The Lord is the Defender of all the innocent. So rest assured!

---

1. From the Paschal Canon.

204. DO NOT FEAR LIFE'S TEMPESTS

December 1, 1885

With love I am fulfilling your wish, sorrowful N—!. . . Do not grieve that life has become difficult for you, do not be despondent, and do not be troubled! It is impossible for a young person to cross the stormy sea of the passions without storms and fear of the destruction which threatens us at every hour. But all this is for a time; the storm will die down, and the lovely sun will sparkle through, and we will reach a pleasant, calm, and eternally verdant little island.[1] Only, we must endure patiently!

205. A WISH ON THE DAY OF TONSURE

December 17, 1885

I congratulate you, sister in the Lord, Mother N—, namesake of joy, and likewise rejoicing in spirit on receiving the little wedding garment,[2] which is the image[3] of your betrothal to your beloved Bridegroom and God, Jesus, the King of kings.

So be beloved of God not in appearance[4] only, but also in your manner of life. Especially in humility and submissiveness. Jesus was obedient unto death. *Wherefore God also hath highly exalted Him* (Phil. 2:9)! "The assembly of the humble is like the assembly of the Seraphim."[5] Not of simple angels but of the highest celestial orders. Once more I say and I repeat — be humble, be submissive, do not be fond of honor and show — and He Who boundlessly loves the humble will love you!

206. A WISH ON THE DAY OF CHRIST'S NATIVITY

December 22, 1886

---

1. See *The Ascetical Homilies of St. Isaac the Syrian*, Homily 46, p. 224: "As it is not possible to cross over the great ocean without a ship, so no one can attain to love without fear... Thus fear sets us in the ship of repentance, transports us over the foul sea of this life (that is, of the world), and guides us to the divine port, which is love... When we attain to love, we attain to God. Our way is ended and we have passed unto the isle that lies beyond the world, where is the Father, and the Son, and the Holy Spirit..."
2. I.e., the Little Schema.
3. Or "schema."
4. Or "schema."
5. Cf. *The Ascetical Homilies of St. Isaac the Syrian*, Homily 51, p. 245.

I greet you, reverend Mother, with the feasts of the Nativity of Christ and the new year. I wish that you may celebrate not with old leaven (kvass), but with the leaven (kvass) of purity and truth (Cf. I Cor. 5:8). The most delicious kvass[1] is humility and love — to this, treat the mothers and sisters, and treat yourself. And do not forget my main injunction to you: Lord Jesus Christ, Son of God, have mercy on me, a sinner. Save yourself!

XXVI. LETTERS TO A.K.

207. YOU CANNOT BE SAVED WITHOUT TRIBULATIONS

Peace to you, sister! I received your letter. I am very sorry that you grieve unreasonably and torment yourself. After all, one cannot even go through life without woes, and one cannot be saved without them, according to God's word, *We must through much tribulation enter into the Kingdom of God* (Acts 14:22). Why, don't you wish to enter into the Kingdom of God? So endure patiently, being as this is inevitable for us; pray, labor — and you will inherit the Kingdom of Heaven with all the saints... Say your thoughts as much as you can — your heart will feel the lighter. And write to me anything you cannot say to your Eldress.

208. IN YOUR PATIENCE POSSESS YE YOUR SOULS

I received your letter some time ago, much-afflicted one.

Life is hard for you? Why, is there anyone for whom it is not hard? And do those in the world really have no troubles? Be patient, and a comforter will come in time. The Lord said, *In your patience possess ye your souls* (Luke 21:19). If you are unable to do something and your health does not permit it, humble yourself and beg meekly [to be excused] — and above all, be patient. And if you lose patience in some situation, reproach yourself and ask God for help. Peace to you and the blessing of the Lord!

---

1. Kvass — A fermented drink. Kvass is also the old Slavonic word for "leaven."

209. NEW YEAR'S WISHES

January 14, 1881

Peace to you! I greet you with the new year. In this new year I wish you new strength, new patience, new humility, and the best of new, blooming health. That is, of course, if this is pleasing to the Lord and profitable for us. Otherwise, better to creak along as before, if only we might be saved. . . Be humble, and the Lord will never forsake you.

210. DO NOT BE IN A HURRY TO ENTER A NEW CONVENT

May 27, 1884

Peace to you, S.! I see that you are bent on entering a new convent, but you do not know as yet where would be best. Now look, you will be asking to be received back again — after all, you don't know the Superior yet! Wait! Look before you leap![1] In any case, it is Batiushka Amvrosy who is in charge of accepting people.

211. DO NOT GRIEVE OVER BEING TRANSFERRED FROM YOUR CELL

April 29, 1892

Truly Christ is risen! I received your letter in which you tell of your sorrows and your not getting along with certain sisters. I sympathize much with you. But do not grieve over being transferred from your cell. This means that it is necessary for you to suffer this and humble yourself before God, which will be beneficial for your soul. You should not be angry with others to the point of having remembrance of wrongs. Compel yourself to pray for all who hate and wrong you, in accordance with the Lord's commandment!

---

1. In the Russian, "Ne sprosás brodú, ne súytes v vodú!" Lit., "Don't venture into the water without first finding out about the ford!"

212. CONCERNING BEING EXCUSED FROM AN INAPPROPRIATE OBEDIENCE

June 11, 1892

I received your letter. . . If your obedience in the chapel is harmful for you, you may try asking your Mother Abbess to be excused from it, citing your poor health: that sitting in the shop is beyond your strength and not profitable; you become distracted a lot and get carried away by thoughts, and you are sick besides.

Perhaps she will find someone older and more stable than you. But if she keeps you in this obedience, you should devise to guard your seeing so as not to see human vanity and fleeting worldly allurements and enticements. . . Ceaselessly exercise yourself in the Jesus Prayer and in meditation upon death and upon the recompense after death to each according to his works. Say often the prayer, "O Theotokos and Virgin, rejoice." Call St. John the Theologian and the Martyr Thomais[1] to your aid. The Lord is mighty to deliver you from the snares of the enemy!

XXVII. LETTERS TO A.B.

213. TO HEAR THOUGHTS IS BEYOND YOUR CAPABILITY

September 1, 1875

I received your letter, sister in the Lord! I conveyed the appropriate message to Batiushka. He sends you his blessing. Maybe he will also send you a note. For the meanwhile, he directed me to tell you that to hear thoughts is beyond your capability right now, and you might be harmed yourself. Now if this is done with Matushka Abbess' blessing, it will be a holy work. And may God bless you. But in any case, this work requires sobriety. In case of extreme need, of course, it would be on our conscience if we were to turn away our neighbor, refusing to share his load, his burden. But still, with discretion.

May the Lord bless you! Batiushka, too, sends you his blessing!

---

1. These saints are especially invoked in the struggle to preserve one's purity.

214. DO NOT FEAR BECOMING POOR

January 16, 1877

I read your letter of unknown date. And only now have I digested it, that your grief is not so much for yourself as for your relatives. You fear lest they become poor — lest they walk in the way of our Saviour, the apostles, the righteous, and almost all the saints. You fear also for yourself lest you die of hunger, of cold, forgetting that He Who governs the world does not forsake a single little bird — He feeds all, He warms all. And if you have a mind, just look at these baby birds: the size of a thimble, her little leg like a piece of straw, and imagine — no boots!. . . Not only no storeroom or barn, but not a seed, literally not a seed. This little bird gets up on a frosty morning, and all there is, is these skinny little legs and this little bill and a good appetite. And not a seed in the barn. No barn in fact. . . Now, you and I are monastics. . . Practically in despair she is. But why? Are they robbing our convent? Taking away our last clothing? Snatching away our last piece of bread? No! "What if my parents become poor! They won't have enough. And I won't." Child! *Behold the fowls of the air: for they sow not, neither do they reap; yet your heavenly Father feedeth them* (Matt. 6:26). Sister, do not anger God!

As for your thought that [where you are] you are not on firm footing in the spiritual arena — this only indicates your childish spiritual infirmity! Where do you think you can go to where you could escape from yourself?[1] You see, this is diabolical pride shaking you. And it won't be satisfied until it leads its prisoner down to the abysses of hell. What you should do is try your best to emulate Him Who said, *Learn of Me, for I am meek and lowly in heart, and ye shall find rest. . .* (Matt. 11:29). But I hope to see you if the Lord wills, and then we will talk. . .

215. A WISH ON THE DAY OF PASCHA

April 6, 1877

Christ is truly risen! I thank you, sister, and all the sisters of one soul with us who greeted me through you with the radiant feast of the Resurrection of Christ. And I in turn greet all of you with a joyous "Christ is risen!"

Christ is risen, and death is put to death! Christ is risen, and Hades

---

1. Perhaps here, as in Letter #220, A.B. is contemplating leaving her convent to go elsewhere.

is abolished. *But we are risen and are set upright* (Ps. 19:8). For meet it is that the Heavens should rejoice, and that the earth should be glad, and that the whole world should keep the feast! For Christ, our everlasting Joy, hath arisen.[1] "Thy gates shall be opened, O Jerusalem, continually, and shall not be shut day nor night" (Cf. Is. 60:11).

Because thou hast been forsaken and hated, and there was no helper, therefore I will make thee a perpetual gladness, a joy of many generations (Is. 60:15).

And thou shalt no more have the sun for a light by day, nor shall the rising of the moon lighten thy night; but the Lord shall be thine everlasting light, and God thy glory (Is. 60:19)!

That is what the Prophet Isaiah prophesied concerning the Resurrection of Christ and concerning us, the feeble ones.

Peace to you and blessing from the Lord! Batiushka Father Amvrosy greets you and blesses you.

216. TRIBULATIONS WILL MAKE YOU WISER
March 17, 1880

That is not at all the reason I have not been writing to you, reverend sister, perpetually grieving and perpetually jealous of N— and perpetually the object of N—'s jealousy!. . . I am very sorry for your poor heart: how sticky it is! It stuck to Father X—, and to the Father Economos,[2] and to. . . And to people of every sex and age — it just sticks like anything. And so awfully hard you can't yank it off afterwards! Well, naturally you are going to feel pain! And consequently you will acquire some sense too. *Give instruction to a wise man, and he will be yet wiser* (Prov. 9:9). I console myself with this, at least, that although you will grieve for awhile, you will become the wiser for it. And all the tribulations will pass — but the knowledge will remain. So we won't lose heart, if you are going to become the more precious through bearing afflictions. Now every muzhík[3] knows that he who has been broken by afflictions is more valuable, for one broken [animal] is worth two who have not been broken.[4] And the Holy Scriptures say the same thing, "An untried man is unpracticed."[5] But I would like for you to be practiced. Peace to you and the blessing of the Lord!

---

1. From the Paschal Canon.
2. Economos — The steward of a monastery.
3. Muzhík — Peasant.
4. Lit., "beaten."
5. St. Barsanuphrius, Answer #255.

217. Y— OPENS THE HEAVENS!

December 10, 1880

Peace to you and blessing, reverend [sister]! I do not know what kind of person you have become now in your deeds, but in your words you are simply a Prophet Elias: she shuts up the heavens, and she opens them by prayer and brings down, not rain, but snow at least! O marvelous wonder! I, the sinner, after living 30 years in the hermitage, can in no wise manage to get up the strength to begin praying about my sins — whereas Y— opens the heavens. Woe to my wretchedness! Pray that the Lord might open unto me the doors of repentance. (Nevertheless, I wish the same for you!)

218. I WON'T PRAISE YOU FOR BREAKING OFF YOUR RELATIONSHIP WITH YOUR ELDRESSES

July 10, 1881

Reverend sister, Peace to you and the blessing of the Lord! From your last letter I see that you have decided to break off your relationship with the Matushkas, your Eldresses, but you did not explain the reason — was this a whim or something valid. But in any case, I won't be in a hurry to praise you for this. And I won't hesitate to scold you the moment I find out the reasons you have preferred a self-directed life to the guidance of eldership.

I thank you and all who greeted me for your greeting and for remembering me. . .[1]

219. YOU DO NOT UNDERSTAND WHERE YOUR "HOME" IS

October 26, 1883

A few days ago your father visited us. He complains that you keep asking to go home. How dense you are, Matushka! So many years now you have been living at the convent, and you cannot seem to understand where your "home" is. . . Get some wisdom, sister!

Forget about your relatives. *Let the dead bury their dead* (Matt. 8:22). Without you they will be saved, if they desire it!. . . You trust your heart

---

1. July 3 was the Elder Anatoly's nameday.

and your own understanding!. . . But where is the witness of the purity of your heart? Where is the proof of the correctness of your understanding? Humble yourself, Mother! Peace to you!

220. IT IS SAINTS WHO BECOME FOOLS!

You have simply lost your mind! Miserable she is! And life is just impossible! And she wants to become a fool for Christ! And to go off to another convent! Any other convent! Humble yourself!. . . Batiushka said to tell you that "it is saints who become fools" — that is, for these people their afflictions among the brethren are not enough, and they go seeking them out amid the crowds in the world! Now [does that sound like] you?! Humble yourself!

221. IT IS ALL RIGHT TO CRY, BUT WITHOUT CONCEIT

I am not in the grave yet, Matushka, not quite in the grave. But, alas, I was laid up in bed and went nowhere for two weeks. . . And then it was time for confessions — almost the entire monastery, the farm — and how many lay people there were! You know Batiushka's health is so-so — and he keeps getting weaker.

It is all right for you to cry. May God bless. As much as your little heart desires — all day if you wish. But to become conceited, that is, to think that here you have tears, that this is saving, that this is from God — God forbid. In that case better restrain them.

And your idea to end your life is also good. Your slothful, irrational life that is, and to begin a new one in the image of the angels — good, good!

May the Lord grant you this! I very much wish the same for myself also!

Blessed are they whom Thou hast chosen and hast taken to Thyself, O Lord! Unto ages of ages shall they praise Thee! How beloved are Thy dwellings, O Lord of hosts! My soul longeth and fainteth for Thee, O Lord! For the turtledove hath found a nest for herself — even Thine altars, O Lord of hosts, my King and my God (Cf. Ps. 64:4;Ps 83:1,3-5)! Save yourself!

XXVIII. LETTERS TO M.S.

222. EVERY OBEDIENCE IS BENEFICIAL

December 24, 1876

Sister, you write that you are burdened by your obedience of sewing for the sisters, and you would like instead to chant and to read. An obvious demonic temptation!

Everything which is given to us as an obedience is pleasing to God and beneficial for us — but it is precisely this that you do not like. Do not listen to the Devil, who seeks to destroy us, but listen to our Lord Jesus Christ, Who was obedient to His Father even unto death. Thus you too, be obedient to your Mother given you by God. And you will follow after Christ and behold His glory!

223. A DIFFICULT OBEDIENCE IS MORE BENEFICIAL THAN A GRATIFYING ONE

April 16, 1882

No, I will not turn you away, and if you come, I will do my best to spend some time with you. Attachment is love according to passion, impure love. Every obedience is saving and therefore almost always difficult, according to the measure of its profitableness; but a gratifying obedience is not as beneficial, and sometimes even harmful. St. John of the Ladder says, "If one who is under obedience, in performing his obedience fulfills his own desire, he is a fornicator."[1] Remember this!

224. DISCLOSURE OF THOUGHTS IS APPOINTED BY THE HOLY FATHERS UNTO SALVATION

Peace to you! Are you saying your thoughts now? Disclosure of thoughts has been appointed by the holy Fathers that we may be saved the more easily. For the path to salvation is in general difficult, but he who strives for his salvation with disclosure of thoughts and consultation of his elders makes this difficult path much easier for himself! Save yourself!

---

1. Cf. *The Ladder of Divine Ascent* 27:62: "For the monk under obedience, self-will is the fall"; and 4:31: "I fell into the fornication of disobedience."

225. THE PASSIONS ARE UPROOTED GRADUALLY

Christ is risen! You grieve much that passions overcome you and that you are not able to resist them. Grieve over this you should, but you should also know that the passions are uprooted gradually, and that one must work on oneself for a long time. Meanwhile, let us be patient and humble ourselves. I do not compel anyone to go to Matushka [to say her thoughts]. I only recommend it, because I have learned from experience that saying one's thoughts lightens the burden on one's soul. As for uprooting your passions, begin with self-reproach and with awareness of your own (and not your sisters') weaknesses; and consider yourself to be deserving of afflictions.

Such a manner of life will bring you peace. *Amen, amen, I say unto you, That ye shall weep and lament, but the world shall rejoice: and ye shall be sorrowful, but your sorrow shall be turned into joy. And your joy no man taketh from you* (John 16:22).

226. WE HAVE AN OBLIGATION TO LOVE ALL, BUT WE DARE NOT DEMAND LOVE FROM OTHERS

You are mistaken in fearing to say your thoughts to Matushka: it would make things easier for you. But I do not compel you. Do try with all your might to humble yourself. And your thought that you are not loved is purely demonic. Besides, we have an obligation to love all — but we dare not demand that others love us. Peace to you. Save yourself. Be patient, and you will be saved. As for your being prone to anger and insubmissive, that comes from pride. Pray, be patient, and it will pass.

227. THE PASSION OF FORNICATION WARS AGAINST EVERYONE. OUR LABORS WILL BE VALUED AT THEIR WORTH ON THE DAY OF THE DREAD JUDGMENT

No, I have not forgotten you, it is just that I myself have had an awful time. I had no rest during the entire fast. The passion of fornication wars against everyone. And at the toll-stations, the demon of fornication boasts before all the princes of darkness that he has brought more prey to hell than all the rest. Endure patiently and ask God's help. It is good to speak for the profit of the sisters, but even better to keep silence. And better still to pray for them while reproaching yourself.

Learn to honor and love those in authority. As for our labors, they will be meetly and rightly valued at their worth on the day of the common Judgment. Constrain yourself, sister, for the Kingdom of Heaven is of them that constrain themselves. You should say those thoughts which oppress you with particular frequency. Concerning mental prayer, it is too early for you to know as yet. For now say the oral prayer: Lord Jesus Christ, Son of God, have mercy on me, a sinner.

228. CONTINUAL CONSOLATION IS HARMFUL. VAINGLORY RUINS ALL OUR FRUIT

Christ is risen! See, now you have understood how the Lord is always mighty to console us. But continual consolation would harm us: just as if the sun were to blaze continually, or the rain to pour down continually, everything would burn up or rot. But when they alternate, that is good. See, that is how it was with you also. First, things were fine, then later not so good. I have not read that at night one should make three prostrations, but I have read in the Holy Scriptures: *Pray without ceasing* (I Thess. 5:17). Also, all the scriptures and the Fathers command us to humble ourselves without ceasing. For this you may have our blessing as your Elders. As for what I do not know — well, I do not know it. Flee vainglory; it will ruin all your fruit. . . Ask God for discernment you may. But it is more profitable for you to ask [your Elders] your questions because, look, you are still feeble. If the Lord grants, we will see each other. Just remember Jesus Christ. And instead of those three midnight prostrations, you may chant in the morning, "Let us arise in the deep dawn and instead of myrrh, offer praise to the Master: and we shall see Christ, the Sun of Righteousness, Who causeth life to dawn for all."[1]

229. BLASPHEMOUS THOUGHTS ARE FROM PRIDE

Blasphemous thoughts are multiplied and strengthened due to pride and condemnation of others. Therefore, beware of both, and the

---

1. From the Paschal Canon.

blasphemous thoughts will wither. Disdain them as you would barking
puppies because they are not yours: it is the enemy who is blaspheming,
and you will not answer to God for them.

In affliction ask God's help, because not in vain is it said in the Holy
Scriptures: *Call upon Me in the day of thine affliction, and I will deliver thee,
and thou shalt glorify Me* (Ps. 49:16). Peace to you and God's blessing.

230. CONDEMN YOURSELF AND NOT OTHERS

One should not believe in dreams. It is sinful to condemn others.
But to reproach and humble oneself is very soul-saving and profitable.
Say what is necessary to your sister, only not often, or you will make her
sick of you: but speak always after having prayed, and with meekness
and love.

231. YOU ARE BURDENED BY YOUR OBEDIENCE BECAUSE OF PRIDE

To you it seems that you have a bigger obedience than everyone
else; but to me it seems that you have more pride than everyone else.
Otherwise such a thought would never have entered your head. But that
it is hard for you, of this I am certain. For it is hard for everyone to save
their souls. With regard to your lack of moderation, for this you yourself
will suffer carnal warfare. Against blasphemous thoughts, read the little
book[1] which I left with you.

232. DEPRESSION IS FROM A HIGH OPINION OF ONESELF

Peace to you! The reason you become depressed is that you have a
high opinion of yourself and criticize those who are weak.

If anger and murmuring are so strongly evident in you, it is a sure
sign of a proud soul. Humble yourself, reproach yourself, and the Lord is
mighty to give you a helping hand and to comfort you.

---

1. Probably *Spiritual Medicine*. See Letter #182.

XXIX. LETTERS TO M.M.

233. PRACTICE THE JESUS PRAYER. YOU DO NOT LOVE YOUR [SPIRITUAL][1] MOTHER BECAUSE OF PRIDE

March 24, 1884

I make answer to your letter: first, try with all your might to practice the Jesus Prayer — it is all our life, all our beauty, all our consolation. Everyone knows that it is difficult at first; but in return, it is afterwards priceless, all-joyous, all-dear.

Second, the reason you do not love your [spiritual] mother is pride, which you do not recognize in yourself but with which you are abundantly filled. If she were of noble birth, you would love her and put on airs on this account. Remember the fifth commandment!

As for me, I won't forget you, whether you are high-class or not! But if you will live well, in a monastic manner, it will be much more pleasant and joyous for me.

You may read an akathist if time permits.

234. FLEE JEALOUSY

April 21, 1884

I am writing to you, M., just for company, so that you[2] do not become offended with me! I seem to see that you are beginning to be taken with a pernicious disease: jealousy. If it is there, leave off. You will both disturb your own peace and grieve me, repaying my concern for you with ingratitude. I take comfort in the hope that now you know better, and will be more discreet and more humble. Be the first to show respect for those who are older, and care for those who are weaker.

---

1. From the context it seems likely that a spiritual mother is being referred to here, as in Letter #290.
2. Beginning with this sentence the rest of the letter is written in the plural.

Love is higher than everything else. . . Do not be ungrateful to the choir directress. . . It is not she who needs you but you who need her. In your free time do not abandon your books — there is our knowledge, there our salvation!

Do not forget the Jesus Prayer when possible. Above all, do not hide things from me. It is both ungrateful and ruinous for you to repay my sincerity and concern with deliberate secretiveness, the fruit of which you have reaped but, it seems, have not chewed well as yet.

235. OBEDIENCE IS A GREAT AND HOLY WORK
October 26, 1884

M. is afraid lest they draw her away from me. One can quickly tear a person who is full away from his kasha, but not a hungry person. As long as you are vigilant and careful and do not lose your love and devotion, no one will pull you away. Especially if you keep your promise, which gladdens me, "to do nothing according to your own will." Then no one will separate us. Read in the book of Abba Dorotheos the story of young Dositheos. Neither man nor the enemy of our souls has power to assail such devotion. And why? Because the Lord has said, *Where two or three are gathered together in My name, there am I in the midst of them* (Matt. 18:20). So when God is between the two of us, who can be against us? Only hold more firmly to this great and holy work — obedience. You want to be obedient, but you regret not being able to "train yourself in this, not seeming to bring yourself around." Why, if M. managed this with love and ease, then we would call her Matushka M., and living as you are, we would stand you in the icon corner; but being as you still resemble us sinners, just sit by the seashore and wait for fair weather.

Show S. the rule, and fulfill it yourself according to your strength. You embarrass me: I keep praising my M., and she keeps giving in and climbing on the stove ledge[1] to sleep. We will get our fill of sleep — there will be plenty of time. But for now let us labor. If you will be humble and heedful, everything will come in its time. For now seek consolation in guarding your eyes, in humility (in word, in gaze, in step, and so on) and in crying out: Lord Jesus Christ, Son of God, have mercy on me, a sinner.

---

1. Russian stoves, made of earthenware, provided steady heat for the home and had platforms for sleeping.

236. BE PATIENT WITH ONE ANOTHER

November 20, 1884

M., be patient! The Lord endured patiently and enjoined us to do the same. Take pity on Matushka! If only you knew how she loves you, how her heart pains for you! She can not go in several directions at once! Both I know and she knows that your situation is distressing — but what is she supposed to do, throw M. An. out into the snow? If one were to throw any one of you young ones out into the cold, even then [it would be cruel]. . . But she is an old woman.

Your convent is young, all four of you are young — be patient with one another. Why, all of you are the same age! Nevertheless, the convent has become your cradle, your mother, committed to leading all four of you to the Jerusalem on high. But you, for the sake of smoke, refuse a Kingdom.

And moreover, what a Kingdom! *Thy Kingdom is the Kingdom of all the ages* (Ps. 144:13)! All the kings here below are mere servants there, whereas you are future queens! And you, daughters of Jerusalem, refuse eternal royal dignity. What strange characters you and Duniasha are, and the rest of you!. . .

237. A REBUKE FOR INCONSTANCY.
WHETHER TO ASK FORGIVENESS

March 31, 1885

That I should live to see even M. start running away from me! So much for devotion! So much for constancy! Even she turns away from me, on whose account I am disparaged for spoiling her too much! Where now to seek justice, I can not imagine! I don't even know from what angle to approach you now. You are angry.

You ask whether to ask Magd.'s forgiveness? Of course you should, if you have wronged her in some way! But if she is grumbling through no fault of yours, what are you going to ask forgiveness for? If she is angry for no reason, well, let her be. For you, it is enough if you will be patient with her weakness. Probably she also thinks that you complained about her to me — whereas I did not so much as see you here!

What is one to do with you people!

238. THE LIGHT-BESTOWER IS ABLE TO ILLUMINE US
December 22, 1885

Thy bridal chamber, O my Saviour, do I behold all adorned, and a garment I have not, that I may enter therein. Illumine the garment of my soul, O Light-Bestower![1]

Do you see? Our garments should be light. And only the Light-Bestower is able to illumine that which is dark. The bridal chamber, too, is light — unspeakable, unimaginable light, sweetest light, most loving, most captivating. One who has beheld it but once in his life will never forget it. Love for this light, for this bridal chamber, for this Light-Bestower, is so sweet, so ardent, inexpressible, endless, that rivers and seas cannot quench this ardor of love. That is why St. John of the Ladder says, "I have seen some possessed by the flame of carnal lust, who transferred this love to their heavenly Bridegroom and outstripped those who had previously been ahead."[2] Therefore, you and I will not despair: the Bestower of Light is able to illumine us also and grant us wisdom. Of ourselves we can do nothing. But our patient endurance according to our strength, our grief, our perplexity, our very decay He can cleanse, adorn, illumine, make more fragrant than incense and the sweet-smelling censer. Not for nothing was there shown to you in sleep the bright bridal chamber of the wise virgins, so that you would take heart and draw strength therefrom in your struggle against the enemy. Our warfare is *not against flesh and blood, but against principalities, against powers, against the rulers of the darkness of this world* (Eph. 6:12). You struggle, you grieve, you near the breaking point — and the Lord looks straight into your heart, strengthening you invisibly, while the angels praise the feeble little girl who is struggling and weave for her incorruptible crowns, one little blossom of which is worth more than the entire world. Peace to you!

---

1. Exapostilarion of Holy Week.
2. Cf. *The Ladder of Divine Ascent* 5:26: "I have seen impure souls raving madly about physical love; but making their experience of such love a reason for repentance, they transferred the same love to the Lord; and, overcoming all fear, they spurred themselves insatiably on to the love of God."

239. GREAT IS THE REWARD FOR THOSE WHO STRUGGLE AGAINST THE ENEMY

January 8, 1886

I received your letter, M. Only you did not sound happy. . . Do not shirk your struggle against the enemy. Great, O how great, is the reward for those who contest. Eternal light, joyous light, living, life-creating, gladdening, in exchange for all these sorrows. The Lord said to His beloved ones, *In the world ye shall have tribulation, but your sorrow shall be turned into joy. And your joy no man taketh from you* (John 16:20,22,33). In other words, it will be eternal. And the sorrows will be dispersed as smoke, as dust.

240. DO NOT BE ANGRY; BE PATIENT

February 17, 1889

Peace to you, M. Save yourself! Do not be angry, my dear! Nothing can come of heat, save heat. But from patience come peace, light, grace. Why, all of this will pass like the early morning mist the moment the sun comes up. And our sun will dawn very, very soon. *In your patience possess ye your souls* (Luke 21:19)!

241. DO NOT BE IN A RUSH TO EXCHANGE THE MONASTIC LIFE FOR LIFE IN THE WORLD

December 1, 1892

Peace to you and salvation! I received your letter and I marvelled: such a long time you have lived at the convent, and you have not gotten yourself one bit of intelligence. The Lord arranged things for you so that without a contribution or special petitions, He received you into His holy convent, gave you a cozy nook, an honored obedience near to God, and all this means nothing to you — it is better to become a nanny! Unreasonable one! Just look how many now seek a situation like yours without obtaining it!

Even now there is living at Optina a nice young girl who is asking to join you, but Mother is not accepting her.

Why, if only you understood what a pain you are asking for, you would be horrified by your foolishness! Right now there are thousands galore of nannies and cooks in Petersburg, and no one honors or respects them — whereas the nuns you can count on your fingers. And these are respected and honored. But this you cannot fathom. Do you know how many tares they will sow in your soul [in the world], piling in ill-smelling poisons — and you, and no one else, will have to uproot them [these tares] from your heart, you will have to drink this cup of worldly enjoyments. "All the sinners of the earth shall drink the dregs thereof" (Cf. Ps. 74:8). But you are a chosen sheep of Christ's flock — not for you are these "dregs" prepared. Concerning you and those like you, the Lord has said, "Fear not, little flock, for it is My Father's good pleasure to give you the Kingdom" (Cf. Luke 12:32).

But you, foolish one, are ready at any moment now to exchange a royal crown on your noggin — to look after geese!. . .

Forsake foolishness and ye shall live! Go in search of understanding that ye may live (Prov. 9:6)! What manner of a man was King David? Comely he was, and glorious, and rich — but what does he chant? "I have seen iniquity and unrighteousness in the cities. Lo, I have fled afar off into the wilderness. Who will give me wings like a dove" (Cf. Ps. 54:6,7,9,10)? But you are in a hurry to yourself clip your dove wings, in order to live the life of rats and mice! Pitiable one! You ask me to permit you to stay longer in Petersburg. I do not have the authority to do so, and I would be liable to answer for it before God and man. Even for permitting you to visit in the big city I am already catching it. You may add one little week and return without fail to your sisters. May the Lord save you!

XXX. LETTERS TO A.L.

242. NEW YEAR WISHES

December 31, 1888

Peace to you, A.! I greet you with the new year, new health, a new, holy life. I trust that you will try to fulfill all this. That is, that starting tomorrow you will live giving thanks to God, saying the Jesus Prayer always, and not murmuring, starting no arguments, and accounting yourself as inferior, as not good, so as to be good in God's sight and in time to become holy, a bride worthy of Christ the heavenly Bridegroom. And in this will be both my joy and yours. Save yourself!

243. LEARN TO SAY YOUR THOUGHTS

January 27, 1889

Peace to you and God's blessing! I received your letter. You did well in disclosing to me your feelings on seeing the Mother who frightened you with her gaze. Now be careful, for she can do you much harm. Avoid her as much as possible. Do not go into her cell, and if you are alone, on no account let her into yours. It is your Guardian Angel who showed this to you in time. I am very pleased that you are learning to say your thoughts. If you will continue to do so in future, you will escape many calamities and woes. For this purpose many travel hundreds of versts[1], spend their last hard-earned kopeck, in the face of such adversities, in the cold, at inns, nothing to eat or drink — all in order to receive instruction and help. Read about disclosure of thoughts in Abba Dorotheos. Even great elders went to older and more experienced fathers in order to learn the spiritual life. The great Anthony, at 95 years of age, went to Paul of Thebes, who was 115. But who are you and I? Learn, my dear daughter. Or else you will be too late, even should you wish to. Write more often, especially if something is weighing on your conscience, or if you have some question or sorrow — write everything. May God's blessing be upon you from henceforth and forevermore!

244. ON SPIRITUAL HEAVINESS

November 7/8, 1889

Peace to you! I congratulate you on your nameday.[2] Today are celebrated all the heavenly angelic orders, together with their Commander, Michael the Archangel. And since you and I bear this angelic order, we, too, exult together with the heavenly ones, believing faithfully and steadfastly that sooner or later, by repentance or by humility, by faith or by someone's prayers, we will be communicants with them and co-dwellers with them and beholders of the trinally-radiant God.

I received your confession written in your last letter. God will forgive all the sins you have confessed. And I, the sinner, forgive and absolve you. Regarding your misgivings about disclosing your thoughts

---

1. Verst — 3500 feet (about 2/3 mile).
2. Lit., "your Angel's day."

to others, they are needless. As for your sins, I tore them off the letter at once and destroyed the scrap of paper on which they were written. . . It is a pity that you have weakened toward God and toward prayer. However, the same thing has happened with me sometimes. It would come and go. Hope [to the end]! I am very sorry about your poor health. After receiving your letter, I too was taken so ill that I have only just now come to. Even today I am not serving for my Angel's day. You had "inexpressible depression and weariness," and I had such heaviness, darkness, delirium, confusion, and weakness, that day and night all I did was moan and toss about. And it was then that I pictured to myself the torments of hell! Where can this endless torment possibly come from? I ask, "Is it 10:00?" They tell me, "4:00." My dear! Why, how am I going to get through the night? So I wait. It seems to me that by now it must be past 10:00. I ask, "What time is it?" They say, "It isn't 5:00 yet!" Yes, it is a fearful thing to go into hell!

10:00 AM, November 8 — Even though I did not sleep tonight, I did not suffer either. Glory to Thee, O Lord! At 10:00 in the evening I saw Masha off, who is sick. I lay down to sleep — I could not go to sleep. At 12:00 I began reading the service to the Angels. Again I lay down, again I did not fall asleep, and so I languished all night. Now, thank God, I am all right! Only just like you, I can neither pray nor work. And such a wonderful service to the Angels! Peace to you and salvation!

245. YOU HAVE TO THINK OF OTHER PEOPLE TOO
November 8, 1892

Oh dear, A.! I do not know what in the world to do with you!. . . So foolish N— said something or other, called you proud — and immediately we are in despair, ready to leave the convent. . .

I told you, didn't I, that all this rearrangement might not work out. Didn't I give you the entire upstairs — and still you are cramped. Well, you just have to think of others too; the others would like to be saved too, but don't know how to go about it. Both the enemy plots against them, and they themselves have weaknesses — and you and I abet the enemy, and in moments of disturbance we finish off those who are weak instead of helping them out. "If thou turn the ungodly from his way, thou shalt be as My mouth."[1] See how lofty is the portion of those who save others. But we lose these precious opportunities because of our roughness and stupidity, and we think only of how to please ourselves!

---

1. Cf. Jeremias 15:19: *If thou bring forth the precious from the vile, thou shalt be as My mouth.*

How to preserve our honor (our false honor, that is — our love of honor) — and we are left with nothing, profiting neither before God nor before men! Peace to you!

246. ILLNESS HEALS THE SOUL. DO NOT JUSTIFY YOURSELF BUT REPROACH YOURSELF

March 25, 1893

Peace to you! Glory be to God, if so be that you received Holy Communion. As for your being ill, it is no calamity; for sinful people this is a purification: as fire purifies iron from rust, so illness heals the soul.

As for my opinion of you, it would be superfluous to confirm it for you, as my deeds confirm that I have nothing against you. But if I notice failings in you, I speak frankly. That is my responsibility, and yours is to accept both the good and the bad with faith from your [spiritual] father. Do not be in a hurry to justify yourself, as you have read in the Abba that the Devil joins himself to him who is righteous [in his own eyes], that is, to him who justifies himself. Better try instead to reproach yourself. That is saving in every instance. . .

Save yourself — that is, endure patiently!

247. DO NOT BE DESPONDENT

Save yourself, A., young monastic, reverend novice of God, favorite and handmaid of our Lord Jesus Christ! Do not be despondent, young struggler! The enemy wants to intimidate you at the very start — but do not listen to him. And say, "It is God Whom I have come to serve, to bear afflictions and tribulation for the sake of Him Who died for me; I came to the convent to endure and to suffer for awhile, in order to reign eternally with our sweetest Jesus and to revel and dance with all the saints who have ever lived, and with the angels." And so let us endure patiently here for a time so as to reign there unto the ages, and unto the ages of ages!

248. ADVICE FROM ST. PETER OF DAMASCUS

Peace to you and salvation! Do not talk to anyone about your dream, but do tell Batiushka Amvrosy. And do not be carried away with overmuch joy. St. Peter of Damascus teaches, "When joy comes, represent sorrow to yourself; and when you are encompassed by sorrow, try to awaken joy." Thus you will be safeguarded both against deception and against despair.[1] And now pray to God and make five prostrations, repeating, "O holy five wise virgins, pray for me, a sinner!" And then, having fortified yourself [thus], sigh to the Lord Jesus Christ and His Most Pure Mother, and write down this dream! And send it to me.

XXXI. LETTERS TO E.S.

249. ON THE LORD'S THEOPHANY

January 5, 1889

I greet you and all our Matushkas and little sisters who are of one soul with our entry into a new year and with the forthcoming great feast of the Theophany of our Lord. A great event is Theophany. It is celebrated by the Holy Church throughout the world. It is celebrated, too, by every Orthodox soul (especially every monastic soul) when, by means of afflictions, patient endurance according to one's strength, and humility, the soul is cleansed, little by little, from the passions, and especially from demonic pride, and finds peace: that is when it is deemed worthy of Theophany.[2] That is, God Himself is seen by the soul and dwells within it. *His place hath been made in peace.* And the words that follow — *and His dwelling in Sion* (Ps. 75:1). You are still far from this latter. One needs much understanding and many struggles to ascend to this level. But peace you can find: first in your soul, then with the sisters, and then also with God. That is when we will have Theophany. And so try to acquire this longed-for peace. Of course, you cannot do so on your own, but ask God and He will give you the *peace which passeth all understanding* (Phil. 4:7).

---

1. Cf. St. Makarios of Alexandria, First Syriac Epistle (quoted in *The Ascetical Homilies of St. Isaac the Syrian*, p. 455): "In a time of joy let us expect affliction, and in a time of affliction let us expect help."
2. Theophany means "manifestation of God" in Greek.

250. ON HIS OWN ILLNESS

April 1, 1891

Peace to you! Yesterday I wrote to Batiushka about my poor health and asked him not to tell anyone so as not to worry you, my little children, unnecessarily. Now I am writing freely, because I am feeling better. And if I do not inform you now, you will expect me tomorrow as I promised, and if I do not come, you will worry. So now, do not expect me tomorrow. My last year's guest came to visit me — influenza. Last night was miserable for me — nausea, vomiting.

But especially the dizziness such as I have never experienced in all my life. Your eyes become heavy, but the moment you close them, the dizziness begins — and how! It seems like heaven and earth and all my brains and joints are about to turn right over. And the moment this passes, again the eyes become heavy, and again the same awful thing. . . Today N— spent the night with me; I asked him to keep me and some others under observation, because there is influenza on the way. N— thanked me for this. He says that from the symptoms of my illness he decided upon a prescription recommended by X—, namely "homeopathic aconite for dizziness." After two drops of it, I haven't once been dizzy for two hours so far. And that is the main thing and what's scary. . . As for the rest, I will tell you what we find out.

Now they do not lead me about my cell anymore, but I walk myself with a cane. How I wish you could see me, a tottering little old man with a cane!

XXXII. LETTERS TO M.

251. STOP MISBEHAVING AND STOP LAUGHING!

November 29, 1881

Peace to you! Still you are misbehaving over there! And laughing boisterously! Is that how people behave in a hospital?[1] Is that how

---

1. See *The Ladder of Divine Ascent* 1:19: "Let no one, by appealing to the weight and multitude of his sins, say that he is unworthy of the monastic vow. . . The healthy do not go to a hospital."

monastics save themselves? Do those who have put on the garment of repentance and humility sleep like that and laugh like that? N. is a novice, and her vows are little ones. But just look where you are now! A nun! And, moreover, you condemn her for putting eau de cologne on her tongue. Mayhaps this was prescribed for her as a remedy against overmuch talking! Ask her and she will put some on yours too! Save yourself!

252. BE DISCREET IN CONVERSATIONS

January 29, 1882

Peace to you! I am very glad that you have now been pacified! Only, mark my words: bridle your tongue.[1] Always be careful in your conversations. Otherwise a contrary wind will start blowing, and you will grieve, but you won't be able to take back [what you have said]. Above all, remember that humility can save us even without works, but works will not save us, no matter how great they may be.

253. LOVE THOSE WHO OPPOSE YOU

April 22, 1886

Truly Christ is risen!

M., do not be angry! M., humble yourself![2] You are simply being a crank! You have heaped abuse on all the little girls and you ask, "Maybe this is from the enemy?" Well, do you really think it is from grace? Oh dear, some nun you are! Little kids, village girls, she calls to account "by the book" — whereas she herself tramples upon the law of the monastics. "A tooth for a tooth." Oh my Matushka, my saint, all in silver, all in gold! So they are no good — but are you so very good? Crash, bang, "the so-and-so's, the such-and-such, repulsive, I can't stand the sight of them." Why, in what way are you better? They know how to call people names like that too, and how to get mad. Why should you deserve respect? Because you are older? Why, that makes it worse for you! The

---

1. In the Russian there is a saying here which rhymes: "Yesh piróg s gribámi, a yazík derzhí za zubámi." Literally, this translates to "Just eat your mushroom pirog (pie), and keep your tongue behind your teeth."
2. These two sentence rhyme in the Russian: "M., ne yarís! M., smirís!"

Lord said, "Whosoever will be senior, let him be the slave of all and the servant of all" (Cf. Matt. 20:26-27). But you carry on like an angry baroness: "they're repulsive, I don't want to even look at them." Humble yourself! Don't lose your mind from pride and rage. . . Instead, with God's mercy, be patient, in a Christian, monastic manner — give the little girls a good example, love those who oppose you, and the Lord will love us sinners!

254. HOW TO LEARN THE JESUS PRAYER

You have greatly comforted me by wishing to learn the Jesus Prayer. Begin with the oral prayer. But before anything else, lay down as a foundation patiently to endure afflictions. Then it [the prayer] will quickly become part of you. Fast according to your strength. Prayer also requires strength. God will forgive you all that you have confessed. Only, I do not like people who talk in church. All right, thoughts you can't escape — but is anyone moving your tongue for you? And you are a temptation to others too. Save yourself!

255. BE STRAIGHTFORWARD. DO NOT BE ANGRY

You write that you want to disclose to me the details of your temptation but fear disturbing me. Do not be afraid. Write everything you have on your soul. It is your duty to do so, you are a monastic; and it is my duty to accept everything from you. When you write, we will analyze the situation, and I will answer in more detail. But for now I will say: it is sinful to be angry with G. or with anyone else. It is said clearly, *Whosoever hateth his brother is a murderer* (I John 3:15). Humble yourself. Reproach yourself — yourself and not others. You will not answer for G.G. and N.N., but you will certainly answer for yourself.

XXXIII. LETTER TO N—

256. REJOICE THAT YOU ARE WALKING IN THE WAY OF CHRIST, AND DO NOT EXALT YOURSELF

June 28, 1880

Peace to you! And may *the Lord bless thee out of Sion, and mayest thou see the good things of Jerusalem all the days of thy life* (Ps. 127:6). I rejoice with all my soul that you remember my injunction: you do not forget God as far as is possible, and you keep His commandments. The Lord is your helper, and I, the unworthy one, will always be with you in spirit.

Do not be disturbed because they forbid you to perform works of piety; it has always been that way. The word of God proclaims, *All that will live godly shall suffer persecution* (II Tim. 3:12). And our Saviour Himself, leaving His beloved disciples behind in this world and departing to His heavenly Father, said to them, *In the world ye shall have tribulation, but your sorrow shall be turned to joy, and your joy no man taketh from you* (John 16:20,22,33). And He said to them also, "If ye were of the world, the world would love his own. But because ye are not of the world, but I have chosen you out of the world, therefore the world hateth you, even as it hated Me before it hated you" (Cf. John 15:18,19). And so rejoice that you are walking in the way of Christ. Only, do everything with humility, remembering the word of the Lord, *When ye shall have done all those things which are commanded you, say, we are unprofitable servants* (Luke 17:10). Above all, do not exalt yourself and do not think that your life is better than that of others but, on the contrary, think that it is worse. If you will walk thus in the way of piety, you will find yourself within the gates of the Kingdom of God before you know it. There you have a first exhortation. If you have a question about anything, write to me.

XXXIV. LETTER TO P.

257. BLESSED ARE THEY WHO HAVE UNDERSTOOD THE
FALSEHOOD OF THE WORLD AND OF THE DEVIL
February 15, 1876

I read your letter, P., and I was comforted that you do not find it tedious in the convent. For those who are unintelligent and fainthearted, this world is all their life, all their joy. But for the sons and daughters of the Jerusalem on high, this world is a prison. A fraud, a deception — such are all its joys and pleasures! Isaac the Syrian writes, "This world is a harlot; when they carry a man out of his house, then will he understand that the world is a harlot."[1] One finds out, but too late. And therefore blessed, a hundred times blessed, are those who have understood in time the falsehood of the world and of the Devil, and hastened to enter with the wise virgins into the bridal chamber of the heavenly Bride-

---

1. Cf. *The Ascetical Homilies of St. Isaac the Syrian*, Homily 37, p. 164: "This world is a harlot... When the world has stripped a man of everything and thrust him from his dwelling in the day of his death, then only will the man understand that she is verily a deceiver and a beguiler."

groom. *Praise and beauty are before Him, holiness and majesty are in His sanctuary. Bring sacrifices, and go into His courts; worship the Lord in His holy court* (Ps. 95:6,8).

Sion heard and was glad, and the daughters of Judea rejoiced: a light hath dawned forth for the righteous man, and gladness for the upright of heart (Ps. 96:8,9,12). And there is very, very much that is comforting in the services and readings of the Church. Just read Psalm 44 in the Psalter: verses 10, 11, 12 and the rest of the verses of this psalm — and maybe the next psalm too. . . I thank you for your greeting for Lent, and I in turn wish for you that you may pass this gladsome season[1] of the fast in peace and with profit for the soul. "Fasting is the mother of chastity."[2]

XXXV. LETTER TO O.

258. ILLNESS IS FOR YOU A PRICELESS TREASURE

Peace to you, Sister O.! Finally I received a letter from you. I thought that since you were not writing, you must be happy. So it turns out otherwise. So you are getting along just like us, and like all who are saving themselves. Well, at least that makes it easier for us to humble ourselves. For all things, glory be to God. Illness is for you a priceless treasure. Endure patiently. The Jesus Prayer, as it becomes part of one, is unfailingly accompanied by pains in all who are passionate. From the oral prayer, the first thing that aches is the lips. This will pass. Drink as little tea as possible and as weak as possible, and drink cold water more: this will alleviate both your chest condition and the burning of your heart, and ease your suffering. Only the water should not be too cold. As for all the sins you have confessed, may God forgive you.

XXXVI. LETTER TO N—

259. UNLESS YOU EXERT YOURSELF, YOU WILL NOT BE SAVED. AFFLICTIONS MAKE US PRACTICED

With chastisement hath the Lord chastened me, but He hath not given me

---

1. From the Lenten Triodion.
2. Ibid.

over unto death (Ps. 117:18). And for what purpose? So that we would repent. And settle down. But it looks like you and I will decay in the grave before we come to our senses. So we don't like the gloom of the passions You don't say. We would like others to humble themselves (smiryális), while we laugh (smeyális). And in spite of everything, give us consolation. Unwise novice: why, herein lies the whole secret — in wearing us out. As much as our outward man perishes, so much is the inward man renewed day by day, say the Holy Scriptures (II Cor. 4:16). But you and I would like to just roll into Paradise, fat and all. However, I have no time to write right now. I will just say briefly: the Lord wishes not only to grant us eternal life but also to make us practiced — and without afflictions it is impossible to do this. Christ is risen from the dead, by death hath He trampled down death. Therefore we, too, if we wish to put our own death to death, must die by volition. The Apostle, too, says this, "A seed is not quickened, except it fall and die" (Cf. I Cor. 15:36-38). Consequently the Lord loves you, for *whom the Lord loveth He chasteneth. But if ye be without chastisement, then are ye bastards, and not sons* (Heb. 12:8). And so that is why you are worn out, and you feel "ready to lie down and die."

XXXVII. LETTER TO A.

260. THE CROSS OPENS THE ENTRANCE INTO PARADISE

November 18, 1878

Finally, I have gotten around to writing to you, much-afflicted Mother, reverend A. If the word of God is true, *that we must through much tribulation enter into the Kingdom of God* (Acts 14:22), then I cannot but comfort myself with the hope that you will walk right straight through the doors of the Kingdom of Heaven. The holy Fathers relate that when the thief of the Gospel, too, came to the gates of the Kingdom, the Archangel with the flaming sword wanted to chase him away, but he showed him the Cross. Immediately the fire-bearing Archangel himself withdrew and permitted the thief to enter. Understand here not the wooden cross. But which? The Cross in which the chief [Apostle] Paul boasts and concerning which he writes, *I bear in my body the marks of the Lord Jesus* (Gal.

6:17). See of what honor you have been deemed worthy! So do not be despondent! But chant *Open unto me the gates of righteousness; I will enter therein and give thanks unto the Lord. This is the gate of the Lord, the righteous shall enter in thereat* (Ps. 117:19,20). Well, A. and I are righteous too, because although we are actually very, very sinful. . . but. . . we repent.

And St. Dimitry of Rostov, our comforter, wrote, "If a sinner repents, already he is not a sinner, but a righteous man. And I inscribe him together with the righteous."

XXXVIII. LETTER TO N.

261. *DO NOT DISREGARD YOUR DREAM*

January 17, 1879

I read your letter, Sister N., and I read the whole dream to Batiushka Father Amvrosy. Everything would be fine, but it is a pity that the Bridegroom did not give you a wedding garment. Entreat Him, "Illumine the garment of my soul, O Light-Bestower, and save me."[1] You must not disregard this dream. Say the Jesus Prayer more often, and humble yourself. Be patient. And know that the royal garment consists not in the rassa but is sewn from light. And do not be overly concerned about the outward garment. . . The important thing, I say, is to ask the Bridegroom for the royal garment. That is, ceaselessly say the prayer, "Lord Jesus Christ, Son of God, through the Theotokos, have mercy on me."

XXXIX. LETTER TO S.

262. *ONE IN WHOM THAT WHICH IS CORRUPTIBLE HAS NOT DIED WILL BE UNHAPPY EVEN IN THE KINGDOM OF HEAVEN*

You write that despite the improvement in your life, you are still sad. And that you do not have much of a liking for certain people. But I

---

1. Exapostilarion of Holy Week.

will say to you, S.: put you in the Kingdom of Heaven, and you will be unhappy there too. And why? Because that which is corruptible, that which is passionate, has not yet died [within you]. That is why the holy Apostle Paul writes, *A seed is not quickened, except it fall and die* (I Cor. 15:36). Likewise all that is earthly, until it pays its debt to the earth (until it suffers through all that is earthly), cannot but suffer. Therefore, you are suffering from the usual infirmity of human nature — well, so endure patiently. Of course, one who turns to God with all his heart and prays to Him often escapes many sorrows; but now if we do not desire voluntary labors, then we must patiently endure involuntary sorrows so as not to be excluded there from among the saints. It is said that nothing defiled will enter into the Kingdom of Heaven (Cf. Rev. 21:27). This means that if one is to enter this Kingdom, he must exert himself without fail. Well, so you are exerting yourself. And in return for this, you will enter with the wise virgins into the bridal chamber of Christ!

XL. LETTERS TO N.

263. ONE MUST LOVE GOD NOT IN WORD BUT IN DEED

Peace to you, N.! Again you are sad? Still you do not wish to patiently endure your spiritual maladies? So you do not wish to enter into the Kingdom of Heaven? After all, the Scriptures say *that we must through much tribulation enter into the Kingdom of God* (Acts 14:22). So much for our love for the heavenly Bridegroom! In words we love Him and we desire Him — but when it comes to putting it into practice, we go and cry. Do not be fainthearted. After all, you are not a little eight year old girl. I assure you that your troubles are not at all as great as the enemy makes them out to you to be. At home you would have suffered much greater ones, but the enemy would not have broken you up over those so much. However, since you are bearing these for the sake of God, for our sweetest Jesus, therefore the Devil torments you. Well, so are you hungry? Without clothing? Injured?

Save yourself, sister in the Lord! Endure patiently whatever God sends. And believe God's word, that He will not send you any temptation which is beyond your strength! But in the measure in which you will grieve and suffer, in that same measure you will also see the glory of God. Not only there, after your death — but in part, here as well.

264. LIVE SIMPLY. ABOUT THE PRODIGAL SON

Save yourself, N. Peace to you and the blessing of the Lord! You did well in starting to write to me. Live simply. Write when you need to. If I do not answer, do not grieve. I read this letter of yours also: I sincerely sympathize with you and would like to do everything possible for you — but then, would you benefit? Better let us accept everything from the hand of God. If He sends consolation, we will thank Him. And if He does not send consolation, we will thank Him. You cite the case of the prodigal son — why, he did not remain forever in his father's arms either: his father caressed him, fed him some nice hearty veal — and then went with him out to the field with the servants as before. Of course, he did not work — but still together with them he baked out there in the sun. And probably they had more than one run-in with that older brother. But in spite of everything, they remained as an example, and via the Gospel their story has gone throughout the world. Let us likewise not lose heart and despair when everything does not go our way. In spirit I am always with you. And I pray for you. Save yourself!

XLI. LETTER TO A.

265. IF YOU WISH TO BE WITH JESUS, FOLLOW AFTER HIM

Sister A., Once more, Christ is risen! I am glad you got what you wanted! You quit your difficult chanting obedience! But again, a new woe! They reproach you for this. In other words, you would have liked them to praise you. [But] a soldier who flees from the battle is not decorated with medals.[1]

Why, you believe — and I know it well — that you have entered the bridal chamber of the heavenly Bridegroom, the angelic company of the monastics, not in order to pamper yourself and to follow your own whims, but to gaze upon your Bridegroom and follow after Him by His

---

1. Lit., "with crosses." In Russia, the medals awarded in recognition of distinguished military service were crosses, as also in France (the Cross of the Legion of Honor), Britain (the Victoria Cross), etc.

holy path. But how did He walk? He did not sit upon thrones, did He? Or seek honors? Although He deserved them and could have done so, He did not. He just did that which His Father commanded Him: He did good. And in return for this He heard from those He had benefacted, Thou hast a devil, Thou art a Samaritan (Cf. John 8:48). And similar things. And it was for this that God highly exalted His name above every name (Cf. Phil. 2:9). If you wish to be found together with Jesus, follow after Him. It is a sin to be petty!

XLII. LETTER TO N.

266. HE WHO REMEMBERS JESUS HAS A GLAD HEART
I do not know how long ago I received your letter, N., because in it you indicated neither the date nor the month. With regard to the rule I assigned you, I will say this: perform it in whatever way is convenient, only try not to omit it altogether, and for your mind to be occupied with prayer and with God. Because, see, you have tightness in your chest, your heart aches — whereas he who remembers Jesus has a glad heart. Do not believe your dreams, or you will get mixed up. If one is particularly important, you may write it down for me, but beware of interpreting and explaining them on your own. Save yourself, sister!

XLIII. LETTER TO O.

267. DO NOT GRIEVE OVER YOUR SISTER'S ILLNESS
Matushka O., my dear benefactress,
I kept comforting myself with the thought that my new pupil had finally stumbled onto the right path and become acquainted with the way of humility and salvation. But now I hear that O. is going out of her mind because N. has become very ill. O. is going out of her mind because

the Lord has sent N. His mercy, His precious Cross, a serious illness? Silly! Why, look, our Grand Duke, the Commander-in-Chief, has placed his beloved son in the front lines in order to procure a medal[1] for him, though God only knows whether he will receive it. Because very likely he will receive death instead! Whereas you faint because the Lord Himself has come to your sister and placed a cross upon her. My dense pupil. At least from now on be reasonable, and try to comfort the sick one by a cheerful countenance even more than by serving her.

However, I do have faith that you will become wiser. And come to dwell with the wise virgins in the bridal chamber of the heavenly Bridegroom!

XLIV. LETTER TO A.

268. AN EXPLANATION OF THE WORDS OF ST. SERAPHIM OF SAROV. ON WARMTH IN PRAYER

Now Matushka A., you really have acquired too much of a taste for letters. I wrote to you not long ago, and already she is sitting there waiting — "impatiently," yet. It is time, Matushka, to pray, "But a spirit of chastity, humility, patience etc. bestow upon me, O Lord and Master of my life!"[2]

You ask for an explanation of the words of the great Elder:[3] "A broom sweeps dirt and litter out of the house." And what sweeps impurity and the stench of sin out of the house of the soul? Guess!

It would be odd to ask, how does one heat water? Of course, one lays out the coals and lights them and blows on them. The water of tears, which is born of warmth of feeling, is also heated with burning coals, with fire. *Our God is a consuming Fire* (Heb. 12:29). So you see, when the water (tears) cools, hold more tightly to God, to Jesus Christ, the Son of God, and the water (tears) will come to a boil.

We will explain the breathing through the nostrils later. But here is just a little for now: what do you breathe with? Your ear?. . . Of course, with your nostrils! Well, there you have it! So unite prayer to your

---

1. Lit., "a cross." See footnote, Letter #265.
2. Cf. Prayer of St. Ephraim the Syrian.
3. St. Seraphim of Sarov.

breathing, as St. John of the Ladder teaches[1] — and there you have breathing through the nostrils.

As for what comes next, it will become apparent to you. But just this is enough for now.

XLV. LETTER TO M.

269. THE REASON THE SAINTS ARE GREAT IS THAT THEY LEARNED WISDOM THROUGH EXPERIENCE

May 18, 1880

Truly Christ is risen! Reverend Sister M., I do not know how many letters you have written to me, but I have only one on hand. . . Those letters have started to disappear in quantity. But although letters may somewhat alleviate our afflictions and misfortunes, they cannot entirely deliver us from them. The best remedy for them is not consolation (uteshénye), but patience (terpénye). I do not say this so that you would not seek advice, but I impress upon you that all the wisdom of Solomon cannot help one for whom it is needful and beneficial [simply] to suffer affliction. Because wisdom and counsel may teach, but affliction [actually] dislodges passion or sin. And it teaches man not by words but in practice. That is precisely why the saints are great: they learned spiritual wisdom through experience and pain of heart. Give blood, it is said, and receive the Spirit.[2] Peace to you and the blessing of the Lord!

XLVI. LETTERS TO O.P.

270. THE MONASTIC LIFE IS NOT CARNAL BUT SPIRITUAL

August 18, 1876

Out of my pile of letters I am tackling a second one, and I make reply, novice of God, to your letter of August 11.

Peace to you, sister in the Lord!

---

1. See *The Ladder of Divine Ascent* 27:61: "Let the remembrance of Jesus be present with each breath."
2. See footnote, Letter #145.

Needlessly do you grieve over not having before you an elder to whom you could disclose your thoughts and actions, in accordance with the teaching of the holy Fathers. Seek! Can it be that God is not true, Who said, *Seek, and ye shall find* (Matt. 7:7)?

To have your teacher before your eyes is not the important thing! Judas, the ungodly one, was almost inseparably in the presence of Him Who is eternal Truth incarnate, in the presence of Jesus — and he did not profit by this. Therefore, it is not enough to look into the eyes and gaze upon the lips of one's teacher. For the Apostle Paul did not see before him the One Whom Judas saw — but this did not hinder him from being a chief apostle. So do not grieve, remembering Paul, and take comfort in the thought that Jesus our Bridegroom, Who is full of love, did not disdain us, but hearkened unto us and called to Himself us who, impure as we are, are beloved of Him. For He died for sinners. Therefore let us who are sinners not despair.

Your understanding is childish. You anxiously wonder when you will visit us. But I reassure myself precisely with the thought that I am always with you in spirit. Why, you are worse than that Samaritan woman who entered into a debate with the Lord, asserting that one ought to worship in the mountain of Samaria. But the Lord brought her, and us through her, to the understanding that *God is a Spirit* (John 4:24), and so on. Our soul, too, is a spirit. It follows that he who communicates with another spiritually, lives and acts in a manner worthy of a Christian. For our life, especially that of monastics, is not carnal but spiritual. Thus, Abgar the King of Edessa did not see the Lord either, but he loved the Lord and was loved by Him in return.

Now, since thoughts are not a hand or some other object, you can convey them in writing as well, and the Lord will receive this just as He would if it were done orally. . .

You permit despair to enter your heart; that is not Christian. As we approach the Dread Mysteries of Christ, we say, not with reservations or hypocritically, but sincerely, "I believe and confess that Thou art the Christ, the Son of the Living God, whereas I am chief among sinners. . ."[1]

You may write everything always. I will receive it with love.

---

1. Cf. the "Prayers before Holy Communion."

271. HE WHO ATTENDS TO HIMSELF SHALL BE SAVED. BE PATIENT WITH YOUR WEAK SISTER, AND YOU WILL EXTINGUISH CARNAL PASSION

December 20, 1876

I see your sorrow over your spiritual infirmities and failings, and I have good hopes. Because he who attends to himself, and regrets his feeble manner of life, and seeks help from God, will automatically walk in the path of the publican who is praised in the Gospel.

How bad you are! You cannot bear afflictions; you cannot calmly accept reproofs even from those who are older: a whole pile of weaknesses. You have entirely taken after me!

Well, so what are we to do? Should we just throw up our hands? No, Matushka! Let those who practice virtue sit back and relax — but we who are weak absolutely must cry out to Jesus, Who came to call not the righteous but sinners to repentance. And so, having neither works, nor the spiritual strength for struggles, we must cry out without fail, "Lord Jesus Christ, Son of God, have mercy on us!"

The reason you are ashamed to ask forgiveness is that you are not used to it. But when a person becomes accustomed to this work, making a public prostration is as easy as cracking open a nut. And the reason you desire death is that, in the first place, you do not understand what death is and what awaits us there. And in the second place, Matushka, you are pleasure-loving — that is, you do not wish to patiently endure tribulations, as you understand neither the purpose nor the value of tribulations. "The mercy of God is hidden in sufferings."[1]

However, if you will humble yourself, you will in time accept all of this in your heart and understand.

At one and the same time you complain about your incompatible neighbor and of carnal passion. What a funny girl you are! What a slow-witted nun! On the right she is burned with fire; on the left she is doused with cold water. Well, silly, take some water and pour it over the fire! That is, be patient with your weak sister! And the carnal passion will be extinguished. After all, this passion is kindled by and thrives on the hellish fuel of pride and impatience! Endure patiently, and you will be saved! The enemy and the flesh may oppress you, but I will not cease from repeating to you the psalmic words, *Wait on the Lord; be thou manful, and let thy heart be strengthened, and wait on the Lord* (Ps. 26:16)!

---

1. St. Mark the Ascetic, "On Those Who Think That They are Made Righteous by Works," #139.

272. CARRY THE CROSS GIVEN YOU BY GOD

January 25, 1878

Sister, you write that you are exhausted by illnesses and afflictions and do not know how to be saved? It is very simple: carry your cross, ready-made and already placed around your neck by God, by God Himself Who wishes *all men to be saved and to come unto the knowledge of the truth* (I Tim. 2:4). But you, Matushka, have completely lost this true knowledge[1]! Because wrongly do you feel grieved with the Mother Abbess. She does well, very well, in not permitting you to wander about the town. That is completely unmonastic. How in the world did they put up with it before!

At least now be a little wiser: humble yourself, judge yourself, and endure patiently and, as far as you can, gratefully, the treatment which is sent to you by God. That is very simple and even the easiest thing for you, since you yourself admit that you are able to undertake neither voluntary struggles nor prayer. And remember the holy words: the strength of God is made perfect in weakness (Cf. II Cor. 12:9). Peace to you and God's blessing.

273. WHAT IS THE USE OF HEALTH WHEN THERE IS NO PROGRESS IN THE SPIRITUAL LIFE

October 12, 1880

Peace to you, sister! I received your letter, and I am writing you "a line" according to your wish. I see that your health is improving, but there is no improvement in the area of monastic struggles. Well, so what is the use of our health? We did not enter in at the monastery gates for the purpose of preparing our carcasses for display. So why did we come? In order to adorn ourselves with afflictions, illnesses, reproaches from others, fasting, prayer, humility! There you have our purpose in leaving the world! However, I trust that you will gladden me with some good news [one of these days]. As for the attraction of the lusts of the flesh, that is an inevitable conflict for feeble strugglers; otherwise chastity, too, would be easy to come by. . .

---

1. Or "lost your mind"; there is a play on words here.

XLVII. LETTERS TO E.D.

274. [SPIRITUAL] GIFTS ARE GIVEN NOT
FOR LABORS BUT FOR HUMILITY

December 21, 1878

I greet you with the feast of the Nativity of Christ. He who spends this great feast with understanding finds great consolation.

A strange and marvelous mystery do I behold: the cave is a Heaven, the Virgin a cherubic throne.[1] And all virgins who suffer from demons and men for the sake of preserving their purity also, like the Most-holy Virgin, serve as a throne for the Most Pure Son of the Virgin, our Lord Jesus Christ. That is precisely why the enemy so hates those who live in virginity and tries in every possible way to defile them. As for us, let us not become despondent even if we are plunged into impure thoughts, but let us hasten quickly to the pure water of repentance and self-reproach — and the merciful Lord will forgive us. Do not be discouraged. Although you are warred against by passions despite, as you write, your advanced age — as you are already over twenty — still do not be discouraged. Sometimes the passions war against us even at 30, and 40, and 50, and 60, and 70. Purity and passionlessness are bestowed not according to our years — *wisdom is the grey hair unto men* (Wis. 4:9) — but according to our humility. St. John of the Ladder teaches that gifts (and hence purity) are given not for labors (even less for age), but for humility.[2] Let us humble ourselves, and the Lord will cover us, and we will become holy. But until we humble ourselves, and [thus] make God merciful, our passions will not abate, even if we break our forehead against the floor doing prostrations.

275. YOU CANNOT GO THROUGH LIFE WITHOUT
THOUGHTS

February 2, 1889

I received your letter. You cannot go through life without thoughts.

---

1. From the Katavasias of the Nativity of Christ.
2. Cf. *The Ladder of Divine Ascent* 22:32,33.

Just as you can not grow [grain for] bread without manure. For him who is wise, they weave a crown. *Give instruction to a wise man, and he will be yet wiser* (Prov. 9:9). But let him who is tripped up (opletáyetsa) by them repent (káyetsa), arise, and save himself (spasáyetsa).

The monastic life is not torturous, but radiant, holy, and saving. . .

276. THE PASSIONS HUMBLE US

Peace to you and the blessing of the Lord! From your letter I see that your complaint is as before, that is, that you are growing older, but your passions are not leaving you despite your venerable 25 years. It is a great pity that you have lived in this world for so many years now and not destroyed the passions! But then again [if you had destroyed them], what would there be left for you to do now at your venerable age of 25? By what means could one then humble you? But as it is, digging around as you are in this stinking dungheap of passions, you can not raise your eyebrows very high. And you would have to be awfully clever (umudrítsa) in order to take pride in yourself (pogordítsa).

Even though you are sinful, at least be humble. And you will be at peace. The Lord looks precisely upon the humble.

277. THE LORD KNOWS BETTER THAN YOU HOW TO SAVE YOUR MOTHER

The sisters of N— are nagging me. "Write to E., do write," they say, "She is awfully sad." Why, I wrote to you not long ago. And still you are grieving? Why? On account of your mama? If so, that is doubly bad. *He that loveth father or mother more than Me is not worthy of Me* (Matt. 10:37). She is poor, you say: well, so what if the Lord wishes precisely through this, through poverty, and not through ease and plenty, to bring her into His eternal Kingdom? But you foolishly pine away — why does Mama have to go straight into the Kingdom?

Now what if God were to do as you wish and provide for her another path, the one you desire — and your mother were not to enter the heavenly bridal chamber? Then what would you do? Humble yourself, little girl! Not only is God wiser than you, but He is also a thousand times more merciful. You have not died for your mother yet, whereas He, the Holy One, died for us sinners. It is precisely on account of your insubmissiveness to the will of God that passions torment you. . . Sister, learn monasticism. You still have time at your disposal. If something is bothering you, write to me or to Batiushka. Save yourself!

XLVIII. LETTERS TO E.K.

278. DESPAIR IS A TERRIBLE THING

October 2, 1883

Peace to you! You wish to receive a letter from me — I praise your wish. Only you have to do as you are bidden, even if you do not like it. Sincere, childlike honesty is likewise essential. Then we will understand one another. You acknowledge that you are at fault in having murmured and nearly decided to end your life — that is un-Christian. That is terrible. It means you have absolutely no conception of what awaits us in the future life. Your woe passed, but neither the woe nor the joy there will ever pass away unto ages and ages. And perpetually there will only just be beginning either a springtime of life and gladness, or the horrors of death and torment. So live as best you can. Batiushka and I will not forsake you. We will write letters when possible. As for you, write as much as your little heart desires. Save yourself!

279. HOW SAVING IT IS TO DISCLOSE ONE'S THOUGHTS

August 21, 1884

I received your letter. I read your bad thoughts with pleasure, not because I like them, but because you are saying them, albeit with constraint due to false shame — but still you are saying them. And according to the word of God, *Whatsoever doth make manifest is light* (Eph. 5:13). And because the Devil trembles like an aspen[1] leaf in the wind whenever anyone hastens to disclose his sinful thoughts. You write, "For a long time I hid this thought inside, and it was the hardest thing to say." Why, it is precisely in this that the Devil's skill and cunning lies, in that he uses what is to our profit to frighten us. "It is good to confess unto the Lord".[2]

---

1. The aspen leaf always trembles. There is a popular Russian saying that this is because Judas hanged himself on this type of tree.
2. See footnote, Letter #177.

O confess unto the Lord, for He is good, for His mercy endureth forever.[1]
Whereas the enemy tries to use this[2] to instill false fear, false shame: "just
try saying [this thought], and that will be the end of you." But see, it
wasn't the end of you: I came to love you the more for your honesty.

Well, that is precisely how M. has won my favor — she poured out
everything openly, and the Lord apparently helped her. And she
returned a new person. Do you think that if you do not disclose your
weaknesses to me, I will take you for a saint? That will be the day!... You
write, "For M. you can do anything, but you have no sympathy for me."
And you add, "Perhaps this is from self-love." No, it is much worse: it is
from the Devil's pride! You are as ready to get into mischief as the next
person — but she wants everyone to think and speak well of her. Judge
yourself, and do not blame either me or M. I have already assured you
that you are the one who has seen much more favor and kindness from
me — but your pride, which so ill befits both your age and your calling,
conceals everything from you by the gloom of jealousy!

280. REJOICE THAT YOU LIVE WITHIN THE FOLD

For three days D. kept thinking, "What a miserable life! Not to dare
to go past the [convent] enclosure!" O [poor], thrice-miserable one!...

But especially if someone she knows should come to the guest-
house and wish to see his poor dear — he will keep looking so touch-
ingly out of the little window, and here. . . here it is "Don't you dare go
into the guest-house!"

O miserable life! We just have to go past the enclosure. The girls
have to run over to see the visitors more often, ask about their health,
entertain them. . . Right?

But I rejoice precisely because D. is inside the fold, because any old
wolf cannot carry off Christ's ewe-lamb; he will show his teeth to some,
out beyond the gate, and off he goes into the forest. While you are in
God's temple! *How beloved are Thy dwellings, O Lord of hosts! My soul
longeth and fainteth. . .! Blessed are they that dwell in Thy house. For better is
one day in Thy courts than thousands elsewhere. . .* (Ps. 83: 1,5,10) *For He hid
me in His tabernacle in the day of my troubles, He sheltered me* (Ps. 26:5). *I was
glad because of them that said unto me, Let us go into the house of the Lord* (Ps.
121:1). *I went round about and I sacrificed in His tabernacle a sacrifice. . .* (Ps.
26:7). How many consolations, how many joys for a believing soul dwell-

---

1. Psalm 135:1. The word "confess" in the context of this psalm signifies "give
thanks."
2. I.e., confession.

ing in the house of the Lord! But D. feels stifled! She is not allowed to go past the enclosure!

No, you give thanks, a thousand times give thanks that they protect you from wolves, that they watch over you, that they keep vigil for you. And accept with joy any chastisement that they may mete out. *Blessed is the man whom Thou shalt chasten, O Lord* (Ps. 93:12)!

Be more discreet from now on. You[1] have started early to hang around the guest-houses. Our treasurer S. is himself an elder, but the Abbot did not at all like his going to the guest-house. But you are not great eldresses as yet. Learn [the monastic] life, learn unmurmuringly. Why, even life in the world is an absurdity without training. It is all the more so with the spiritual life. Why, you are just like sheep: just take your eyes off them, and in a wink they are past the bushes and off into the forest, looking greedily about.

I have explained to you that laughter is something carnal.[2] From now on after any disorderly silliness, say 33 times [the prayer], "O Theotokos and Virgin, rejoice." Peace to you and salvation, my beloved children!

281. DO NOT REPROACH MATUSHKA

November 20, 1884

When are you going to understand that you are being tested? We see that you have become a bit worse, and you yourself notice it a little. So why do you not wish to be healed? And even if you were innocent, if you were holy and righteous — why not hasten to reproach yourself instead of Matushka? Well, so let us assume you are not stupid, maybe even quite clever! What would you do if you were placed in Matushka's position? I think you would all be barefoot, naked, and hungry. Why, the poor thing was forced into becoming a mother for you. And I, the sinner, am more responsible for this than anyone else. I begged her practically with tears to take pity on my little children, to take them under her wings. . . She listened to me, the sinner, and now she is to blame and before her, I, the sinner. . .

Believe me, we pain for you[3]— so do you pain with us, too. Why, all of us suffer, not for the sake of gain or for the sake of honor, but so that you would be full, so that you would not lose your mind, so that

---

1. The rest of the letter is written in the plural.
2. Or "of fornication"; see also Letter #93.
3. The rest of the letter is in the plural.

you would be at peace, and holy, and pure, and righteous!. . . That is what we busy ourselves about, that is what we suffer for. That is what we entreat God for. So you pray, too. And do not grumble!

282. LOSE NO TIME — LEARN THE PRAYER
March 4, 1885

Peace to you! What is this that has happened to you? I can not understand it. Fever and chills and all kinds of awful things. I am very, very sorry for you, poor little thing. . . I see that for you, the blessed time of being laid up has come. So lie there. Just lie there and say the little prayer: Lord Jesus Christ, Son of God, have mercy on me, the sinner, the infirm one. Otherwise, look what might happen: you would be glad to say it, but you won't have the strength: the doors will be shut. And those who have managed to light their lamps in time will be dancing with their sweetest and most longed-for Bridegroom with the unceasing sound of them that keep festival. And the lamp is precisely this prayer. The heart is the wick, the prayer is the fire — and unspeakable joy in the prayerful heart is the action of the Holy Spirit: delight in the bridal chamber with the heavenly Bridegroom. Therefore I exhort you and I beg you: do not slumber, do not waste time in laughter and jokes, time which will never return — all these fleeting consolations will turn into burning coals, into loathsome stench, into unbearable torment, and there will be nowhere to flee. Therefore the Lord also said to His beloved ones, *Watch and pray, that ye enter not into temptation.* . . (Matt. 26:41) Peace to you!

283. THE SOLE MEANS OF BEING PEACEFUL AND HAPPY IS THE JESUS PRAYER

I received your second letter as well. . . Great is your affliction! And after all, the Lord said, *In the world ye shall have tribulation, but your sorrow shall be turned into joy. And your joy no man taketh from you* (John 16:20, 22, 33). So you, too, sit by the seaside and wait for fair weather. . .

As regards your heaviness of heart, I have both told you and will tell you again: the sole means of being peaceful and happy is the Jesus Prayer. Without this precious gift, seek no consolation in monasticism, expect none. But how to seek Jesus? I have read to you from the Bible, and you have read yourself.

284. THE LORD SEES OUR PATIENCE

I received your letter. You say you are depressed. You do not wish to bear this burden either? Why, what then are you preparing as a dowry for your Bridegroom? After all, He is the King of kings and the Lord of lords! How is it that you do not wish to understand that the only thing we are able to offer to this most beloved Jesus is to endure patiently. More comely than all the sons of men (Cf. Ps. 44:2), day and night He beholds us — "I stand at the door of your heart," He says, "and knock" (Cf. Rev. 3:20). As an army commander stands in an elevated place and observes who is fighting, and where, and how, and crowns those who merit it, even so the Leader of us monastics, the Comeliness of Angels, is always by our side. Only listen to me, say the Jesus Prayer more often. Yea, you will be grateful [for it]! For encouragement and consolation, read chapters 81, 87, 73, etc., and actually it would be good to read the entire book, On Virginity by St. John Chrysostom. So you do not understand yourself! Well, so thank God both for what you are and for the fact that you do not understand what you are. But your lot is a high one. Fear not, My little flock, for it is God's good pleasure to give you the Kingdom (Cf. Luke 12:32)!

XLIX. LETTER TO A.D.

285. YOU DESIRE HEAVENLY GLORY, BUT THRUST AWAY THE MEANS OF OBTAINING IT

August 20, 1881

Reverend novice, Sister A., I must have received all your letters, but I have not been careful to answer them all. I asked Batiushka about your last letter, and I have received an answer now, which I am enclosing for you. As regards your great afflictions, it seems that, like me, you are not very fond of them. Like me, the sinner, I see you came to the monastery to seek heavenly glory and the eternal delight of Paradise, but you thrust away the means for obtaining this. You want to get to the gold ore, but you do not wish to dig in the earth. No, Matushka, nowhere in the world do things happen like that, and they cannot. *He that shall endure unto the end, the same shall be saved* (Matt. 24:13)!

L. LETTERS TO O.O.

286. LET US BEGIN WITH SELF-REPROACH AND OBEDIENCE TO THOSE WHO ARE OLDER

December 7, 1879

Skete of Optina Hermitage

I received your letter. It is nice to see that you are so grateful. You are greatly comforted by my letters. And I do not mind writing to you, either. Only on the condition that you will also comfort me. Now, I do not demand anything special from you, just what you have promised, that is, that you will try to fulfill my advice. That will be the best proof of your gratitude and the best consolation for me. However, they tell me that after returning from the Elders, O. has become more irritable, more disobedient, more petty!

Of course, I do not believe all of this, because I know you and your sincere promise to humble yourself, to obey, to constrain yourself in the monastic life. But probably there is also some truth to these rumors. And so, O., do not be angry with me, but take my honest advice to heart: judge yourself, and try to correct yourself. But we cannot correct ourselves unless we begin with self-reproach (and not with reproaching others) and with obeying those who are older as much as we can. Because — you are small. If you will try to do this, that is when the business of monasticism will go forward. And all good people will love you. And God will love you. For He Himself says, "If any man will keep My commandments, I will love him and will Myself come unto him" (Cf. John 14:21). "I and My Father will come unto him, and make Our abode with him" (Cf. John 14:23). This means that They will live right there in your heart. This, O., is what I desire for you more than anything in the world. Because it is precisely for this that we were born into the world; it is for this that we live; it is for this especially that we have come to the monastery. That is, in order to patiently endure afflictions, malicious talk, labors, illnesses, and humiliation — and there to receive unspeakable good things which *eye hath not seen, nor ear heard, neither have entered into the heart of man. . .* (I Cor. 2:9).

Peace to you and the blessing of the Lord!

287. IN ORDER TO FIND CONSOLATION WE MUST LOOK
WITHIN OURSELVES AND STUDY THE WORD OF GOD

April 19, 1880

I thank you, O., for your greeting. And I also greet you with a joyous "Christ is risen!". . . You wish a word of consolation from me, the sinner. You dense little girl! Why, just take that canon of St. John Damascene: there you have profound thoughts, there you have light, there you have consolations without end. "Let us purify our senses and we shall behold Christ, radiant with the unapproachable light of the Resurrection."[1] Thus, in order to find genuine consolation, what is needful is not to stare about, or to whisper to your friend, or to misbehave — but to look within yourself, to comfort yourself with the word of God, and to conduct yourself as I have told you personally. Otherwise, no consolations will be of any help to you. And your mindset is childish: she gazes at hats, at fancy clothes — why, your own clothing is regal! Resplendent not with colored fabric but with heavenly significance! *Let my soul rejoice in the Lord, for He hath clothed me in the garment of salvation and covered me with the robe of gladness. He hath placed upon me a crown as upon a bridegroom, and adorned me with ornaments as a bride* (Is. 61:10). And further on: *For the Lord hath taken pleasure in thee, and as a young man liveth with a virgin, so shall thy sons dwell with thee; and it shall come to pass that as a bridegroom rejoiceth over a bride, so will the Lord rejoice over thee* (Is. 62:4,5). Your true Bridegroom Jesus, and not some ragman, some petty shopkeeper!. . . May the Lord preserve you and teach you to distinguish the [delusive] sweetness of Gehenna from the pure joy of Paradise!

288. SPECIAL APPLES

December 9, 1880

O., I remember your wish to receive a line from me, and especially a treat; I am sending you three special apples. For more than a week they were lying on my window sill and looking out at the skete, and at the little birds, and at everything in the skete. Save yourself. Labor. Pray. Above all, do not be vainglorious, and guard your eyes!

---

1. From the Paschal Canon.

289. CLEVER LITTLE GIRL

October 12, 1881

Yes, O., it is true, I have not written to you in a long time. But I kept being about to. And I would even hurry to send off a letter or a treat, but circumstances were always inopportune. . . As for [writing you] three lines, I am doing so with love. I read your letter. What a huge number of sins you have listed there! She is so little, I thought, and here she has scraped together so many great big sins! Now, that is not such a big thing, that a sinful person should have sins — just like a nut tree has nuts, a turnip plant has turnips, and so on. But the unusual thing is this: where can a little person collect a whole tightly-packed basketful of troubles? Those troubles are even so great that O. just tucks her head under her pillow, and she thinks. . . "Why was I born?" Really, that is some question there: Why was O. born? And why does she go on living? [What], why does she go on living, yet?! That is really some question! Why, such a thought only enters the mind of a rare philosopher. It seems to me that it never did enter mine. . . What a clever girl you are! One thing, though, you apparently do not know, and that is what St. John Chrysostom says: what is most distressing and unbearable here on earth cannot even be compared with what is least so there.[1] Save yourself! Peace to you! May the Lord forgive all the sins and weaknesses you have confessed. And may He, our All-merciful Saviour, and His Most Pure Mother, help you to correct yourself. But our correction is humility, that is, the acknowledgement of our weaknesses. And remember the saying that a sinner who repents and humbles himself is dearer to God than a righteous man who is conscious of his own righteousness. Now since you repent before me and before God, and abase yourself, and are ashamed of your weaknesses, the Lord will both have mercy on you and save you. And you will see the good things of Jerusalem (Cf. Ps. 127:6)!

---

1. I.e., in hell.

LI. LETTERS TO A.G.

290. A PASCHAL GREETING AND AN
EXPLANATION OF THE PASCHAL CHANTS
April 20, 1883

Truly Christ is risen! At long last you remembered me with a greeting. And I in turn greet you with the joyous greeting. "O Thy divine and beloved and most sweet voice! Thou hast truly promised that Thou wouldst be with us unto the end of the world, O Christ! O Wisdom and Word and Power of God! Grant that we may partake of Thee fully in the unwaning day of Thy Kingdom!"[1]

What does this "fully" mean? Read concerning this in the Gospel of St. John, chapters 14, 15, and 16, and in the Ladder, Step 30, chapters 10, 11, 12, 13, 16, 17. And perhaps you will understand a tiny bit. But it would take me too long to explain. And besides, my mind isn't very capable of it. But you will understand at least a tiny bit anyway. "Father, I pray not for the world, but for them which Thou hast given Me. That they also may be with Me, that they may behold My glory which I had with Thee before the foundation of the world" (Cf. John 17:5,9,24). "As I am in Thee and Thou in Me, so they also may be with Us" (Cf. John 17:21).

Why, it is even awesome to think of what awaits us there: *it doth not yet appear what we shall be* (I John 3:2). And so patiently endure afflictions and heaviness. It is said that, "everyone that shall leave father, or mother, or wife, or brother, or sister, shall receive an hundredfold, and shall inherit eternal life" (Cf. Matt. 19:29).

I have been thinking much about your temporal well-being. . . I am having the thought, why don't you get together with A.S. She is a humble girl. She also wishes to build a cell, she is not fussy, not willful; you have different Matushkas,[2] but this cannot interfere with your concord: I don't think you would go and be a temptation to one another by dragging each other to your respective Mothers. There is only one possible

---

1. From the Paschal Canon.
2. Spiritual mothers, in this context.

problem — what if you become attached to each other? Then it would be difficult to pull you apart. However, in you I have hope. I do not think you would quickly go off in that way. I am only speaking by way of cautioning you. Peace to you!

291. YOU HAVE SIMPLY GOTTEN LAZY!

November 21, 1883

Finally the fleas have gotten to Annushka. Because she was just sitting there, being quiet. And who knows how she is getting along. Now I see they have gotten to her — she hollered! And thank God! Remember: a repenting sinner is more pleasing to God than a self-satisfied righteous man. And whomever God loves, I love also.

You write that you have developed an aversion to everything sacred — no, you do not understand yourself: you have simply gotten lazy and come down to the same level as me. Because I am just exactly like that. I myself am ashamed of it, but I cannot master my slothfulness. Even my teeth ached in exactly the same way — well, God willing, they will heal. Why, it seems that in your case everything has begun to ache — your feet, and the small of your back, and you have weakness — too bad there is no fresh nettle, or I would cure you. . . As for the thoughts, there is nothing new there. I would be surprised if you didn't have any. Then I wouldn't be able to handle you. But as it is, involuntarily you will humble yourself. In the other case one would even be afraid to love you, you would be so holy — but now one cannot help loving you, and as the saying goes, "Birds of a feather flock together,"[1] and I love you for your childlike frankness. . . Peace to you, save yourself! Write, without being embarrassed because you are not nice: I am much worse than you. But see, kind people still love me.

---

1. More literally, "Like automatically befriends like." (Svoy svoyemú ponevólke drug.")

292. DO NOT WORRY ABOUT YOUR CELL
September 26, 1884

Peace to you, A.! You, dear, have become so embittered against me that you believe your thought that I do not read your letters. Now aren't you ashamed to slander me so, in return for all my love for you! Why, it is precisely your letters that I have been reading!. . . Do not worry over-much about your cell! S. fixed herself up beautifully — but she is more depressed than you! And that precisely because she became tied up with her cell. Remember God's word: *Our conversation is in the Heavens* (Phil. 3:20). But these cells often draw the mind and the heart far away from the abodes on high, and result in many vain cares and worries for the soul. What did the Lord say: "Behold the fowls of the air, which gather not into barns, yet your heavenly Father feedeth them. Are ye not much better than they" (Cf. Matt. 6:26)? You doubting Thomas! Come to your senses!

293. HAVE FAITH IN PROVIDENCE
December 12, 1884

Do not be despondent, A. I am glad that God sent you an occasion to recognize your weakness in time. Be thankful to God for this lesson, and try to profit from it. *Give instruction to a wise man, and he will be yet wiser* (Prov. 9:9). Do pray for your father, but have faith that everything which God sends is beneficial. We must have faith in divine Providence and give no place to faintheartedness and our own reasonings. Today is the sun's turn toward summer; I wish that you also may attain to a turn toward warmth and joy. Peace to you!

LII. LETTERS TO S.

294. ON THE FEAST OF CHRIST'S NATIVITY —
A WISH FOR PATIENCE
December 22, 1877

Skete of O.H.

I greet you, Seraphimochka, with the approaching feast of the

Nativity of our Lord and Saviour Jesus Christ. Never is it more appropriate to wish someone peace than during these days, for it is for this that Christ was born, to bring peace on earth. Therefore, anyone who murmurs and is discontented with his situation does not experience this feast. So if you should notice in yourself this illness of unbelief, leave off. And the Lord will reward you. I consulted Batiushka Father Amvrosy about you also, and he bids you to wait. Have patience, my dear. Impatience, on the other hand, brings no profit to anyone. After all, you are not out in the snow like some Bulgarian[1] — you are sitting nicely in your parents' home among your near ones. And always God is with you, and He keeps looking into your heart: what are you thinking in there? Do you love Him? And are you willing to patiently endure everything for His sake, for the Merciful One? Now, if you find an occasion, I suppose you may come to us. Only, we haven't put a spot in order for you as yet. So be at peace! And God will be with you unto the ages. Desiring this for you, I remain your sincere well-wisher.

295. BE PATIENT IN TRIBULATIONS, AND BE STRAIGHTFORWARD

March 27, 1878

Much-suffering S., In the world all you had was tribulations, and now you have tribulations. In the Holy Scriptures too it is said, *We must through much tribulation enter into the Kingdom of God* (Acts 14:22). Now wouldn't you like to enter in there? Be patient, Matushka; thank the Lord that He has deemed you worthy to taste of His cup of sorrows. And He will save you.

I am sorry for you because you still do not trust me, S. You still do not want to reveal your infirmities and needs. But it is time you were straightforward. . .

Peace to you!

---

1. I.e., like a wanderer, like a Gypsy.

296. DO NOT BE ABSENT-MINDED, AND WRITE ABOUT EVERYTHING HONESTLY

July 19, 1878

Reverend novice S., Peace to you and blessing from the Lord! I have read all your letters, both new and old. And from all of them I can see that you are not listening to me. That is, you are not indicating on the letters when they were sent — neither month nor date. And so I am writing to you, correct yourself! And indicate the date and month from now on. And write about yourself sincerely and unhypocritically — that is, if things are fine, then write that they are fine, but if they aren't quite fine, then write it the way it is.

As regards [chanting on] kliros, do so while you have the strength. When we see each other, then we will talk it over fully.

297. SALVATION LIES IN PATIENCE AND HUMILITY

January 4, 1879

I greet you with the present feasts and with the new year. From my heart I wish you, much-ailing and much-suffering sister in the Lord, patience and humility; in these consist our salvation. I grieve much for you, that you are suffering so. But the Lord suffered also, and how He suffered!

As regards showing a doctor your ailment: may God bless! I would not have advised you to do this with your previous illness, but with a serious one you may. Only let the doctor examine you with Elikonida or someone else present.

298. THE MERCY OF GOD IS HIDDEN IN SUFFERINGS

July 11, 1879

It has been arranged by God Who saves us that no one can avoid tribulations, because the Lord would like to save all, whereas without tribulations it is impossible to be saved.

"The mercy of God is hidden in sufferings!"[1] So the holy Fathers teach. Be patient, and you will be saved.

---

1. St. Mark the Ascetic, "On Those Who Think That They are Made Righteous by Works," #139.

299. DO NOT FORGET THAT WHICH HAS BEEN ENJOINED YOU

October 15, 1879

Save yourself, sister in the Lord! Do not forget that which has been enjoined you. Especially the Jesus Prayer and the commentary that "the mercy of God is hidden in sufferings."[1] And so that means the more painfully, the more deeply something clutches at your heart, the more benefit to the soul, the more mercy from God. Know for certain and believe that it is inevitable for all who are to inherit the life of Paradise to taste of the bitter tree of temptations — but for all this a reward will be rendered a hundredfold. According to the multitude of sorrows Thy consolations, (O Lord), brought gladness unto my soul (Ps. 93:19).

300. SELF-REPROACH IS THE EASIEST VIRTUE

October 17, 1879

Save yourself! That is, humble yourself, be patient, love your neighbor — and before you are in the mantia, you will be in the angelic choir. But if you should fall short in something, reproach yourself, and the Lord will receive even this in the place of struggle. That is why Pimen the Great said, "Self-reproach is the easiest virtue." And Isaac the Syrian says, "Humility, even without works, can save a man". . .[2]

Pray, labor, be patient, and above all humble yourself and, I repeat, you will be a seraph. St. Isaac the Syrian writes, "The assembly of the humble is an assembly of the Seraphim."[3]

301. YOU GRIEVE FOR SOME UNKNOWN CAUSE

January 11, 1880

Reverend, heroic, much-suffering, much-ailing [sister in the Lord]... I received your letter, only I must admit I do not understand what these great woes of yours might be. It seems that most of all you grieve for some cause unknown to yourself, to me and, it seems, to anyone; as for

---

1. Ibid.
2. Cf. *The Ascetical Homilies of St. Isaac the Syrian*, Homily 69, p. 338.
3. Cf. *The Ascetical Homilies of St. Isaac the Syrian*, Homily 51, p. 245.

what might happen, that is, you might be transferred somewhere, you might get sick, etc., etc. — these things could happen to me just as well or to anyone, but no sensible person cries over this ahead of time, but awaits whatever the Lord may send him. And whatever the Lord sends, good or bad, he receives it with joy and does his best to endure patiently. And if he cannot endure patiently, he repents of his faintheartedness. But you and I get fainthearted well ahead of time, before even seeing any disasters or sorrows, and we are in distress before any distress appears. You are a Christian, so live in a Christian manner. Have faith in God, Who fashioned you and Who has numbered you among His chosen little sheep. Among His beloved brides. And as such, you are now written in the Heavens. As for your present troubles (as I recently wrote to someone else), they are your dowry for your beloved Bridegroom Jesus. So don't kick when there is being thrust at you a whole stash of precious dowry.

302. CONCERNING TRUE FASTING. CONCERNING DEMONIC THREATENINGS

March 13, 1880

Reverend sisters, new strugglers, lying not upon the earth but reclining upon your beds, save yourselves!

Chant once more in third tone, "The springtime of the fast hath dawned forth, and so, too, the blossom of repentance. Wherefore, O ye sisters, let us purify ourselves from every defilement whilst chanting unto the Giver of light."[1]

Little sisters, did you read this or no? Well, I have written it for you. Here is something else you should chant in third tone (you just missed it since you weren't in church on Monday), "Let us fast with an acceptable fast, pleasing unto the Lord. A true fast is the estrangement from evil, restraint of tongue, refraining from anger, separation from lust, slanders, lies and false oaths. Abstinence from these things is a true and acceptable fast."[2] So there is hope of not perishing even if one is lying on one's bed? Yes! Keep what is indicated here, and you will not perish. Now, that really would be nice and marvelous: to ride into Paradise on one's bed. Nevertheless, one can say for certain that he who humbles himself will ride into Paradise. Only let him reproach himself and not others. One cannot demand anything from those who are sick. As for those scary,

---

1. Cf. the Vespers Aposticha, Wednesday of Cheesefare Week.
2. From the Vespers Aposticha, Monday of the First Week of Lent.

ever so scary things that knock on your window, break cups, and shatter oil bottles — I have discussed it with Batiushka. Batiushka has blessed you to have a moleben served to all the saints to whom all of your church altars are dedicated; that is, first to the Precious Cross, the Protection of the Most Holy Theotokos, and so on in order. Add to them the holy Martyr Conon. And I suggest that you add also the Hieromartyr Cyprian. And be at peace — soon everything will pass! All this murky power means nothing and will accomplish nothing. It only scares you like children. The whole legion did not dare touch the swine — is it about to touch you, God's novices? As for you, S., who have no patience, at least lying down cry out, "O Lord and Master of my life. . . a spirit of chastity, patience, love bestow upon Thy handmaid."[1] Now is an opportune time to pray thus. And so, save yourselves. Serve Sasha right now while she is sick — but the most important service is to carry each other's spiritual infirmities, and then you should also serve one another by deeds, *in honor preferring one another* (Rom. 12:10).

And you, Sasha, maybe you have gotten well by now? If so, you also learn patience, humility, fasting. And above all, both of you, flee competition with one another. Where there is peace, there is God. I, too, am with you in spirit. . . All of us are equal before God.

303. HOW IS YOUR SPIRITUAL BUSINESS? PRACTICE THE JESUS PRAYER

April 7, 1880

Last week I received a letter from your mother in which she asked

---

1. From the "Prayer of St. Ephraim the Syrian."

us to decide whether Olga (is that your aunt?) can fully trust her husband with business. Her husband has stopped drinking. Batiushka's decision was to wait a year.

And how is your spiritual business, Seraphimochka? Have you acquired much? That is, have you patiently endured many sorrows? Have you tried much to be a consolation to the sisters living with you? Have you reproached yourself much? And inwardly praised your sisters? If you have labored in these things at least a little — well for you! But if you have not thus trained yourself, reproach yourself and make a beginning. If your body will not endure fasting and labor, then turn your attention to your soul, that is, your heart and mind. Practice them in the Jesus Prayer. And your gain will be greater than that of those who labor with the body. Above all, hold to the Jesus Prayer, sometimes orally and sometimes with the mind. In time you will come to love it, but in the beginning, it is true that it is sometimes difficult.

And as you two perform outward prayer and reading according to your strength, since you are of one soul, you need not feel too shy in front of one another. If one of you becomes exhausted and lies down, the other, without the least embarrassment, should go ahead and do prostrations, or read, or say the Jesus Prayer. The one lying down also benefits from prayer that is said aloud.

304. HOW TO LIVE AT HOME

June 1, 1880

Peace to you and the blessing of the Lord! I received your letter from home, but a little late — I was expecting it earlier. Glory be to God that you arrived safely. Rest, catch up on your sleep, don't go to Matins for now, drink milk, and comfort your mother.

I see that thus far your letters are not becoming more frequent, so you are not depressed. May the Lord grant that it is so, for you just kept sighing and grieving. Nevertheless, write often, Matushka, if you please, whether things are going well for you there or not — and when you become sad, pick up St. Abba Dorotheos, crawl into a hole, and read. And that little prayer, don't forget the Jesus Prayer. *Behold, now [is] the accepted time. . .* (II Cor. 6:2).

305. HOW TO LIVE IN YOUR CELL

September 3, 1880

Peace to you[1] and blessing! Now God will bless An-sia to go to Moscow. And you, Matushka Seraphima, remain as a cell-attendant, a real cell-attendant for Sasha. And you, Sasha, be a helper, a real helper for Seraphima. And so there will be peace. Seraphima did well in helping An-sia (the elderly cell-attendant) — it was with this very intention that I placed an elderly one [with you], so that the two of you would not be overly pampered by having a cell-attendant and look on with your hands folded as she ran around and did the cleaning. In such a case you would have felt a bit embarrassed, too — but instead, it is "No, no" — and you'll sweep the stairs yourselves, and fetch water, and get your-selves some small pitchers so as not to strain yourselves. And if you are ailing, have a whole barrel brought up, pump some water, and go to sleep. And let Sasha not fall behind the others, even though it is hard for her old bones to bend over and wash dishes — it still is better than suf-fering so from despondency. But if she will listen to me, then her life will be happier, too. I see now that you do not remember my advice, and so I am reminding you once more in a note of the rules you were given. . .

306. CONGRATULATIONS UPON RECEIVING THE ANGELIC ORDER

November 24, 1880

Reverend sister, Mother Seraphima, I congratulate you with your new title, new rank, new life — the angelic conversation. *Let my soul rejoice in the Lord, for He hath clothed me in the garment of salvation and cov-ered me with the robe of gladness. He hath placed upon me a crown as upon a bridegroom, and adorned me with ornaments as a bride* (Is. 61:10). Blessed art thou, daughter, that the Lord hath chosen thee, loved thee, crowned thee with the angelic garment as His bride, and numbered thee with His hon-orable and chosen flock: Fear not My little flock, for it is God's good pleasure to give you the Kingdom (Cf. Luke 12:32).

Hearken, O daughter, and see, and incline thine ear; and forget thine own people and thy father's house. And the King shall greatly desire thy beauty. At Thy right hand stood the queen, arrayed in a vesture of inwoven gold, adorned in varied colors. The virgins that follow after her shall be brought unto the King,

---

1. This letter is generally written in the plural.

they shall be brought with gladness and rejoicing, they shall be brought into the temple of the King (Ps. 44:8,9,10,13,14).

You wish a rule for your new life. But what kind of rule can one give you who are sick? With all your strength cleave to Jesus, your beloved Bridegroom, and that will be enough. Say the Jesus Prayer with your mind, with your voice, in a whisper, any way you can. As for readings and prostrations, do them when you have the strength.

307. A GREETING ON THE NATIVITY OF CHRIST
December 24, 1880

Christ is born, give ye glory! That is, chant thus with your voice and glorify Christ. And then reflect: how is it that the Uncontainable One has been contained in a manger, how is it that He Who is awesome to the Cherubim and Seraphim is held in the Virgin's embrace? How does He Who holds the Heavens in His hand now lie in a cave? Truly, a strange and marvelous mystery![1] And so in this way, give ye glory to the Lord! And then give ye glory by deeds, that is, by love for one another!

308. DO NOT FEEL OPPRESSED BY SCOLDINGS
January 15, 1881

"Who is he that loveth me, but the same which receiveth sorrows from me?" (Cf. II Cor. 2:2) — thus wrote the holy Apostle Paul to his disciples. And thus I wanted to try out the new nun: how would she receive "sorrow from me"? It turned out Mother Seraphima is not gracious to me when I bring sorrows but loves me only when I bring consolations. The moment I gave her a lecture and became severe — "it is Sasha's fault," and other people's. Why, how have I offended you? How have I disgraced you? Can it be that you cannot take scoldings even from me? And all for nothing — after all, are we penalizing you? Are we reporting you to anyone?

All right, let us assume that they told on you to me and that they had no grounds for what they said — but whom have we told? Now, how can I give you reproofs and admonitions any more, when they make you ill? Did I reprove you in order to do you in? What I expected was that you would take it with humility, and hasten to reproach yourself and not others — but it turned out otherwise.

---

1. From the Katavasias of the Nativity of Christ.

Well, I won't offend you, that is, reprove you. I have told you before that you do not understand yourself — but you consider yourself so wise that you place your own opinions above those of others. And on what account have you become so angry with Sasha? All right, she made a mistake — all right, she lied — but still you cannot say she wishes you harm. She made a mistake — and you are infallible?

No, I have not taken offense. You made that up yourself; as before, I am sincerely well-disposed toward you. Of course, I didn't think you would quarrel so quickly — you haven't even lived together for a year — and this pains me; but still I know well your weaknesses. It is a pity that you yourself do not notice your touchy personality, which I had some experience of even here; I would say something innocently or jokingly, and you would flare up and I would be embarrassed. But still I say, that's human, and I haven't changed toward you. Only I ask you: stop whimpering. Your tears are not only unprofitable but even silly. . . Leave off silliness, tears, and anger. It is a sin! Peace to you!

309. WHAT IT MEANS TO SAVE ONE'S SOUL

January 25, 1881

Peace to you and salvation!. . . I had become used to receiving letters from you [two] often; but now, not having received any for a long time, I do not know how you [two] are getting along there. Peaceably, may God grant. *His place hath been made in peace* (Ps. 75:2). Where there is peace, there God is also.

Where God is, there is also peace. And the opposite of this is self-evident: where there is envy, enmity, impatience, self-love — there the Devil is also. Where the Devil is, there is everything destructive, proud, hostile. *In your patience possess ye your souls* (Luke 21:19). And so do not slacken, do not grow despondent when you meet with an opportunity to possess your soul. To possess one's soul means to give it that preeminence and position ordained for it by God: that is, for it to be sovereign. Godlike, righteous, holy. But to fall away from this means to destroy one's soul. What is a man profited, if he shall gain the world and lose his own soul (Cf. Matt. 16:26)? And so always put first your own spiritual profit and that of others, and only then what is necessary for the body — comforts, tranquility, and perhaps sometimes consolation. *Let Thy mercy, O Lord, be upon us, according as we have hoped in Thee* (Ps. 32:22)! You may visit the sick sister now and then.

310. ONE WHO IS NOT ENDURING TEMPTATIONS FROM
THE SISTERS WILL BE TEMPTED BY THE DEMONS

October 12, 1881

You are troubled by demonic temptations. One cannot be without this. One who is not enduring temptations from the sisters must endure them from the demons. Read about this in St. John of the Ladder.[1] If it were otherwise, then those who at present are rubbed this way and that by others would in time appear bright and white — whereas those in reclusion would appear just as they were before. . . Endure patiently, Matushka! Endure everything patiently, and you will be at peace with yourself, and you will bring peace to others! But if you begin reckoning up scores, you will lose your peace, and your salvation along with it. . .

311. HE REPROACHES HER FOR
PERPETUAL DISSATISFACTION

April 9, 1883

I received your letter. Always you are forgotten. I don't write to you every week. Why, where am I to find the time? I wrote you two a letter — "no, that was to Sasha — mine should be separate, as you know." Why, you yourselves say that you love and pity me, but at such a time just reading your letter is already toil and travail. And such letters as yours, too! Perpetual dissatisfaction, perpetual upset. How many times have you yourself repeated: from now on I will be patient and leave her alone — and then in actuality, you yourself annoy her. So she is lying down, just let her lie! As if what is between you isn't enough, you reproach me as well for leaving you at the convent, for promising and not coming through. [And] I think: I myself travelled to Livna and Kaluga in search of my daughters! And I had great hopes for them! Now, I assured both you and Sasha that I sincerely desire the very best for you, that is, the same as I desire for myself. I saw that you could live on my allowance, as very many live, and as I lived: but no, you need comfort. Your cell-attendant isn't capable: N. wasn't capable, and P. wasn't capable. Turns out you are the only capable ones! The only solution is to give each of you a maid. The old ones are no good — they know too much; the young ones are no good — they know too little. Give you one who knows everything

---

1. See *The Ladder of Divine Ascent*, 4:30.

and does everything just so. But you educated know-it-alls cannot yourselves please one another. So begin yourselves to show an example of pleasing one another and of love. Begin with yourselves!

312. YOU REPROACH OTHERS BUT DO NOT CORRECT YOURSELF

April 14, 1883

I received your letter, S. You keep worrying and grieving about P., how in the world to teach her — and I keep being concerned about how in the world to teach you. How many times have I told you to learn composition and how to form your letters at least tolerably well — nothing of the sort: it is going from bad to worse. And let's not even mention spiritual matters: not a drop of humility and patience has materialized. It is constantly, "P. doesn't know how to. . ." — so why don't you know how? Sasha hasn't complained once about her. But N. didn't please you — she knows too much; P. is young — she knows too little. As for you, you know everything, but you don't even do what is most essential — spiritually, that is. You've even exalted yourself above me — "Don't write so sternly to me, or else I'll become ill." Some nun!

I don't forbid you to teach; it is a good work — live and learn. Only begin with yourself. You are more dear to me than P.! P. can simply be sent elsewhere, but you are always with me. Peace to you! Now are all things filled with light; Heaven and earth, and the nethermost regions of the earth. Let all creation, therefore, celebrate the arising of Christ![1]

313. DO NOT GRUMBLE ABOUT THE MONASTIC LIFE

March 27, 1884

Again it's my fault that I've shut you up in the convent. But for this I expected gratitude. That at least you would thank God for such a great mercy of His shown to you!. . . With regard to your sinning in thought, God will forgive you for this when you repent; but now when you grieve over having preferred our sweetest Jesus to a husband — for this you will suffer. You keep picturing how your husband would feed you blini and pumpkin — but the other bitter side you do not wish to see.

And can a husband, no matter how good,wures and delights than

---

1. From the Paschal Canon.

the Creator of Heaven and earth?. . . Don't grumble! And try to see your own failings! Be grateful to God, and be patient and loving with Sasha!

314. YOU CANNOT BEAR THE TRUTH BECAUSE OF VAINGLORY

Glory be to God that you have gotten better! Only be sensible in the future. I told you even before this, do not insist on forcing yourself to go to church. It is not out of laziness that you stay at home, and God will not require church attendance of one who is ill. Fulfill your rule, too, in whatever manner you are able, even if it is in ten installments. When your head is not well, do not do prostrations. I do the same myself. As regards reproaches from the sisters, I have said, and I will repeat it a hundred times: without them you would be lost. If you are vainglorious to such a degree that you cannot endure to hear the truth, then what would happen if this weakness were not observable in you. After all, truly you are not rich, truly you are weak! But you bristle — "Don't you dare say things like that!" It depends upon you whether to live peacefully or not. Show patience, and there will be peace. But if you begin returning evil for evil, then both peace will leave, and God will forsake you for taking justice into your own hands. Where there is peace, there is God. *His place hath been made in peace* (Ps. 75:2).

315. DO NOT TRUST IN YOUR RELATIVES, BUT LOOK TO GOD

Do not grieve over those at home or be grieved by them. You have come to God, so look to God. He is more dependable than all princes and sons of men (Cf. Ps. 145:2). And do not be overly enamored of this present life. When you are at peace, give thanks to God, and when you are sorrowful, again give thanks to God. And ever await God's mercy.

316. WITHOUT SORROWS YOU WILL NOT LEARN MONASTICISM

Matushka S., you are dense! So when are you going to resemble a nun? A hundred times I have told you that your troubles are the size of a mosquito bite. But you carry on as though your life were hanging by a thread.

You see, you are learning, and I will express for you what it is you want: you want precisely to learn monasticism, but sorrows you do not want. So how are you going to learn?

No, Matushka, the Holy Scriptures say, "Give blood, and receive spirit."[1] But I see you have a fondness for gold crosses which are hung around the neck: my beloved one, if you love this Cross, first yourself hang upon a cross. Jesus, Who is God, Himself first suffered and only then was glorified. Can it be that you are better than He?

317. LEARN MONASTICISM. DO NOT PINE FOR YOUR RELATIVES

Christ is risen! My Matushka, my light Seraphimochka! Up until this minute, I thought that you were a no-kidding, real, genuine, angel-like nun. But you are simply a little girl, and not just any little girl, but a real little village girl, who in order not to cry absolutely must have a gingerbread rooster or a lollipop. So how will you be numbered with the angelic choir? And how is one to address you now? So your relatives have forgotten you, and your spiritual batiushka too! But I do remember you and I remember you a lot, so the sin is on your part! So when are we going to learn monasticism? Or are we just not going to? No, Matushka, we must! You have made a vow, so keep it; do not give joy to the enemy, the Devil. Do not seek what is not given you. What kind of consolation are you seeking from the dead? *Let the dead*, that is, those in the world — even if they are your relatives, still they are in the world — *bury their dead* (Luke 9:60). As for you, sit in your cell and weep over your dead, that is, yourself: because you have assumed the clothing and ways of a monastic, and yet you are not a monastic. He that loveth father or mother or sister or brother is not My disciple (Cf. Luke 14:26), said our Saviour. But are you not His disciple? Have you not vowed to follow after Him forever? It is said in the Scriptures, *Forsake foolishness, and ye shall live* (Prov. 9:6).

So, forsake your pettinesses. You see, you imagine you are tormented by your relatives' indifference, whereas you are simply jealous that Sasha has been supplied with everything and you haven't. That is why I exhort you to preserve simplicity with Sasha; although she is a bit petty, still she is a quiet, sober, reverent girl. And it is a sin on your part if you cannot get along with her. For you two not to have any disagreements or misunderstandings is impossible, so do not seek the impossible. But know that to the degree you are patient with her, you will both have peace.

---

1. See footnote, Letter #145.

318. SAY THE JESUS PRAYER, AND YOU WILL BE WELL

You are sick again? That means you do not remember my medicine. I told you, constantly say the Jesus Prayer, and you will be well. After all, I did not give you this advice lightly, but having had thorough experience of it in practice. True, it is beneficial for a young person to be ill for a time. But it is even better for him, being healthy, to serve God in body and in spirit.

319. THE VERY BEST FAST. BE MORE FRANK

I received your letter. And I am answering it right away. I congratulate you on your new home. See how Matushka loves you. But if sorrows are needful for you for the sake of your eternal salvation, no one will be able to deliver you from them, and you cannot escape them by going somewhere else. Well, so you have left Sister A.E., and they have given you another nice one: but your hand has begun to ache, and your head. So is your situation any better?

And so endure patiently, and you will be saved. What did we just chant in church in the Aposticha? "Why, as one slothful, O my soul, art thou enslaved to sin? And why, though thou art ailing, dost thou not hasten unto the Physician? Behold, now is the accepted time; behold, now, of a truth, is the day of salvation."

"Arouse thyself; wash thy face with the tears of repentance, and make thy lamp bright with the oil of good deeds, that thou mightest find forgiveness and great mercy from Christ God."[1] Now, for a new little nun, the very best fast, the very highest virtue, is to patiently endure all that God may send. Another thing — be frank. How is it that you are suffering there and not writing to me, "fearing to offend God." Why, my Matushka, if you offend God but then repent to your spiritual father, He — God, that is — will simply forgive you for having sinned and offended Him. But instead you suffer and do not repent — and the end result is not good. Sure enough, you ended up getting hysterical!

So do not aim high, but try to live humbly and also openly. After all, you came in order to learn monasticism — so who is going to condemn you if you do slip? You ask me to ask God for some patience for you — why, how illogical you are, Seraphimochka! You ask a little handful of patience for yourself, and here you yourself have a whole stash of this precious virtue! For to learn patience does not mean to read and to inquire, but very simply: to pain. Pain a little, and you will be patient.

---

1. From the Aposticha of the Praises, Tuesday of the Second Week of Lent.

And you will be a genuine nun! Indeed, this is why the Lord said, *He that shall endure unto the end, the same shall be saved* (Matt. 24:13)! Peace to you! Be an angel not in name only, but also in your manner of life, and there, you will be with the Seraphim unto the ages of ages.

320. IN WHAT A TRUE FAST CONSISTS

Peace to you, S.! Once more I greet you with the fast!

With the true fast! You have already tasted fasting food, which maybe isn't much to your liking. But what to do. Even meat-eating beasts and predatory hawks and how many other innocent animals, small and great — and how many countless thousands of them there are — also fast. They say that sometimes wolves don't eat for a week and more at a time. So how can we Christians, heirs of the eternal Kingdom, not fast? And now is the most appropriate time. *Behold, now is the accepted time. Behold, now is the day of salvation* (II Cor. 6:2).

"It is the gladsome season of the Fast; wherefore, having abundantly taken our fill of radiant purity, sincere love, enlightened prayer, and all manner of virtue, let us cry out joyously: O all-holy Cross of Christ, which hast blossomed forth the bliss of life, count us all worthy to worship thee with a pure heart!"[1]

Do you see, Seraphimochka! You are no longer a worldly young girl but are numbered among the monastics — among the brides of Christ. And so, you should know not the letter only but also the mysteries of the Kingdom. For not to eat bread and not to drink water or anything else is not yet fasting, for neither do the demons eat or drink anything at all. And yet they are evil and hateful to God. But fasting for us is, as the Church chants, "the estrangement from evil, restraint of tongue, refraining from anger, separation from lust, slanders, lies and false oaths. Abstinence from these things is a true and acceptable fast."[2] But S. and I are lacking not only in these great virtues, but even in patient endurance of what God sends! Yes, Seraphimochka, in your impatience you have entirely taken after me. Life is hard for such people. That I know from experience. It is all true. Nevertheless, I will also be telling the truth if I say that by God's mercy, I have somehow managed to live in the monastery for a quarter century. Who knows, maybe you will live in one even longer, despite all your impatience. Yes, you will. You will for sure, if you humble yourself — that is, if you say to yourself and to God, "I am weak;

---

1. From the Stichera for "Lord I have cried," Tuesday of the Second Week of Lent.
2. From the Vespers Aposticha, Monday of the First Week of Lent.

I cannot be a nun, for I am just too weak, but I do want to be a nun — help me, O Jesus!" And call upon the Most-holy Mother of God as often as possible — and you will be saved. As for external sorrows and unpleasantnesses — they will fly off you like dried-up mud from your clothes. . .

321. ON THE HIGH CALLING OF A BRIDE OF CHRIST. SEEK SPIRITUAL PEACE

I congratulate you, S., on being united to the chosen flock of our beloved Lord, on being numbered with God's brides. Watch over yourself, live worthily of your new calling; this is a high calling, of which the Apostle says, "Ye are citizens of the heavenly Jerusalem, a royal priesthood, an holy nation, a peculiar people" (Cf. I Pet. 2:9). "Your conversation is in the Heavens" (Cf. Phil. 3:20). But by what means can one attain to dwell or, more precisely, to reign in the Heavens? The Holy Scriptures say, *We must through much tribulation enter into the Kingdom of Heaven* (Acts 14:22).

So if you are surrounded by tribulations, rejoice — for then you are walking on the unerring path. And he who does not run away from tribulations but bears them according to his strength — he it is who will receive the eternal Kingdom.

On her way back, your mother visited us and gladdened us [with the news] that you are at peace and even joyful. Try as much as you can to be spiritually at peace, for it is said of God, *His place hath been made in peace* (Ps. 75:2).

This means that God Himself dwells in the person who has a peaceful heart. The most important thing is to consider yourself inferior to all; do not seek either love or honor from anyone, but yourself have them toward all — and thus you will lay hold of peace! But the moment you begin seeking for others to notice you and discover in you good qualities and some virtues — goodbye spiritual peace!

Batiushka Father Amvrosy sends you his blessing!

LIII. LETTERS TO T.

322. ON RIGHT TEARS. DO NOT FORGET TO PRAY

August 17, 1886

Peace to you, T. It is Sunday; I just opened my eyes and tackled your letter. You write asking me to write you "a line," and here I have not started the letter yet and I am already on the tenth line. But I wanted to write you more and do a better job. So you started to cry from grief because I am not writing to you: well, it doesn't hurt to cry. Only know that your tears are not right. Now, for them to be right, St. John of the Ladder teaches us to direct them to God concerning the forgiveness of our sins — of which you can probably discover not a few. As for this nun speaking wrongly of you, do not grieve over it, just try in actuality not to gossip. Do not forget to pray. Remember the Russian proverb, "Without God one can get nowhere."[1] Constantly say the Jesus Prayer. In church stand or sit silently — and if you do not obey, I will never write you one little word. I have a terrible dislike for blasphemous women who have no respect for the Holy Church. After all, there isn't even any excuse for these foolish causers of offense: well, so someone ate or drank to excess —[as if] nature demanded it; or else they overslept — but those who talk and laugh in church, now is anyone moving their tongue for them? I repeat, have reverence for the Holy Church, our common mother.

323. SEEK NOT LETTERS, BUT PRAYER
AND THE WORD OF GOD

December 14, 1887

Peace to you, T. Sure, it is true, I have become callous.[2] Now, don't exaggerate — you are not a dog, you are a handmaid of God; you are my devoted disciple, although you are a little dense. Because one cannot teach you patience. All she does is rebel! Now, I do think of you all the same. I think of you, but I cannot help you. And why? Here is why: you want me to fulfill your wish, to write to you — but I would like for you

---

1. Lit., "not even to the threshold." In the Russian, "Bez Bóga ni do poróga."
2. Lit., "wooden"

to take delight not in letters but in prayer and in reading the Holy Scriptures. And in sorrows to quickly have recourse to the Lord. "Entreaty do I pour forth unto the Lord, and to Him do I proclaim all my sorrows."[1] So learn, T.! It is about time you got some sense. . .

324. LIVE NOT AS YOU PLEASE BUT AS GOD COMMANDS US TO

March 1, 1888

Peace to you and the blessing of the Lord! I greet you with Cheesefare Week and with the approaching Fast. . . May the Holy Church teach you to live as God commands us to and not as you please. You and I have been living in a monastery, but we have not learned patience. Still you keep reproaching me for not writing to you: why, now wouldn't I answer you if I saw a real need as with others? But your desire is simply childish: she received a letter, and that does it! As for your wish to part company with me, I cannot make this decision on my own, because I did not take you in spiritually on my own, but with an elder's blessing. And so, if I am burdensome to you, you should address yourself to him. As for me, I will not turn you away. . . May the Lord save you, and may He help you to tame your untameable heart. Pray for me also, that the Lord may correct me, the slothful one.

325. SALVATION LIES NOT IN LETTERS BUT IN FULFILLING THE COMMANDMENTS

November 4, 1888

Peace to you and salvation! I received your letters full of reproach and indignation. And I was very grieved. I see that my instruction is not profiting my beloved children. And so I just had the idea of going into seclusion. Otherwise, I see that I will bring no one anything but sin and trouble. I teach humility without having any myself, and so my teaching is useless. . . It would be better to retire. . . And then they will give Tania a nice elder who will turn out two letters in answer to every one of hers. .

Now, how many times have I told T. that salvation lies not in letters, but in fulfilling that which is enjoined, either by me or by another, but especially by our holy Fathers. However, T. is in no hurry to fulfill. Instead, give her letters, lots of letters. And make them long, and make

---

1. From an heirmos (Plagal of Fourth Tone) of the Sixth Ode (based on the Prayer of Jonas the Prophet).

them nice. Look, go read the holy Fathers — where will you find disciples demanding letters from their elder? But everywhere you will find them showing respect for their elder!

St. John of the Ladder writes, "If your director should take out your right eye, [even then] you should have no evil thought about him."[1] But I have never given you so much as a single bruise, and here you have become so embittered against me! Well, forgive me! I wish to correct myself!

326. IS IT TRUE THAT YOU WON'T BE SAVED?

February 15, 1889

Peace to you, T. . . You write that at some point I said to you that you will not be saved. Why, T., that is really a slur. Not only no elder, but even no angry old half-witted monk would say that. The Lord calls all, He loves all, He shed His most holy blood for all, in order to save and not to destroy man. And we see how the Holy Church chants in praise of prodigals, thieves, publicans, robbers who have been saved — and with the Holy Church we pray, "O Lord, number me together with the publican, and the thief, and the harlot."[2] See what kind of people are saved! But you have accused me of [saying] such nonsense, that supposedly you won't be saved. Even if you were worse than me — even then we would not lose hope that the Lord would save you.

Now by your despair you just gladden the enemy, and anger God, and deprive yourself of His aid. *Forsake foolishness, and ye shall live* (Prov. 9:6), says the word of God. Now you will be approaching the Holy Mysteries, and you must needs say, "I believe, O Lord, and I confess. . . that Thou camest to save sinners, of whom I am chief."[3] The foolish person will think: I am lost, for I am chief among sinners — but the Christian will humbly reproach himself and glorify God's mercy and His love, and in peace he will communicate Christ, which is something I desire for you with all my heart!

---

1. Cf. *The Ladder of Divine Ascent*, 4:27: "A soul attached to the shepherd with love and faith for Christ's sake will not leave him even if it were at the price of his blood. . ." See also 4:110, "About Saint Acacius": "And he endured so much from this elder, that to many people it will perhaps seem incredible."
2. Cf. Sessional Hymn of Compunction, Monday, Grave Tone.
3. From the "Prayers Before Holy Communion."

327. THE WEAPON OF SALVATION

March 3, 1892

Still you keep lamenting because I do not write to you. May the Lord Who comforts the humble comfort you also. Only, have the true and sure pledge of humility: self-reproach; and add to this patience, and arm yourself with the Jesus Prayer along with remembrance of death — and then the yoke of the Gospel commandments and the rules of the monastic life will become easy for you, and the burden of obedience will henceforth be light. I really cannot write often due to extreme lack of time and due to my poor health. Peace to you and God's blessing!

And to thy spirit!

LIV. LETTERS TO E.D.

328. THOSE WHO ARE AFFLICTED HERE WILL REJOICE AT THE DREAD JUDGMENT

April 3, 1880

I greet you, reverend Sister D., with the ending Fast and with the passing winter, and likewise with the coming spring and the radiant Resurrection of Christ, which I wish that you may at last meet with joy and in good health.

When we reach this day, it will be as though the Fast had never been (although those who have truly fasted do receive greater consolation). So it is also with the coming of the Great Day, that is, of the Dread Judgment — it will be as if we had never even seen any afflictions. Everything will be swallowed up by unspeakable universal rejoicing.

Of course, at that moment those who ran away from afflictions here will grieve a little. There, those afflictions crown those who were afflicted — and there, every tear, every wound [sustained by] the soul will shine forth more brilliantly than precious diamond. Still, the common rejoicing will be so great that just looking at our neighbors, we will have consolation and gladness.

So comely will they be there — all those souls who have suffered here. But you keep not wanting to suffer affliction — it is here she keeps wanting to be happier. But won't we die? Can it be that you have discovered some secret to escape the gates of death? So if you do not know this secret, humble yourself. Pray. As for me, I know this secret. Love Jesus, and you will understand the power of the troparion, "Christ is risen from the dead, by death hath He trampled down death, and on those in the graves hath He bestowed life."

329. A MONASTIC WITHOUT AFFLICTIONS IS A FIREBRAND

I received both of your letters, reverend sister in the Lord E. You keep wanting to arrive directly in Paradise without afflictions. No, Matushka: without afflictions, a monastic is a firebrand. But what we desire for you is eternal gladness. Do not be despondent; everything will pass. All the saints walked by this way, that is, the afflicted way. Peace to you and the blessing of the Lord!

330. WHAT THE NATIVITY OF CHRIST TEACHES US

December 24, 1881

Reverend novice of God D., I greet you and our ailing M[other] M. with the approaching festal days of Christ's Nativity. May God grant that you may celebrate these days with understanding. And what is this understanding? The Lord, having just seen the light of day, saw Himself in a manger of dumb beasts. His neighbors were asses and oxen. It was cold in the cave.

I sympathize very much with you in your sorrows. But they are not our doom. What did the Lord promise His beloved disciples: "In the world ye shall have tribulation, and the world shall rejoice, but ye shall weep. But your sorrow shall be turned into joy, and your joy no man taketh from you" (Cf. John 16:20,22,33). Now see for yourself: if you wish to rejoice with unspeakable joy, endure patiently the afflictions which are sent you by God, and you will not regret it. Peace to you and to our ailing M[other] M.!

331. THOSE WHO SUFFER WITH CHRIST ARE ALSO GLORIFIED WITH HIM

April 7, 1883

Christ is risen! Why are you sad? Do you not believe in God Who visits us? Can it be that He Who died for you does not love you enough? You have not as yet proved your love for Him in any way, whereas He has proved His love for you by word and deed and by a promise. He Himself taught us to patiently endure afflictions, and He walked by the afflicted way, and He died a shameful death for us. And He left His beloved ones this testament: "In the world ye shall have tribulation. But your sorrow shall be turned into joy. And your joy no man taketh from you" (Cf. John 16:22,33). But the joys here are fleeting. Therefore, rejoice, and suffer together with your Bridegroom, Jesus.

"Yesterday I was buried with Thee, O Christ, and today I arise with Thine arising. Yesterday I was crucified with Thee; (for this) do Thou Thyself glorify me with Thee in Thy Kingdom."[1]

"Glorify me with Thee" — do you understand this? That is, make me radiant with that same light with which Thou Thyself art radiant, O Almighty One! Clothe me with that same divine royal garment in which Thou Thyself shinest forth, sitting on the right hand of Thy Father on the throne of the Majesty in the Heavens.

Jesus Himself asks this of His Father: "Father, that they whom Thou hast given Me may be one in Us, as We are one. Thou in Me, and I in Thee, that they also may be one in Us" (Cf. John 17:11,21). Amen.

LV. LETTERS TO E.Z.

332. IT IS NOT TRUE THAT YOU ARE OF NO USE TO THE CONVENT

September 16, 1876

I received your letter long ago, sister in the Lord E., but the almost continual services, my own infirmities, and other circumstances left me no time to write a letter until today. And now I am writing, having just served the Liturgy at the monastery. I am saying all of this so that if this

---

1. From the Paschal Canon.

happens in the future also, you will not account the chance delay as lack of concern for you. Twice I gave your question to Batiushka Father Amvrosy for a decision, but each time something interfered. I have only now obtained one. Batiushka blesses you to explain to your Mother Abbess concerning the difficulty of your situation. That in teaching the little girls you bring no profit to the convent is incorrect — everything which is done as an obedience is profitable. And you should not even think about what is profitable or unprofitable in the affairs of the convent. As for thinking a little of yourself and your bodily infirmities, that is more excusable.

As regards your relations with me, write everything, without hesitation or embarrassment. I went by this path, and I have not regretted it. Peace to you and blessing from the Lord. Batiushka Father Amvrosy, too, sends you his blessing.

333. DO NOT WORRY ABOUT YOUR IMPOSSIBLE TEMPER.
WHY IT SEEMS TO YOU THAT YOU ARE NOT NEEDED.
PUT WHAT YOU READ INTO PRACTICE.
THE SIGNIFICANCE OF BOOKS

November 15, 1876

Sister in the Lord, most reverend E. I received your letter in a pile of letters after my two month absence from Optina. And I kept hurrying to answer it, but I have only just now managed to get around to it. You write that you have an impossible temper — well, mine is even worse. But I am not overly discouraged, bearing in mind that I came to the monastery to learn and to improve myself. So is it so surprising if we do go off sometimes? But let us do our best. And I have faith that God will help us.

You write that you feel as if you are not needed, even though no one has told you so. And you ask, why? Almost any one of our novices could solve that riddle for you: "Because you are not first." If you had a sense of Christian humility, it would never even occur to you that others have an obligation to remember about you, that you merit being ranked with the rest — in a word, that you are not unneeded. At the same time you ask for advice as to "how to get rid of this [feeling]," and [mention] that you are "impatient" and "irritable." He Who is the Truth long ago proclaimed the way to get rid of it: *Learn of Me, for I am meek and lowly in heart, and ye shall find rest* (Matt. 11:29).

Everyone knows where anger comes from. When you won't give a dog a piece of meat, or you take it away from him, he tears at it and barks. Thus you and I also like to have our own little way. And if people hinder us from having it or won't please us, we (I especially) bark, and perhaps we bite our brother (or sister bites sister). So let us search out the true cause of the evil, and we will understand the matter. And let us hasten to cure ourselves. Or at least, let us judge ourselves and hasten to [join] the wise transgressor — the publican whom the Lord praised.

Matushka, you ask me to teach you patience. . . How peculiar you are! God teaches her! People — the sisters — teach her! All life's circumstances teach her! All of them teach you patience, they teach you by practice, by the thing itself, by the very nature of the ability to endure patiently — and you ask me for a theoretical lesson in patience. . . Patiently endure everything that happens to you — and you will be saved!

You are embarrassed to disclose all your thoughts to Matushka. Say what you can to her, and write us the rest. The Holy Spirit is the same in Kashir and in Kozelsk. By His power we will quickly absolve the penitent. I do not forbid you to turn to me. And the simple reason I do not turn you away is that they did not turn me away either, although I am a hundred times worse than you.

What books should you read? You do not retain [what you read]? Well, memorize something thoroughly, for example, *Thou shalt love the Lord thy God with all thy heart. . . and thy neighbor as thyself* (Luke 10:27). And similarly from another [book] — but not so as to be able to say, "we know," but "we fulfill." The power lies not in words but in deeds.

Let us begin from the beginning. Let us recollect how to call upon God! And let us call upon Him in the manner of children, until He Himself comes and teaches us all truth. I see that you have read much, and that this has not helped you. Try beginning to put what you have read into practice, as far as you are able. And add to this (again, as far as you are able) the unceasing (oral) Prayer of Jesus — and you will see the mercy of God. Lest your zeal be in vain and you become disturbed by the fact that you read and read and the end result is zero, I will tell you a secret discovered through many years' experience: when you approach a book, have as your object first of all to achieve that which, as you say, you lack, but which is essential with every virtue — that is, patiently to await God's mercy with understanding, for the Lord is a God of knowledge (I Kings 2:4), Who giveth wisdom and knowledge (Cf. Dan. 2:21).

In the second place, a book is not the substance and essence of knowledge: it is one of the means of arriving at it. And so, a person can come to know the mysteries of the Kingdom without books, and he may also not know these mysteries even after having read a ton of books. He who has prepared himself beforehand by practice has little need of books. I do not say this in order to divert you from books, but in order to warn you — lest you begin to hate them, if you do not find what you desire by studying them. Third and most important, I will say as an encouragement: to him who inquires after wisdom, wisdom will be imputed (Prov. 17:28). Peace to you and blessing. Forgive the disorganization — I wrote in bits and pieces, and hurriedly.

334. DO NOT BE JEALOUS OF YOUR SISTERS
January 12, 1878

I received your terribly offended letter of January 2, reverend sister. Here everyone got it — M., and M.'s mother, and everyone who possibly could get it, whereas the cause of your troubles and suspicions is solely my wretched self! It is only from your letter that I found out that M. is so thoughtless. That she complains about you. That she is a so-and-so. That she is evil personified. But I always thought, from reading and studying the letters of you both, that you were a good novice of God, heedful, solicitous over your salvation. And that M. was nice too! So much for my impressions!

And to top it all off, up to this very second, despite my endless correspondence with M., I do not recall a single place, a single innuendo about your person, conveyed either personally or in writing! So much for number one.

Number two: you are disturbed by the fact that I did not absolve you. Why, I did not bind you in the first place. And if I do not reproach you for some weaknesses — well, wouldn't I indeed warn you, knowing the perilousness of your situation, if you trusted me? I see that you did wrong. But you repent! And there is no sin which is not forgiven, save the unrepented one.

Look, even if I had found it necessary to torment you by delaying to respond to your wishes and requests — even then, are you about to go judging and condemning me, you who have such trust in me?

As regards your unreasonable competition with M., I will simply tell you, sister: you look at the matter like a little girl who, although not madly jealous, is still very lacking in discernment (that is, when you take only weaknesses into account, without discretion). I know with whom I am dealing. And according to my understanding, I try to do that which is profitable. But you do not believe this. Now if you do believe it, humble yourself, calling to mind the Apostle's words, *Shall the thing formed say to him that formed it, Why hast thou made me thus* (Rom. 9:20)? And so know that I forgave you the instant I read your confession. And you were forgiven by God while you were still writing or, more precisely, when you decided to write and not to repeat the foolish things you had done. — But again, a new calamity. Now M. will find out that I wrote to you, whereas M. who is perishing, dying, persecuted, despised by everyone — I also have despised.

No matter what your thoughts may be, I must write to her, too. I will say to you, Matushka, that as far as I can tell, you would not be able to bear a burden like hers. And all your opinions attributing her sufferings to fastidiousness are far from the truth. I advise you to change your opinion of M. and to pity her. Just like I also always remember you and pity you, and I promise to continue doing so...

Oh yes, and probably N. will find out that you [two] received [letters], and she did not. Then woe both unto me and unto you. I shall write to her as well.

335. IT IS IMPOSSIBLE TO BE
ENTIRELY FREED FROM THOUGHTS
February 17,1878

My Matushka, Sister E., you are in despair because you do not correct yourself, that is, because you imitate me? What then is left for me to do? I humbled myself and the Lord saved me! (Cf. Ps. 114:6), said David. Let us do the same, and thus we shall be saved. You want to be entirely freed from thoughts — that is worse than foolish! The saints did not presume to say this! You have written down tons of passions which war against you. But I have twice, three times, ten times as many — and still I am patient. I advise you to be the same!

Concerning the passion which consumed Sodom and Gomorrah and the surrounding cities in flames, I will say, beware! But there is nothing to be embarrassed about here — I am not some stranger!

336. WHY I DID NOT WRITE EARLIER. DO NOT
BE DESPONDENT BECAUSE YOU HAVE SLIPPED
October 7, 1879

Reverend [Sister] E. is thoroughly offended. How many letters she has filled imploring me not to abandon her — and now she herself is going away. She is thoroughly offended!

However, Matushka, you are too late getting mad, now that

summer is over. After all, you are not unaware that it is only now that my correspondence begins, precisely now, precisely on this date — because today the wind began to blow, the snow and rain began to fall, rivers overhead, rivers underfoot; it is hard to go past the threshold. Therefore, it is precisely today that our time of freedom has begun. . . Starting on this most inclement day, my correspondence begins with everyone near and far — and it is now you balk? All right, peace! I promise to correct myself! But in turn, you correct yourself too! Do not be despondent because you have fallen so low. You have not fallen lower than the Prophet Jonas. If, like him, you too will cry unto the Lord, He will hear you. And the sea monster of despondency will spew you out onto the firm rock of hope, and you will be like a new Peter, aware of your infirmity and condescending to the infirmities of others. So be at peace! Arise, set to work, toil away according to your strength, and walking forward, not hastily but humbly, you will be found among the first.

How is it written there: *and the other disciple did outrun Peter, and came first to the sepulchre* (John 20:4); but Peter, having arrived afterwards, went in first. May the Lord bless you with both peace and spiritual knowledge. . .

337. BE PATIENT WITH YOUR SISTERS

October 17, 1879

In accordance with your wish, I am hastening to reassure you immediately that I am the same towards you as before. . . As for your pitiful status in the circle of the sisters, you will only prove that you are a sister to them, and not some freeloader, when you show them sisterly love and bear patiently with them. It even pains me to see or hear how they all oppress you — well, but what if it is in this oppression that all your future eternal glory lies concealed? And what if to take away all your afflictions would mean to deprive you of life? That is, to commit a crime against you? So endure patiently, *wait on the Lord, be thou manful. And let thy heart be strengthened* (Ps. 26:16), remembering: according to the multitude of my sorrows, Thy consolations brought gladness unto my soul (Cf. Ps. 93:19).

338. LET US FOLLOW AFTER PETER,
AND NOT AFTER JUDAS

Matushka E., Christ is risen! that is, Truly He is risen! Well, how is it that you do not understand, O master of Israel (Cf. John 3:10), that everyone will always and everywhere expect more of you than of another. Whereas you ought to be a lamp, you serve as a rock of offense to both young and old! Right? However, at one point even the chief Apostle Peter was a rock of offense — and unto Whom, yet?! But this did not hinder him from becoming the chief among Christ's chosen disciples. So don't you be despondent either. I have sinned much myself. So what are we to do? Surely not imitate Judas?! Let us rather follow after Peter! All right, maybe the keys won't be given to us like they were to him. . . but what do we need keys for now anyway? We now "celebrate the death of death, the destruction of Hades, the beginning of a new and everlasting life. And with leaps of joy we praise the Cause thereof," Who hath "opened unto us the gates of Paradise."[1]

You have no hope of changing — what an unlovely thought! Why, I am worse than you, and still I do not despair! With regard to the matter you heard which caused you temptation, and with regard to all such things, St. Isaac the Syrian has said, "Watchfulness helps more than works!"[2]

339. NEITHER YOUR MATUSHKAS NOR YOUR
BATIUSHKAS
WILL SAVE YOU — ONLY PATIENCE WILL

I received another letter from you, exactly and precisely like the rest. That is, if only you were not under your temporary supervisor Pelagia, you would be a different person, maybe even happy. I should believe you, but somehow I don't.

If not Pelagia, then I think Akulina or Arina will rub you the wrong way. And neither your Matushkas nor your Batiushkas will save you. Only one physician will save you, the one who has been recommended to you a hundred times: patience.

---

1. From the Paschal Canon.
2. Cf. *The Ascetical Homilies of St. Isaac the Syrian*, Homily 51, p. 249.

340. A HOMILY OF ST. ISAAC THE SYRIAN ON
TEMPTATIONS

I received your letter, reverend sufferer, at a time when there is not a moment to so much as cross oneself. Today I wasn't even at the Canon. And I am writing to you during Great Compline. Well, this means that it is necessary for you to suffer for awhile. I grieved much for you, and I went to Batiushka to tell him of your plight. In response to my complaint, he bade me indicate to you the 79th homily of St. Isaac the Syrian. I have not read it in a long time now, but I do remember the passage which would often be pointed out to me (if not thrust at me) — page 432: "But the trials that God allows to fall upon men who are shameless, whose thinking is exalted. . . are the following: manifest temptations of the demons which also exceed the limit of the strength of men's souls; the withdrawal of the forces of wisdom which men possess; the piercing sensation of the thought of fornication which is allowed to assault them to humble their arrogance; quick temper; the desire to have one's own way; disputatiousness. . . to be despised by all men and to lose their respect. . . to be constantly talking and speaking idly, etc. These are the trials of the soul. To the trials of the body which befall them belong: painful adversities, always prolonged, intricate and difficult to resolve; encounters with wicked men; to fall into the hands of men who afflict us; many times to stumble severely on rocks, and to have grave falls from high places, and similar mishaps which do the body great injury. . ." "Do not be angry with me that I tell you the truth. You have never sought out [humility]. . ."[1] etc. — read it for yourself. However, there is also a cure for this disease. This prescription[2] is at the end of the chapter, on page 435. But without this cure, my Matushka, all the possible prescriptions in the world won't help you. Because if even some all-knowing, all-healing Moscow Aesculapius — let alone one from Kashir — should diagnose your illness and heal the pain in your ankle, then your knee will start to hurt.

And all worldly wisdom will by its treatment only drive the illness closer to your heart. . .

You will come to understand for yourself the consequences of this world's successes. As for the cures which are not of this world, they are: to cleanse the inside of your vessel, and all your outside will be clean (Cf. Matt. 23:26). This our Lord has said. But if you do not succeed... endure

1. Cf. *The Ascetical Homilies of St. Isaac the Syrian*, Homily 51, p. 249.
2. I.e., humility.

patiently! And it will all be [cleansed]!

341. HUMILITY IS NOT ATTAINED RIGHT AWAY. PEOPLE'S FALSE SUSPICIONS [ABOUT YOU] WILL NOT HARM YOU. DESPONDENCY IS FROM PRIDE

For a long time I have been trying to get around to answering you, most reverend sister in the Lord, and I would begin; but I would be hampered by the constant arrival of more people and more correspondence. You complain that you cannot master yourself. . . And you cannot humble yourself in your heart. Why, my clever child, I have both told you and written to you, that if in actual deed you were as good as you are in your desires (vainglorious, of course) to be good, an excellent nun — then we would directly make you an abbess, and instead of putting you to learn patience, we would have you teach others. However, those in authority have not entrusted you with this, advising you instead to do some learning yourself. So learn. Little by little. Little by little. Read again about the ladder in Abba Dorotheos, in the middle of the 14th instruction (p.193 in the Optina Hermitage edition of 1866). Read it and engrave it — engrave it carefully somewhere. And relax. If only you remembered this ladder, you would not quickly become disturbed about not being able to humble yourself in your heart. Come on now, pray tell, where do you think you are climbing to! Why, you are jumping straight up to the top steps. The great Moses the Ethiopian, when he was ordained hierodeacon, said when he was insulted, *I was troubled and spake not* (Ps. 76:4). But our reverend sister of Kashir does not wish to be on a level with Moses. Give her such humility that even her heart would remain undisturbed. Humble yourself outwardly at least. Humility is comprehended and attained not by hunching and crawling, but by the power of the lifegiving Spirit.

Now as regards your having spoken impudently, that was a blunder; but still it is not a sin unto death. You will sin again a hundred times, and a hundred times you will rise again, and each time the Lord will receive you, and forgive you, and will not remember your lapses — only humble yourself as much as you can.

As for Matushka continuing to have that suspicion about you, this will in no wise harm you. And it will undoubtedly serve you as a guardian angel. So do not worry. We look out for you more than you think.

With regard to your having been ashamed even unto death and even more — "It would have been easier for me to die!" — here, my Matushka E.A., here you are simply being a worldly young lady. Your [spiritual] mother, out of the kindness of her heart, and not without causing him pain, tells — whom does she tell? The mayor? A lion led along the street [as a show]? A visiting gentleman? No, she tells her [spiritual] father that this matushka does not adhere to proper monastic order, she does not know how to humble herself! O, the shame! And so you would have liked for me not to know your weaknesses? And for your Mother Abbess' opinion of you to remain a secret? Do you see, my dear, how far you have been carried away by vainglory? All right, enough![1] Let us make a beginning of correcting ourselves! I, too, wish to make a beginning. Help us, O Lord!

As regards my feelings toward you: after this terrible persecution of yours, after this humiliation and annihilation which seemed to you to be "worse than death" — you, sister, have become closer to me. Yes, and I think to God also. God looketh upon the humble (Cf. Ps. 112:5), He looks directly into their eyes, into the very depths of their hearts.

Do not be despondent. The reason you feel miserable is that the nest of the demon of pride has been disturbed; the little root which was sprouting up has been jiggled. And you should rejoice on this account!

Behold, now is the accepted time. *Behold, now is the day of salvation* (II Cor. 6:2). Moreover, it is not only to God and to myself that you have become dearer after your disgrace — you say that Matushka, too, has changed. *This change hath been wrought by the right hand of the Most High* (Ps. 76:10)!

Let us make a beginning, with God's help, and let us endure patiently, and let us humble ourselves! And God will be with us unto the ages!

LVI. LETTERS TO E.

342. *HOW TO BE FREED FROM EVIL PEOPLE*

You ask how one can be freed from evil people? By simplicity of thought and feeling, being as you have come to serve not the Devil, but God. And the Master of Heaven and earth and of the entire universe is

---

1. Lit., "All right, amen!"

not the Devil, but God, Who commands both angels and demons and Who grants peace to our souls. To your postscript I will reply with another postscript: If your afflictions humble you, bring peace to your spirit, and draw you to prayer, then know that your feeling is not delusive. That is why St. Mark the Ascetic says, "The mercy of God is hidden in sufferings."[1]

343. WE DO NOT FORBID YOU TO CHOOSE WHAT IS PROFITABLE. YOUR FEAR OF A WITCH IS THE FEAR OF AN [IGNORANT] PEASANT WOMAN

June 29, 1876

I finished answering almost all my letters and have paused on yours, as I have half a dozen of them on hand. Not that I have been burdened by their quantity, but I fear lest in consoling you [by many letters] I should deprive you of what is most essential for a monastic — patience; and lest I distress you by offering you astringent food. . . I do know you personally and I know your talents, through which with proper guidance you could bring profit to the convent — but what can we do if they do not appreciate you and me? We cannot very well designate our own worth, can we? And show off our good points (although a monastic cannot and should not have anything of his own).

Our opinion is this: if you are unable to carry the burden laid upon you by Providence, we will not bind you, because St. Mark the Ascetic says in his homily on the spiritual law, "Many counsels of our neighbors

---

1. St. Mark the Ascetic, "On Those Who Think That They are Made Righteous by Works," #139.

are helpful, but our own judgment is best."[1]

And so, we do not forbid you, if you find something more expedient for you. . . With regard to visiting your mother, if she is inviting you, well, why not go? In your difficult circumstances this would relieve your spirit not a little. As for your childish fear of falling under the power of the Devil through some witch, you only prove by this that your conceptions of the Christian, of God, and of the Devil are those of an [ignorant] peasant woman.

If the demons did not dare to enter into swine without the permission of Jesus Christ, how are they going to enter into people? And moreover into monastics? Now, if you try to insist upon, for example, assuming the position of sacristan,[2] and enlist her [the witch's] aid — well, then maybe. . . But now do not be afraid. As long as you are suffering affliction for the Lord's sake, He is with you inseparably. Peace to you!

344. IT IS NOT NECESSARY TO GO BE A SISTER OF MERCY[3]

November 16, 1876

Peace to you and blessing from the Lord! Batiushka did not approve your desire to go as a sister of mercy,[4] and I approve even less. You have chosen your path, you have dedicated yourself to God — so be at peace. As for whoever is trying to teach you, let them put their own advice into practice. . . Batiushka Father Amvrosy sends you his blessing!

345. IT IS A POOR MERCHANT WHO REJOICES THAT THERE ARE FEW BUYERS AT THE MARKET

Christ is risen!. . . It is not inappropriate for us to honor this feast with joy and good works: prayer, patience, humility, and especially self-reproach, which requires no labor. I told Batiushka Amvrosy about you and about all your woes.[5] He blessed you to be patient awhile longer. And why hurry! If your afflictions were few, probably your profit, your

---

1. Cf. St. Mark the Ascetic, "On the Spiritual Law," #68.
2. I.e., fulfilling your ambitions.
3. I.e., a nursing sister.
4. The wording here seems to imply a specific destination or mission, perhaps a war or a disaster.
5. This word is plural.

training, would also amount to little. Now, it is a poor merchant who rejoices that there are few people at market and that he is not bothered much by customers and salesmen! Moreover, even you yourself are maturing so much through experience that you become amazed: why is it that those very same troubles seem different now? Be patient awhile, get a little older, get used to [the way things are] — and you will see that in actuality much is not the way it appears to be. Remember Krylov's colt:[1] not only could he not understand others, he could not even understand himself. And when [that cart] started really pushing him, off to the side, and from behind — well, he showed his skill all right, and there went his master's pottery. Similarly, if we make E. an abbess, things will not turn out quite as we expected. . . In all monasteries there are troubles. Believe me. Be circumspect in your relations with the new elder. It would be best to wait. Write to me; don't hesitate.

346. A DAILY CYCLE OF PRAYER

March 3, 1877

Sister in the Lord E. . . All of your infirmities, described [in your letter] of January 20, which drive you to despair, are the usual temptations of monastics. Endure patiently, stand firm, and thank God that he has helped you hold on and not fly away from such a cold and cruel life into the cordial circle of the sisters of mercy. Endure patiently, bemoan yourself, and it will be enough. Instead of Matins read the morning prayers, the Twelve Psalms. Then the Hours. Instead of Vespers: the Ninth Hour, Compline, and as many canons and akathists as you can. Do not sleep

---

1. The Elders Anatoly and Amvrosy were familiar with Krylov's fables (see for example, J. Dunlop, *Staretz Amvrosy: Model for Dostoyevsky's Staretz Zossima*), and would often use anecdotes to illustrate their spiritual instructions. The fable cited here ("The String of Carts") is about a colt who watches the first horse go carefully down a steep hill, mentally laughing at him, criticizing him, and calling him names every step of the way as he impatiently awaits his turn. But the job doesn't turn out to be as easy as he thinks, and his cartload of pottery lands in the ditch... Krylov's fables are a classic and have been translated into many languages, including English.

before midnight; there is no need. It is best to get up early. As for your notion about midnight, it tends more toward deception than something good and profitable. . . Say the Jesus Prayer for thoughts; it is the sole remedy against them. Indeed, we are obliged always to have it on our lips, even if not always openly. Mental prayer as such should not be practiced without permission and guidance.

In your first letter you presented yourself as nice, but in your second as thoroughly bad. You ate five times on Thursday of the first week [of the Fast]! And it is nothing!. . . And despite it all, you managed to find some good qualities in yourself and to put yourself on a higher level than others. What an ingenious girl you are! Batiushka sends you his blessing. Peace to you! Save yourself!

347. DO NOT LET IT BOTHER YOU THAT PEOPLE DON'T PITY YOU

December 24, 1877

I greet you, Sister E., with the feast of the Nativity of Christ and the new year, wishing that you may spend these holy days in a Christian spirit, that is, in peace. For it was for this that the Son of God came down upon the earth.

With regard to people not pitying you, do not let it bother you. Temptation has [now] approached you from this angle. But what has approached will also depart. Only, you cannot escape that which must be. See, even your relatives have changed. When it is needful that a person be humbled, then not only the Superior, the sisters, strangers and near ones, but even all creation, according to the words of St. Isaac the Syrian,[1] will rise up against that person. Moreover, you say that you are worse than everyone else — you are lazy and sleepy — but now that people have started in actuality to humble you, your tinsel humility has gone and come off and revealed your essence. However, all this can be set right. Let us endure patiently some more. And then our worth will be demonstrated in practice. . .

---

1. Perhaps this is the same homily referred to in Letter #340.

348. ST. TIKHON OF ZADONSK LONG AGO ADVISED AGAINST ENTERING A CONVENT IN MOSCOW. SOMETIMES PROMISES ARE NOT QUICKLY FULFILLED

February 28, 1880

I also spoke with Batiushka Father Amvrosy concerning you, and I am enclosing his reply on a separate sheet.

As regards I. — I both told her in person, and I wrote in letters and I continue to write, that St. Tikhon of Zadonsk also long ago advised against entering a convent in Moscow. . . And as regards your present order, Batiushka says that soon there will be a change. I think I already wrote to you about this. Regarding my words that you will not have to live in M., I cannot recall why and on what occasion I said that. But in any case, one must remember the proverb, "Man proposes, but God disposes." I myself also have certain promises from great and truly holy Fathers — but without weakening in my faith in them, I await the will of God, which is unknown to me.

The great Prophet Samuel anointed David for the kingdom, and yet it was after this anointing that the future most glorious king on earth was forced to flee to foreign lands in order to save his life. God Himself told Abraham that his seed would be called in Isaac — and after this an angel [sic] commanded him to slay all this hope, all the expectation of mankind, the sole seed and offspring. Endure patiently, and the Lord will give you understanding. We just chanted in the Aposticha at Vespers, "The springtime of the fast hath dawned forth, and so, too, the blossom of repentance. Wherefore, O ye brethren, let us purify ourselves from every defilement, whilst chanting unto the Giver of light. . ."[1] And also, "By fasting from foods, O my soul, and not cleansing thyself from passions, in vain dost thou boast in not eating. For unless the undertaking is unto thy correction, like a liar hated by God, thou art likened unto the demons who never eat."[2]

I greet you with the approaching fast.

Know that afflictions are our dowry for Christ our Bridegroom. Do not spurn them. Yea, you will come to like them!

---

1. From the Vespers Aposticha, Wednesday of Cheesefare Week.
2. From the Aposticha of the Praises, Wednesday of Cheesefare Week.

LVII. LETTERS TO M.R.

349. DEMONIC THREATENINGS MAY RESULT FROM SELF-JUSTIFICATION

February 9, 1890

Peace to you and the blessing of the Lord! How many times I got ready to write to you, for I knew that it was necessary, very necessary. . . But the moment I would pick up the pen, the obstacles would be right there. Either people, or I had to serve, or a headache. Even now as I write, I have such sickness in my eyes and forehead, just as if someone had poured lead over my eyebrows. And how you are, I do not think I can even imagine right now. Probably worse off than me. I spoke to Batiushka Father Amvrosy about your scares. He attributes them to the fact that when you were with him and told him about yourself, you kept blaming others while justifying yourself, and you did not say quite everything. But, of course, all this will pass. Only know that if the demons threatened me for supposedly snatching M. away from them, then aren't they going to avenge themselves on you even more? But we should not become despondent. The Lord of hosts said to His disciples, *Greater is He that is in you, than he that is in the world* (I John 4:4). *The Lord of hosts is with us* (Ps. 45:11). As for your temporary loss of speech, it is not dangerous. Yesterday they told me that one nun could not speak for half a year, but then it passed. And everything will pass. And it will come to pass that we ourselves will no longer be (here, that is). But we must attend to and spiritually travail over that which unto the ages will not pass away, building for ourselves *a house not made with hands, eternal in the Heavens* (II Cor. 5:1).

And thank God that in His boundless love He has delivered you out of the mouth of Gehenna. The demons are wailing like anything because M. has been snatched out of their mouth.

350. THE DEVIL IS VANQUISHED BY OUR ACKNOWLEDGEMENT OF OUR SINS

March 8, 1890

Blessed is God *Who will have all men to be saved, and to come unto the knowledge of the truth.*[1] I rejoice for you, M., that you have overcome your adversary, even as the host of those clothed in white rejoiced after St. Andrew the Fool laid low the black giant. And it is not just one company but all the countless hosts of the heavenly powers who rejoice, according to the word of the Lord Himself, *over one sinner that repenteth* (Luke 15:7). Peace to you and salvation! And the blessing of the Lord from henceforth and forevermore. "There is no unpardonable sin, save the unrepented one."[2] So the holy Fathers teach. If the whole world were filled to overflowing with your sins, one drop of the Saviour's blood would burn them all up in an instant. Gather together the sins of the world, teaches Chrysostom, and all of them, all of them will appear as a single drop in the boundless ocean.[3] Read the homily of St. Dimitry of Rostov "On the Laudation of the Theotokos," that is, for next Saturday. And thank the Lord Who has snatched you out of the mouth of the lion of hell. Save yourself!

That right now it is difficult and frightening for you — this is the Devil's wonted device to confuse a person and hinder him in his work; but all of this will pass. It cost much to acknowledge your sins and to say them. But now [you have] the mercy of God. I advise and bless you to remain at K. You see for yourself how everything is pointing in that direction. And everyone will be at peace. As for it being far away from me, that is a childish notion. The kinship between you and me is spiritual, and distance is no hindrance to the spirit. Peace to you!

351. SORROW IS AN EPITIMIA FOR SIN

Peace to you, M.!. . . I am very sorry about your spiritual state, but I have told you more than once — and I think written — that this was to

---

1. I Timothy 2:4; exclamation from the service of Holy Baptism, and from the tonsure service.
2. The *Ascetical Homilies of St. Isaac the Syrian*, Homily 2, p. 10.
3. See also *The Ascetical Homilies of St. Isaac the Syrian*, Homily 51, p. 244: "As a handful of sand thrown into the great sea, so are the sins of all flesh in comparison with the mind of God."

be expected. It is a spiritual epitimia. It is not given to you alone. No, the spiritual law has it as the foundation of all rules pertaining to those who sin — for the compassionate Lord has purposed to transform us sinners into angels. So endure patiently, believing wholeheartedly and unshakably that all our suffering (even though we ourselves may have prepared the way for it) will be recompensed a hundredfold.

Remember the Patriarch who, leaving his [patriarchal] throne, labored unrecognized among the workers. And when, exhausted by the heaviness of the labor, he once began to doubt whether he would be rewarded for this, he beheld a beautiful youth walking beside him. When the Patriarch asked him why he was there, the young man answered, "I am counting every step you take as you work, and every sigh."

So you see how things happen in this world!

352. AN EXAMPLE OF THE TORMENT OF SIN

October 23, 1890

Peace to you, M.! I read your letter of October 7, and still it is the same — you are in despair: well, so I am writing you the same thing again, too — that is, I repeat for the hundredth time that suffering is inevitable for your soul, in accordance with God's law. Do not imagine that I do not understand it. I understand it very well. There have been similar cases. Here is one of them; perhaps you have read it also. A certain brother who was mired in sins was dying. The Abbot, together with the brethren, began to pray for him. And he beheld a vision: an enormous dragon was sucking in this brother, but he could not suck him in because his spiritual father was praying for him. However, this brother was so worn out from this spiritual and physical torment that he himself begged his spiritual father to stop praying. "It would be better to let the dragon swallow me up," he said, "just do not torture me." Isn't that foolish — as if he would have been better off in the dragon's belly than halfway down its gullet! But the elder paid no attention to his plea, continuing instead to pray. And he rescued the brother from the dragon's jaws. Your situation is similar to this. Your struggle against the Devil is a matter of life and death. And not for this earthly life but for eternity.

Either to reign together with Christ or to be tormented in Gehenna with the demons unto the ages and ages.

You do not see this and understand it little — but the Devil understands it very well. And so he torments and chokes you, thinking perhaps he can swallow you up. It would be a consolation for him not to be alone there. . .

Peace to you and God's blessing! I cannot write any more!

353. QUICKLY SAY WHAT IS ON YOUR MIND

M., save yourself! I received your last letter. There is something you do not want to say! Make the sign of the Cross immediately and write it! Write everything! Take pity on yourself and on us!

Until you say what is on your mind, nothing in the world will help you! And what if — God forbid — death should overtake you! Death!

LVIII. LETTERS TO THE TREASURER N—

354. THE ENEMY HINDERS DISCLOSURE OF THOUGHTS.
IMMODERATE GRIEF OVER THE REPOSED ELDER IS INAPPROPRIATE

August 19, 1892

I received your letter of August 11 in which you write that you had not been accustomed to taking thought for yourself, but had become used to doing everything according to Batiushka's instructions, not expecting to lose him so soon. You have many times wanted to write to me about your grief, but the only result has been lamentation and tears. Each time you get ready to write to me, you remember Optina, Batiushka rises up before your mind's eye, and then you cry until it is time for bed, and that is the end of that. And now you are unable to ask anything: you have forgotten [what to ask], your thoughts are confused. It occurs to you that perhaps the enemy is hindering you, diverting you from [the path of] eldership (as of now you turn to no one [for guidance]).

It is very possible that it is partly the enemy who is hindering you from disclosing your thoughts, which is something he hates in anyone, whoever it may be — but he especially hates it when a person in authority turns to an elder. He would prefer to keep the subordinates also, through the example of [their superior's] self-guidance and self-will, in the captivity of reticence, of a whole labyrinth of thoughts and desires. So long as the wound is hidden from the physician's view, it is not easily healed. And this, our spiritual leprosy, is precisely what the enemy of our salvation needs in order the more surely to direct the ship of our life toward the all-engulfing abyss instead of toward the calm haven. We may call self-deception such an abyss, and the forgetfulness, ignorance, heedlessness, and judging of others which stem therefrom. Batiushka Father Amvrosy died according to the will of God, and therefore at the proper time for him, and immoderate grief on his account is both displeasing to him and may be spiritually harmful for those who grieve beyond measure. As for your complex and distracting occupation, it should not worry you, because it is your obedience, and every obedience is saving when fulfilled properly, with humility and unmurmuringly.

355. ONE MUST CARRY THE CROSS OF OBEDIENCE AND SHOW CONDESCENSION FOR THOSE WHO ARE WEAK

December 30, 1892

I, in turn, greet you with the new year, wishing you a renewal of life unto salvation. Of course, all this is not attained without labors but with great afflictions and with patience in the conscientious fulfillment of one's obedience. Is there anyone who would not like to rest from his labors? Here I have been carrying the burden of my service for the benefit of my neighbor for 20 years already, and at present my health is poor, and I suffer from shortness of breath and insomnia; but who can on his own authority lay aside the obedience which the all-good Lord has laid upon him for the benefit of his soul and for the benefit of others? Perhaps it is not for us to see the benefit we bring to ourselves and to others, and perhaps it is small — but still the Lord alone knows all things, and He will not leave unrewarded even a good volition and disposition of heart.

According to the Gospel, it should be said that undoubtedly each person is given his own saving cross. This cross has grown on the soil of our heart, and it is only through this cross that we can be saved. From this it follows that if we refuse to carry our cross of obedience for no legitimate reason, we refuse to go by the way of Christ, by the saving way, and we want to invent for ourselves another way, free of labor, for attaining the Kingdom of Heaven. But this cannot be. The Kingdom of God suffereth violence, and the violent take it by force (Cf. Matt. 11:12).

It is a good and saving work to love one's neighbor, and to alleviate the needs of your sisters, and to condescend to their infirmities. However, if the Abbess opposes this, then do good more in secret, and comfort those whom you can, in whatever way you can. Arguing does little good — it would be more likely to bring harm rather than benefit to both parties. . . I did not answer you for a long time both due to illness and due to extreme lack of time. I ask you to generously forgive my exceeding infirmity. . .

LIX. LETTERS TO A.L.[1]

356. PUT INTO PRACTICE THE LESSONS YOU HAVE COLLECTED

December 2, 1880

Peace to you! Peace, and God's blessing!

I received your letter of November 27 from Yelets. So you must have arrived safely. I am glad. Now you have returned from your distant pilgrimages not without a supply of knowledge. . . Let us make a beginning of saving ourselves. You collected yourself a whole stash of lessons at Optina. Fulfill them in practice. Above all, remember the saying I told you of St. Isaac the Syrian, "Watchfulness helps the young more than works."[2] Thus, if you feel in your heart that you are being harmed, flee from your relatives lickety-split. It is said in the Scriptures, Let not the young go out to the battle. . . (Deut. 20:8). You may wear a prayer rope, covered. But so as not to wear it without understanding, know that it is an expression of that which is within the heart, that is, the Name of Jesus. Just as the circle of the prayer rope is unending, so too the Name of Christ is called upon continually.

357. A NATIVITY WISH FOR AN UNDERSTANDING OF THE WORTH OF WORLDLY JOYS

December 21, 1880

A strange and marvelous mystery do I behold: the cave is a Heaven; the Virgin a cherubic throne; the manger a space wherein the Uncontainable One hath reclined.[3]

---

1. Both while she was still in the world and after entering the convent. (This footnote is from the Russian text.)
2. Cf. *The Ascetical Homilies of St. Isaac the Syrian*, Homily 51, p. 249.
3. From the Katavasias of the Nativity of Christ.

Truly an awesome wonder! Even the mind of the Cherubim is sore-amazed — how could this have come to pass? And yet, it happened! And which of these wonders is the most wondrous, the mind refuses to comprehend. It stops. . . Yes, this is a great consolation which the Holy Church has gifted to the intelligent person. One could just gaze into the abyss of these three little lines for a whole century. And how many more pearls there are scattered throughout the spiritual songs of the Church! But the earthly mind does not like these treasures, for it cannot compre-hend them. What good is a priceless ruby to a rooster? He would rather have a pea. As for us, what brings us consolation is to prance around on a parquet floor like some billy-goat; we like to split our sides laughing, put on some ugly face, masquerade, and how many more stupid and unseemly things there are to engross this luminous heavenly gift — our mind. However, I am not writing this so that you, my dear, would fling all those masks and ballroom paraphernalia all over the place and thus offend both your family and others. But I am speaking thus so that you would know what it is you are doing. And so that if you should get into mischief, you would confess it to the Lord. And He will forgive you. There you have my greeting for the new year! Do not grieve if my treat seems hard to your teeth, unaccustomed as they are to such food. I am gladly giving you the best of what I have.[1] And my wealth lies in my sin-cere devotion to you, seeing your great love in the Lord for me, the unworthy one. And I will remain thus devoted forever and in the years to come and unto the ages, only do not lose, do not forget your perspec-tive, remembering that you are a Christian!

358. HOW TO PRAY IN THE PRESENCE OF THOSE AT HOME. CONCERNING TRUE REPENTANCE

January 27, 1881

Are you well? You kept writing and writing, and all of a sudden you are silent. Or maybe your head is spinning from the noise and smoke of fun and holidays? In any case, it is time you showed some sign of life. However, I do have maybe even two letters of yours which I have not answered. . . In your letter of, I think, December 25, you write, "An awful thing happened today" — but you have informed me neither directly nor indirectly[2] about what this incident might have been. I should very

---

1. Lit., "my wealth." The Russian saying here rhymes: "Chem bogát, tem i rád."
2. Lit., "neither historically nor allegorically."

much like to know whether it concerns you? Also, I seem to recollect that you wrote that you find it difficult to complete your prayers and readings, since you do not have a room of your own. In that case, leave the customary order — for example, reading before the holy icons, with a candle, etc. — and go about it more simply: read and pray while walking, or tucked away in a corner, or somewhere in the front room. Once I was travelling along the Dnieper by steamer with some Jews. They comprised a large number of the passengers, and they were not the least shy on our account. One of them would be talking with you, for example, but then the time [for prayer] would come, and without further ado he would turn his back to you, bury his face in a pillar, a wall, or whatever was at hand, and go about his work. But those with you are even your family and not people of a different religion. Of course, you should make an effort not to give occasion for ridicule.

You also have a new revelation for me. You write, "I cannot repent in such a way that it would reach God." Well, how about that — you are a clever one! She has discovered the secret of when her repentance reaches the Lord and when it does not! As for me, I have been repeating the spiritual ABC's over and over for about 30 years now, and I have not yet been able to ascertain when my repentance reaches [God] and when it does not. If you happen to know, tell me your secret. As for me, I thought up until now that the Knower of hearts alone knows the worth of our repentance.

Otherwise, how is it said that "as far as the east is from the west, so far are My counsels from your counsels, and My ways from your ways" (Cf. Is. 55:8,9).

You wish to know whether you have made me sick and tired of your letters? Absolutely not. Especially if you will write big. As regards the correction of your life, do not worry. If you cannot be a good Christian, just say so, "O Lord, I am not good. Forgive me!" And that will be fine. Which I wish for you with all my heart.

359. WHAT THE FABLE "THE DRAGONFLY AND THE ANT" TEACHES US

March 19, 1881

What is wrong with you? You are in despair. . . So much you have read, so much I have spoken with you and written to you, and still you have not understood the simplest, clearest bit of truth: that a corrupt tree cannot produce sweet fruit, nor a bitter fountain yield sweet water (Cf. Matt. 7:18; James 3:11).

Yesterday or the day before, Father M. said that you are still dancing away over there. I suggested to him that he show you Krylov's fable, "The Dragonfly and the Ant." It suits you. The dragonfly, too, loved Cheesefare Week[1] and did not like the Fast, and she kept dancing away. I do not say this in order to reproach you, but so that you would see things the way they really are and not lose your head when an opportunity presents itself — that is, so that you would remember that debilitation follows upon sweetness, depression follows upon worldly gaiety, heaviness and even illness upon satiety — as a shadow follows a body.

How hard a tooth is, and yet even it gives way and crumbles apart like sand in the case of people who eat sweets. That is why the Holy Church, our teacher, chants, "What delight of life remaineth no party to grief? What glory standeth immutable on earth? All are more feeble than shadows; all more delusive than dreams!"[2] Krylov too, a secular writer, has told his "Dragonfly" story not for you and me only, but for the entire world — that is, that he who dances away the summer will have a miserable time in winter. He who in the prime of his life does not wish to take himself in hand has nothing to hope for when his health fails, and infirmities and illnesses come upon him. Your father may be a good man and an intelligent man but apparently only in the area of business, whereas he has never studied the Holy Scriptures, nor philosophy. If it were otherwise, he would not bring up his children in such a senseless way and wither blossoms that are only just unfolding with the scorching heat of worldly pleasures. He is in a hurry to make you into citizens of Yelets — but he does not concern himself over your becoming citizens of the Jerusalem on high. I am not saying this to undermine your love and respect for your father — God forbid — all our care, all our life is dedicated to instilling love and respect for parents — but I am saying it so that if your father shows no concern over your soul, you would show some concern over it yourself. Have recourse to God and to His Most Pure Mother and to the holy Saint of God Nicholas. And may the peace of God cover you; and I, the sinner, remember you always.

---

1. In Russia, Cheesefare Week was a time of merrymaking (sometimes to excess) before Great Lent. Even in pre-Christian times, special festivities had been held at this time of year in honor of the spring equinox.
2. From the "Stichera for the Reposed," by St. John of Damascus.

360. DO NOT MAKE A FINAL DECISION, BUT TRY VISITING AWHILE AT A CONVENT

April 2, 1881

I received your letter. Still you are restless and you are despondent. As though you were being taken off to slaughter! Why, wherever did you get such an idea! Right now you are a perfectly free individual. If you had a husband, the situation would be entirely different. But as it is you are free to choose — free as a little bird in the sky. No one is hurrying you. Well, so don't hurry. But you can always try it out. So do not make a final decision either way. As for your father, who is so reasonable and so loving, it is even your duty to explain everything to him frankly. And if you have a desire for salvation but at the same time have misgivings on account of your weaknesses, just tell him so, and ask him, on the one hand, to give you a chance to stay at some convent for a while as a visitor, and on the other hand, not to let anyone know about this. He is able to arrange both the one and the other. Above all, go about this work with prayer to God, meekly, thoroughly, with the awareness that not only your life but the whole of your eternity depends upon this decisive step. Do not worry overmuch about your infirmities, your [weak] will, and your health. A great teacher, who had experienced everything firsthand, said — or more precisely, He Who is eternal Wisdom incarnate said to this great teacher, *My strength is made perfect in weakness* (II Cor. 12:9). When God is present, our intelligence and our strength become unimportant. Of course, if your father refuses to provide for your material support, you will not have the strength to endure the lack of necessities. But your father is hardly likely to abandon you. After all, he would give you a proper dowry upon giving you in marriage.

And can it be that Jesus, our God, is worth less than a Yelets merchant?

361. TO UNDERSTAND THE VANITY OF LIFE IN THE WORLD IS A GIFT FROM GOD

April 24, 1881

Christ is risen! I am sorry for you, that even these great, bright days of Christ's Resurrection give you no joy. "Now are all things filled with light: Heaven and earth, and the nethermost regions of the earth."[1]

---

1. From the Paschal Canon.

Hades itself is now illumined with the light of the Risen One, whereas you are still dismal, and things are not going well.

Of course, after all that skipping around and all those outings, there is no sense expecting spiritual joy, which is alien to lovers of the world and completely unknown to them. But still, you have the advantage that although you are not a participant of light, the darkness does not deceive you either: already you sense in your heart the meaningless gloom of worldly pleasures. And it is not everyone who is able to grasp this truth, but he to whom it is given from on high. "No man can come to Me, except My Father draw him, and I will raise him up at the last day" (Cf. John 6:44). And this knowledge and this feeling are not given to all, but to those who are chosen, who have been, so to say, begged from God by our Saviour Himself: "I pray not for the whole world, but for them which Thou hast given Me. . . Father, keep through Thine own name those whom Thou hast given Me, that they may be one, as We are" (Cf. John 17: 9,11).

I am confident that your papa is an intelligent and capable man, but only in his own element in which he has been active — in the areas of business, of household management. . . but the spiritual element is of an entirely different nature which escapes the wise of this world.

And that is why the Lord said, "If ye were of the world, the world would love his own: but because I have chosen you out of the world, therefore the world hateth you, as it hated Me before it hated you" (Cf. John 15:18,19). Herein lies the whole secret, the reason why you suffer and shall suffer censure and ridicule from lovers of the world. But do not be downcast, for we have as anchor — the Word! "Fear not, little flock! For it is God's good pleasure to give you the Kingdom" (Cf. Luke 12:32)!

So do not be downcast! Instead, await the mercy of God. Submit to your father; he is responsible for you before God and before society. Only, you must ask him that in this area with which he is not familiar, in the spiritual life, he should not himself decide your fate, but instead seek advice from people experienced in the monastic life who might be better able to figure out how capable you are of it.

Why, surely he knows some monastics in positions of authority! As for those living in the world, even priests, the holy Fathers do not permit us to seek advice from them [regarding this]. For they themselves are unfamiliar with this manner of life. Pray to the holy Hierarch Nicholas the Wonderworker and to the Righteous Euphrosyne.[1] Peace to you and the blessing of the Lord!

362. DO NOT BE A SLAVE OF THE WORLD; SERVE THE LORD. YOU WILL NOT BECOME A SAINT RIGHT OFF. THE GOOD THINGS OF THE WORLD ARE NOTHING

May 3, 1881

Peace to you! I just received your letter, and I am hurrying to answer it because you wrote such a despairing letter that any minute now you will become gloomy with depression. And it is not fitting to entertain such dark thoughts and feelings during these bright and holy days when daily the light of Christ's Resurrection is hymned by the Church. Of course, for one who has not learned to chant or to listen to the church hymns but has been more absorbed in novels and dances, the sweetness and loftiness of the church hymns is incomprehensible — but, after all, you haven't permanently chained yourself to the yoke of thankless service to the world! You had a little fun, you did what you wanted — and it doesn't pay? Well, so leave this ungrateful master and come to your real and true Master, Jesus Christ, and serve Him by faith and righteousness. And our merciful Master will number you among His elect.

He bestows honor with incredible liberality, and He is plenteous in mercy and generous with rewards. "He receiveth the last even as the first. . . He is merciful to the last and provideth for the first; and to this one He giveth and to that one He showeth kindness. He receiveth their labors and acknowledgeth the purpose, and He honoreth the deed and praiseth the intention. Let no one lament his poverty, for the Kingdom is made manifest to all. Let no one bewail his transgressions, for forgiveness hath dawned forth from the tomb."[2] Do you see with Whom we have to do? With what kind of a Master? It follows that your tears and your gloomy thoughts make no sense! But I see that you wish to throw off your fashionable shoes with ornaments and your ballroom dress, and this very minute become holy, righteous, to shine right away. No,

1. Perhaps St. Euphrosyne of Polotsk, who helped and encouraged many to take up the monastic life, including a number of her own relatives.
2. From the Catechetical Homily of St. John Chrysostom read at the end of the Paschal Matins.

Matushka, it does not happen that way with spiritual things. Here, patience comes first and foremost; after that comes more patience; and finally all this is crowned by — patience once more. The Lord, when He was leaving His beloved disciples, said, *In the world ye shall have tribulation. But your sorrow shall be turned into joy. And your joy no man taketh from you* (John 16:20,22,33). There are different kinds of joys. For example, here A. puts on a skirt with a long, long train — now there's a joy for her. She will ride along the street in a troika with bells jingling — ah, joy! And there are a lot of joys — Yelets joys, Moscow joys, Peter[1] joys, all kinds of joys — but this is sheer deception. "What delight of life remaineth no party to grief? What glory standeth immutable on earth? All are more feeble than shadows! All more delusive than dreams! Yet one moment only — and death shall supplant them all!"[2] Well, so Cheesefare Week was here — and now it is gone![3] The pleasures of Cheesefare Week were here, and what remains now? Depression, gloom, hopelessness — one could die! Now the Lord said, *By their fruits ye shall know them* (Matt. 7:20)! Take our Father Abbot.[4] He was more well off than your papa: he had millions [of rubles], houses, hundreds of sales assistants, and a [prospective] bride with five million [more rubles]. But just ask him now if he would agree to exchange his rassa of muhoyár for a sable overcoat. *By their fruits ye shall know them* (Matt. 7:20)! I wanted to write more to you, too, because I can see how important such reinforcement is for you right now, but there is no time — I have to hurry! Save yourself!

You can tell your father, "I will wait a year, and after that I must reach a decision concerning this matter." Regarding the ordering of your life: make six prostrations morning and evening, three to the holy Hierarch Nicholas and three to the Righteous Euphrosyne, with the prayer to the holy Hierarch Nicholas, "Pray to God for me, a sinner, and order my life in accordance with the will of God unto salvation!" "O Righteous Euphrosyne, pray to God for me, a sinner, and order my life in accordance with the will of God unto salvation!" The Elder himself dictated this reply for you.

---

1. I.e. St. Petersburg
2. From the Stichera for the Reposed, by St. John of Damascus.
3. The Russian here rhymes: "Bíla, da spíla."
4. Abbot Isaaky I of Optina.

363. UNTIL YOUR LAST BREATH, DO NOT LOSE HOPE OF CORRECTION

May 27

Peace to you! Well, your aunt is here with us again, but you are not. You missed your chance. Now you will have to wait. I read your letter. Still you are confused. You would like to enter a convent, and yet you would not like to. Why, who is compelling you, and who is asking you to? You are your own mistress — independent, well-to-do. You have everything at your disposal. What is there to worry about? If even you have abandoned the spiritual life, even this should not frighten you; instead, let us try to correct ourselves — and if we are not able, let us try to reproach ourselves and humble ourselves. I myself live negligently — well, so what am I to do, just bewail the situation? Never! Until your last breath, do not lose hope of correction and salvation! In this, the thief is a guarantee and encouragement for us sinners. Just imagine: such great saints of God as Noah, Abraham, Daniel, Moses, David the King, and a great multitude of other great ones were still in Hades — and the thief was already in Paradise! And after all, you are not a thief, just a so-so, feeble, mixed-up girl! You may take the medicine drops for your health and eat non-fasting food! But be more discriminating on fast days — it won't hurt you not to eat [special food] for one day! Rejoice in the Lord!

364. DO NOT START UP ACQUAINTANCES WITH YOUNG PEOPLE

October 25, 1881

Peace to you and the blessing of the Lord! My, how suspicious you are! Again you have brought forward a slander against me — allegedly I am displeased with you. Why, even if you really had taken a fancy to someone there, how could I fail to forgive you? I myself am a sinful man. But you did not even take a fancy to anyone, you simply made friends. Well, both God will forgive you, and I forgive you. But still, in future do not start up friendships with young people. And your frankness gives me even less cause to be grieved; no matter what you may write, I am certain that you are being sincere — and that is enough. As for squabbles or no squabbles — that does not depend on us but on the places and people surrounding us. And these we cannot change. So don't worry. I remain the same toward you. . .

Prosper in the Lord, and do not forget the proverb, "Without God one can get nowhere!"[1]

365. I WILL NOT ABANDON YOU
IN YOUR SPIRITUAL ISOLATION

October 31, 1881

Peace to you! Not long ago I sent a letter in which I conveyed to you in writing the forgiveness of all your sins and weaknesses, and assured you that I was never angry with you, nor do I now harbor the slightest trace of indignation — rather I was always peacefully and sincerely well-disposed toward you. And I still am. But now I have received another letter from you and see that you did not receive mine. I am sending another by registered mail. And I hasten to reassure you that I have never so much as thought of abandoning you — on the contrary, I want to help you in any way I can and to be of service with advice and, if possible, actively as well.

I very much understand the feelings which are oppressing you, and I am ready to sympathize with you both in your joy and in your sorrow... I wish for you to take comfort. And from now on, write everything without the least hesitation. I will lay everything to heart and do my best to comfort you. Only know and believe that I am sincerely well-disposed toward you and will never abandon you.

I myself can see your sincere devotion to me and your spiritual isolation. If I must be friendly and sympathetic towards all, must I not be the more so toward you? May the Lord bless you! May He preserve you from all the wiles of the Devil! May He teach you His eternal truth and righteousness! Peace to you and salvation!

366. THE SOUL IS OF MORE VALUE
THAN THE ENTIRE WORLD

October 16, 1882

Peace to you! I am sending you a second registered letter. The first one was addressed to your father, and perhaps you did not receive it. . .

---

1. Lit., "not even to the threshold."

There is too much that I would need to write in order to help you in your distress, and so I would advise you to come here with your aunt. . . But now, be careful, do not be stubborn. Right now you can still be helped, but if this penetrates deeper, you will not be able to uproot it even with difficulty. The heart is not something trivial,[1] nor is the human soul something cheap; it is of more value than the entire world. All the treasures of the terrestrial globe, all the world, is not worth as much as one Christian soul. So the holy Fathers teach. If they do not give you money for the journey, do not worry — just get here somehow. God is not without mercy!

367. CONGRATULATIONS AND BEST WISHES UPON ENTERING THE MONASTIC LIFE
March 20, 1886

Peace to you and God's blessing, reverend sister in the Lord! I congratulate you upon entering your new way of life. This is that narrow way extolled by the Lord, along which few walk. But it leads to a Kingdom — and not to a temporal, fleeting kingdom but to an eternal one: this Kingdom is the Kingdom of all the ages (Cf. Ps. 144:13). I counsel you from your very first steps not to turn aside from the right way. Otherwise you will have difficulty. To this end, by all means beware of forming special friendships. That way you will avoid many tribulations. Do not be discouraged — the enemy will attack you, as you are already experiencing. It is handier for him to attack a new monastic, just as it is for an experienced wrestler to attack someone who is unsteady. And so as not to be that way, that is, inept and shaky, without fail read Abba Dorotheos or John of the Ladder daily. Their books are a great treasury of lessons in the spiritual life. And if, according to your strength, you will walk by the path they indicate, you will not be lost, and you will inherit the eternal Kingdom.

368. REJOICE THAT YOU ARE NOT LOVED
February 18, 1891

Peace to you and God's blessing, reverend sister! I just read your letter and I rejoiced in spirit, for I have faith in the indisputable truth of the words of Him Who is eternal Truth: *Blessed are ye, when men shall revile*

---

1. Lit., "a splinter."

and persecute you, and say all manner of evil against you falsely. . . Rejoice and be glad, saith the Saviour of our souls, for your reward is great in the Heavens (Matt. 5:11,12)! I rejoice for you! As regards your father not loving you very much, that is more profitable for you than his love and affection. Remember that great saint of God, the young struggler St. Barbara the Great Martyr. Her father did not love her very much either. But did she lose anything on that account? Yea, she gained a hundredfold. Not only that, but even now she continues to shine in the Christian world like a brilliant star, helping the weak. And your lot is not far removed from hers. She died a quick death, aflame with love for her heavenly Bridegroom — and you by slow and prayerful suffering are going to the same place. Rejoice, sister in the Lord! You say that I have forgotten you. I have not forgotten you, yea, I have not forgotten you. And I was very surprised that you were silent for so long. I would ask your relatives about you and receive the answer, "She is living at the convent." And now I am comforted that you remembered me yourself. From a worldly point of view you have a sorrowful life. But from a Christian, a monastic viewpoint — [you are going by] the genuine monastic path! The unerring, reliable, calming, comforting path of the ascetic. For the path which is free of sorrows is dangerous. *We must through much tribulation enter into the Kingdom of Heaven* (Acts 14:22)! And the Lord, the Setter of our contest, comforting His beloved disciples, teaches, *In the world ye shall have tribulation, but your sorrow shall be turned into joy. And your joy no man taketh from you* (John 16:20,22,33). Remember how you and I read those comforting chapters of John of Karpathos from the Philokalia.

Turn to the Mother Treasurer Melitina with your perplexities. She has spiritual knowledge and understanding, for she is a disciple of the Optina Elders. Greet her with a bow for me. Peace to you!

LX. LETTERS TO T.

369. DO NOT FORGET THE MOST IMPORTANT THING: READING AND PRAYER

January 31, 1886

Peace to you, T.! What a pity that you could not come with V. Well, we drank [tea] here, and chanted, and read, and made caramelized sugar, and treated my ailment. We rubbed our hands sore. Well, your day will come. For now, I take comfort in the fact that with Matushka gone, you will rest a little and catch up on your sleep.

Now, it is fine to sleep, and it is fine to run around [working] — only do not forget the most important thing: do some reading. And practice saying the little prayer according to your strength, even if it is while walking or while lying down. Otherwise you and I will turn out to be dishonest servants, whereas the genuine servant is he who sits at the feet of Jesus, that is, he who repeats His prayer. He, our true God, has said regarding such a servant, *Where I am, there shall also My servant be* (John 12:26). And He sits on the heavenly throne, at the right hand of the Father.

370. LIVE AS GOD BIDS US, AND SERVE YOUR ELDERS

December 26

My T-ochka wants to hear from me, but she is afraid to ask. So I am afraid to answer. If you are going to be afraid, I am going to be afraid, too. But if you will write more simply, you will find peace.

I thank you for your greeting and best wishes and for the little picture. And I am sending you a little one like it, so that you won't forget me. Because already you are getting all set to be an old lady and think you are going to be forgotten. You have a little place of your own, so that must mean you are not forgotten. And if you wait a bit, you will fix yourself up even better. And for now, your room is in the nice section. So just make a note of that.

And for now, let us live along as God bids us, little by little. There is no higher obedience than to serve those in authority. The Son of God Himself says, "I came not to be ministered unto, but to minister" (Cf. Matt. 20:28). Now, He fashioned both the world and these servants — sinful and wicked people — and He Himself, their God, their King, and their Creator, came to earth to serve them. *Wherefore God also hath highly exalted Him, that at the name of Jesus every knee should bow to Him — of things in Heaven, and things in earth, and things under the earth* (Phil. 2:9, 10).

LXI. LETTERS TO V.

371. STOP STEALING AND EAVESDROPPING
November 22, 1882

Peace to you, V. I have been receiving lots and lots of letters from you. And in them are piles and piles of sins. Well, one cannot be a nun unless the Lord humbles us and casts down our pride — but now what have you been stealing for? Why, they send thieves off to Siberia. And you pilfer poor O.'s apples. Really! Well, for deeds proper to mice you will get caught in a mousetrap! Stop stealing and eavesdropping; these base passions will be your ruin. And so each time you slip, do prostrations. The holy Fathers say, "Every sin can be tolerated in monks, but expel a thief from the monastery." As for your passions not having been extinguished yet, there is nothing surprising about that. Read chapter 43 of Callistus and Ignatius in the Philokalia.[1] May God forgive you all the sins you have confessed. I, the sinner, forgive you also. As regards your chanting, not a soul has praised you to me as yet.

Therefore, the evil one is tricking and flattering you. When carnal thoughts oppress you, do some prostrations according to your strength. Without warfare not a single soul has entered Paradise. But the victorious are crowned.

---

1. See footnote, Letter #155.

372. DO NOT BE UNTRUTHFUL AND SLY, AND DO NOT BE PUFFED UP ON ACCOUNT OF YOUR VOICE

February 19, 1884

Peace to you and the blessing of the Lord, reverend Sister V. I received and read all your letters. May God forgive you all [the sins] you have committed. Only, He will forgive you in the hope that you will correct yourself. I have told you again and again, and I repeat: do not be untruthful and sly. You will repent of it but too late. It is written in the word of God that *Evildoers shall utterly perish.* [1]

Now, for becoming puffed up on account of your voice and your chanting and other similar things, even things you do not have — for this you will suffer. *Whosoever exalteth himself shall be abased* (Luke 14:11).

May God forgive you in these days of forgiveness, and forgive me, a sinner!

---

1. Psalm 36:9. The Slavonic word for "evil" generally means "sly" in modern Russian; hence the use of this quote in the context of this letter.

LXII. LETTERS TO D.

373. A MONASTIC SHOULD BE JOYFUL.
ABOUT KATYA ANDRONOVA

September 17, 1888

Peace to you, D.! Are you all well? Are you happy? The great Elder Apollo would say, "A monk should always be joyful. If he is not, that means he is not living in the way a monastic should live."[1] But you all live a good monastic life and you pray for me, a sinner. I began to have even more faith in your childlike prayers after Katya Andronova's funeral. That little girl simply worked miracles. So many years she fought with her aunt as with a wild beast over Optina. And so she went to the grave without having betrayed Optina. She was ill for several years, very grievously during the last months; and two or three weeks ago she very nearly departed, and they would let no one see her. But Liza, her former helper and her friend, stole in to see her and whispered, "Batiushka is coming to see us." The dying one suddenly came to life and said, "Now I will live in spirit until then." And she really did wait for me. Even more amazing: her aunt had been furious with me and would say, "He (Anatoly) is not setting foot here ever." But when they told her I had arrived, she happily shouted, "Now won't Katenka be glad! Tell Batiushka to come in while I get Katenka ready to see him." And she herself would send for me to come from the guest house. The Lord vouchsafed that I should find Katya still alive. And we spoke much

---

1. "And we observed their joy in the desert, with which nothing on the earth, and no bodily delight, can be compared, for there was among them no man who was sorry or afflicted with grief, and if any man was found to be in affliction, our father Apollo knew the cause thereof, and was able to make known to him the secret thoughts of his mind. And he would say unto such an one, 'It is not seemly for us to afflicted at our redemption, for we are those who are about to inherit the Kingdom of Heaven; but let the Jews weep, and let the men of iniquity be in mourning, and let the righteous rejoice. For they have their happiness in earthly things, and they cultivate the things of earth, and why should not we, who are worthy of the blessed hope, rejoice always, even according to the encouraging words of the blessed Apostle Paul, who said unto us, *Rejoice in the Lord always, and pray at all seasons, and in everything give thanks* (I Thess. 5:16-18).' See The Paradise of the Holy Fathers, Vol. I, p. 350.

together until they locked the gates. As for what happened afterwards, I am sending you Liza's letter, which related everything. As for me, I have been in K. for four days. But I have received no more than 50 [sisters]. And here the lay people are trying to get in, too.

We had a very nice trip after leaving from you. In Dvoriki we stopped to eat your cookies. That's some gardens they have there! Marvelous trees! All red, others white,[1] down to the ground. All apples.

We saw K-n's mansion; we drove past the house itself. And we drove into K. to the ringing of the bells.

There the passport was all ready. And we decided to travel along the Oka [River] straight to K., and from there to T. And so we would not have found Katya alive. But suddenly they announced, "The boat will not run today." And so Katya's wish was stronger, holier than ours — and like it or not, we set off for T. by rail. Here in K. we were received with enthusiasm. They served us [tea], they fed us and fed us. And great was the joy of the sisters. . .

374. A MIRACLE OF BATIUSHKA FATHER MAKARY

May 17, 1892

Peace to you and God's blessing, reverend Mother D. I am very glad that you remember me, and I am hurrying to answer you. There is no time now to collect news. The mailman is already here. And I only received your letter last night. Instead of the news, I will tell you a miracle worked yesterday by Batiushka Father Makary.

A.L.'s teeth started to ache terribly; she suffered all last week. When I was there, she cried and screamed all night. M. Vl-na was spending the night with her in her cell. And so, last night she was wailing terribly. She had shooting pains in the entire right side of her head, her teeth, her entire right side, and her right foot, and she could not walk. Crying, she enumerated all the saints. At last she shouted, "Batiushka Makary! You, at least, help me!" And right away she fell into a light sleep. She beheld as in a dream that she was at Batiushka Makary's dear little grave and was about to eat a little earth. And someone's voice was saying, "Finally you figured out what to do!" And when A. came to herself, not a trace of the pain remained. "Only," she said, "I don't have any of that earth!"

---

1. Some varieties of apples are referred to as "white" ("bély") in Russian, e.g. "bély nalív," "juicy white."

Yesterday M.N. took her some earth. . . It is time you returned to your own little nest. Batiushka Makary would write to [nuns] who were travelling, "It's time, it's really time you returned to your little nest. When a bird leaves its nest for a long time, the eggs cool and the nestlings don't hatch."[1]

LXIII. LETTERS TO A.

375. NAMEDAY WISHES

February 3, 1889

I congratulate you on your nameday. From my heart I wish for you to live in the house of God as long as St. Anna, that is, 84 years. And maybe even longer. Only to live nicely: to be obedient, to remember God often, not to overindulge on sweets, not to condemn others, not to become proud, to love the sisters, to guard your eyes, not to start up any friendships with anyone. God has granted you consolation, and so take delight in it.

You were offended because I said that you supposedly let me down. Well, you did let me down: you did not write the verses (and there was something else, too) — and I was waiting for them. And I am still waiting. Peace to you, my nameday [sister]. As for that thought that I will abandon you — don't believe it. That is the Devil disturbing you.

376. DO NOT BE FAINTHEARTED. A WONDERFUL DREAM (WITHOUT AN ENDING)

August 22, 1890

Peace to you, A. Again you are fainthearted. Again you become downcast with every little gust of the sorrows which are inevitable in this world. And where do you think to escape them? In Kiev or beyond? There are plenty of them everywhere. And eternal glory and honor are due, not to him who quickly flees from them, but to him who faces them dauntlessly.

---

1. See *The Ascetical Homilies of St. Isaac the Syrian*, Homily 48, p. 232. "A bird, wherever it may be, hastens back to its nest to hatch there its young; and a monk possessing discernment hastens to his cell to produce there the fruit of life."

Why, if one just takes an intelligent look at your troubles, it is positively disgraceful! A Christian, living under the guidance of an elder, comforted, loved — and she does not wish to endure an [unpleasant] word. Come on, now, how do others manage to bear their crosses? And moreover, what crosses! After all, you, too, have been baptized (kreschénaya) — but you run away from your cross (ot krestá). Why, how do you expect to enter into the joy of your Lord? Humble yourself. Humble yourself, little girl! Learn some sense. It is time. Otherwise, it will be too late, and you will grieve. May the Lord teach you and soothe you. Peace to you and salvation!

Just this minute someone came from Meshchovsk and related how she had seen a dream in the cathedral in Meshchovsk. "I was alone in the cathedral," she said, "and I saw a very beautiful nun enter, tall, clothed in mantia and kamilavka. She walked past me directly through the northern doors into the altar; she walked past the prothesis table and approached the altar itself, and immediately the royal gates opened. She came out and said, 'Come over here to me" I came up to her, thinking, 'Who is she?' She threw off her kamilavka, and from beneath it tumbled her wavy, thick, white hair. . ."

377. A REPROACH FOR WISHING TO LEAVE THE CONVENT

September 29, 1891

Peace to you and God's blessing! You write that you were waiting "for my heart to take pity on you." Of course, if I had had any hope of being able to comfort you, I would have hastened to try. But I can see it is not so easy. How many years I comforted you — I did everything I could, and still your gaze turns toward your L. or toward the Caucasus. Neither my solicitude nor your troubles have brought you sense; at the very first vexation you are ready to leave the holy ranks of the angels and to turn into a [tough] peasant woman. . . And this despite the fact that the bruises you received on your head from such a one may still not have healed!

Well, why waste words when you pay no attention even to my deeds over many years and my sincere solicitude? As regards the little cow, I am sorry for her, but I won't be sorry for hard-hearted ungrateful people who love no one save their belly. I provided you with everything and tried to see to your needs as best I could — but I won't cater to people who are hypocritical and rude. . .

378. YOUR CELL WILL TEACH YOU EVERYTHING. CONCERNING A TRIP TO FATHER JOHN

October 25, 1891

Peace to you, A. I received your letter. I am very pleased with you — you wrote much and in detail, and you did everything that was necessary.

N— must have made off with the tuning fork and the pictures out of habit. I am surprised she let you have them in the first place! Let those coming for Confession go with God's blessing to Father Th. If I come, it will be the easier for me.

You do well in sitting at home. St. Arsenios the Great taught, "Sit in your cell, and it will teach you everything (good)."[1] Sit there with God's blessing, and Jesus Himself will come to you. Only say that prayer, "Lord Jesus Christ, Son of God, have mercy on me, a sinner."

Do go to church even if you can hear nothing. As for your stupefied and despondent state, there is nothing unusual here — we are all in the same case.[2]

You ask what I am doing? I am thinking about you: what are you doing over there? Are you sad? And what about the other sisters, or rather about the entire convent: how will it survive? Will you have enough bread? There are so many now who are in want, who are hungry. The dumb beasts are dying — they have nothing to eat. As for us, we become despondent while we are still well off. Let us await God's mercy. We have left the world for His sake, so He will not leave us.

You would like to make the trip to see Father John[3] — I really do not know what to tell you. It would be good to go away right now, but on the other hand, it is not profitable for a young one to be travelling around. Pray, and cast lots. Just now a dozen nuns from Belev came; the last ones are leaving. Maybe now I can attend to myself, take a look at myself.

Because Shamordino really has constantly been making my head spin — either I would be going to them, or they would be coming to me. P. was just here with me and she says that our Archimandrite told her that everything will be as it was before. Thus we just have to be patient a bit. Peace to you and salvation!

---

1. Actually, this is a saying of St. Moses the Ethiopian. See Letter #34.
2. The Elder Amvrosy had reposed on October 10, 1891.
3. Perhaps Father John of Kronstadt; he and the Elder Anatoly esteemed one another highly. On October 10, 1892, they served together on the day of the Elder Amvrosy's memorial.

379. WHY YOU ARE SAD

July 7, 1892

Peace to you and God's blessing, sorrowful A. You do not understand why you are so very sad. It is because there is going to be a thunderstorm soon. It has already started over here — right now there is loud thunder and lightning, and the rain is coming down. . .

Another reason for your sadness is that this happens before a time of joy.

And the third and most important reason is that this is the Lord calling your soul to Himself. We do not come on our own, and so He sends His heralds — afflictions, depression, illnesses: "Entreaty do I pour forth unto the Lord, and to Him do I proclaim all my sorrows, for many woes fill my soul to repletion, and lo, my life unto Hades hath now drawn nigh; like Jonas do I pray to Thee: Raise me up from corruption, O Lord my God."[1]

And the Prophet David explains also the cause of sadness: *I remembered God and I was gladdened. I spake in idleness* (that is, I forgot God) and *my spirit became fainthearted* (Ps. 76:3). And the spirit becomes despondent. . . (Cf. Ps. 142:4).

Save yourself, my beloved little child!

LXIV. LETTERS TO CHILDREN[2]

380. YOU ARE UNHAPPY DUE TO SPIRITUAL INEXPERIENCE

April 9, 1884

Truly Christ is risen! And I greet you, my good little children, with this radiant feast of Christ's Resurrection.

"Bearing lights, let us go forth (our young myrrhbearers) to meet

---

1. From an heirmos (Plagal of Fourth Tone) of the Sixth Ode (based on the Prayer of Jonas the Prophet).
2. These letters were apparently written to the little girls of the Shamordino orphanage.

Christ, Who cometh forth from the grave like a Bridegroom. And let us celebrate. . .''[1]

Blessed are you, new myrrhbearers, voluntary recluses, sitting at home like those holy virgins at the tomb of their beloved Teacher and waiting to be told, "Rejoice!"

And for you, this your Bridegroom, Who is more comely than the sun, will arise and appear visibly when the dawn of your morning comes. But at present there is deep night in your souls; little passions disquiet you and muddy the pure wellspring of the heart's consolations. And yet, I repeat that your morning, too, will come — your sun, too, will rise — just be patient. I know that you are unhappy, but that is due to your spiritual inexperience — because even now you are already in Paradise. "Now are all things filled with light; Heaven and earth, and the nethermost regions of the earth."[2] Can it really be that Shamordino is the only exception? When you grow up a little, you will understand better than me.

You say that I have forgotten you: why, all I do is think about you, and I wanted very, very badly to comfort you on the feast, but I have been so busy that I am simply smothered. Besides, the opportunity is lacking. I would even have driven over or even walked, only the weather is not good for my health, and I am still pressed for time.

Right now I will be going to visit some important ladies, and the horse has been waiting for some time already, but I wanted to say a little word to you and to exchange the Paschal kiss with you at least across the frozen snow. "'O great Pascha! O Word of God, grant that we may partake of Thee fully in the unwaning day of Thy Kingdom!'"[3] Let us pray concerning this.

And we will assuredly attain it in the end, if we do not give in to faintheartedness, if we do not cry over calamities which have yet to materialize.

This is the very first time I have taken pen in hand since Passion Week — in order to write to you.

So be grateful, and try to resemble the wise virgins. Save yourselves! I will try to visit you at the first opportunity. . . I am sending you funds for milk. . . Masha, drink your milk, or you will be sorry.

---

1. From the Paschal Canon.
2. Ibid.
3. Ibid.

381. ADVICE TO CHILDREN ON HOW TO BEHAVE

July 18

You are grieved, my little kids! And you are ready to endure the most cruel hardships if only I would get well. All right — I promise. Only, don't you let me down either. I am not going to let loose on you the cruelest of misfortunes — I only ask you to bear one another's infirmities, to be merciful to the weak and the infirm, to obey those who are older not only out of fear but also for conscience sake (Cf. Rom. 13:5).

Why, you are children and silly children at that. Now, where did you get the idea that you could run off and go swimming whenever you felt like it! They let you go freely, and you went and got carried away!. . . Be wise virgins. And your portion will be in the bridal chamber of Jesus, the heavenly Bridegroom!

LXV. LETTER TO THE SISTERS OF K-SK

382. AN EXHORTATION ON HOW TO
LIVE AND SAVE ONESELF

Bless me, holy mothers and sisters! First of all, our most reverend Mother T., and all the reverend mothers and sisters!

I wanted to come in person, but I was overcome by illness. . .

The weather is damp, and you know how my health is; forgive me!

I thank you for your greeting and your love in the Lord. You gave me much joy.

I will bring a good report to our Father and Elder. Struggle!

Before all else, submit to your elders: *there is no power but of God; whosoever resisteth the power, resisteth the ordinance of God, and they that resist will bring judgment on themselves* (Rom. 13:1, 2).

Attend church without fail, those of you who are able; there is our life. Do not miss the common trapeza: at the common trapeza the

Beloved reclines, says St. Isaac the Syrian;[1] but a secret meal is an impure meal.

Keep the traditions of the Fathers; do not go visiting each other's cells; do not see lay people, especially men; do not form special friendships among yourselves: all of us are related, and special bonds are always unlawful.

Forgive me, the unworthy and sinful one, and I, your servant, forgive you in the name of the Lord Jesus. Do not grieve because I am not speaking with you face to face. Believe me, my heart is with you, and will be with you as long as you keep the precepts of our blessed Fathers Makary and Leonid. Peace to you and salvation!

THE END. GLORY BE TO GOD FOR ALL THINGS!

---

1. Cf. *The Ascetical Homilies of St. Isaac the Syrian*, Homily 15, p. 88: "Take for yourself the remedy of life from the table of those who fast, keep vigil, and labor in the Lord, and so raise up the dead man in your soul. For the Beloved reclines in their midst bestowing sanctification and He transforms the bitterness of their hardship into His ineffable sweetness. His spiritual and heavenly ministers overshadow both them and their holy foods. I know one of the brethren who has seen this with his own eyes."

FROM SOME INTRODUCTIONS TO SELECTIONS FROM THE LETTERS PUBLISHED IN RUSSIAN

"All of [the Elder Anatoly's] exhortations are distinguished by simplicity, clarity of expression, and ardent faith, and are imbued with the spirit of genuine monasticism. Since, as the Elder Amvrosy notes, monasticism differs essentially from the general Christian life only by the vow of chastity, the exhortations of monastic elders have universal significance for each Christian.

All who desire salvation have always and everywhere deplored their lack of humility, the difficulty of life, external tribulations and obstacles. It was with such grievances that people would turn to the Elder Anatoly..."

— *From a leaflet published by the Kazan Amvrosiev Women's Hermitage, Shamordino, containing excerpts from the Elder Anatoly's letters (Leaflet #42, 1908).*

"...Like the Elders Father Lev and Father Makary, Father Amvrosy and Father Anatoly were united by ties of close spiritual friendship. Both were disciples of Father Makary, under whom they studied in the same spiritual school; both participated in the translation and publication of the ascetical works of the holy Fathers; and both later became spiritual guides, instructors and elders of many who turned to them for a word of edification or consolation...

...[The Elder Anatoly's letters are distinguished by the ardent vitality of 'seeing' faith and in some passages by poetic beauty of expression, and in general they are permeated with simplicity, sincerity, and humor. In his letters he exhorts mainly to undoubting faith, humility, patience, and self-reproach."

— *From Priest S. Chetverikov, Soul-Profiting Reading, Moscow, 1902, p. 536.*

"...The brief biography of the Elder Anatoly which we have presented here cannot fully capture his likeness or convey even in part the Elder's bright, Paschal spirit and his distinctive qualities.

The fragrance of this spirit is preserved in his letters, written mostly to sisters living the monastic life, struggling in a whole series of convents in six dioceses: those of Kaluga, Moscow, Smolensk, Tula, Orlov, Kursk, and perhaps others as well. All of these nuns, with Father Amvrosy's blessing, turned to Father Anatoly for spiritual guidance... And so a correspondence with the Elder developed, reaching 200 and more letters a day, which he would receive, of course, not only from the nuns but from others as well. And the Elder would answer them in between his daily reception of visitors and the cycle of church services and his monastic rule. He writes in extremely clear, simple language, sincere and captivating.

In Father Anatoly's letters every word is directed toward a single goal: the salvation of the souls of those to whom they are written. Thus the Elder not infrequently goes into all the details of monastic life, giving necessary instructions and supplying the needy with money for postal stamps, a trip to Optina, or other needs..."

— From I.M. Kontzevich, Optina Hermitage
and Its Time, Holy Trinity Monastery,
Jordanville, NY, 1970, p. 319.

A Photograph of Saint Anatoly

THE LIFE OF
HIEROSCHEMAMONK ANATOLY
ELDER OF OPTINA AND DIRECTOR
OF THE SKETE

In the first quarter of the last century, in the village of Boboli of Kaluga Province, there lived the deacon Father Moses Kopyev with his wife Anna Sergeyevna. Anna Sergeyevna was the daughter of the priest of the village of Mokry, where Moses Petrovich had at first been a reader. Matushka diaconissa's parents were pious folk, as were Moses Petrovich's parents. Thus, it is not surprising that Father Moses and his wife were devout people. Accustomed to attending God's church from an early age, they loved the house of God. Being pious, they lived simply, being sufficiently well off according to the standards of that time. This sufficiency, however, they attained only through constant and strenuous labor. They worked the land themselves. They would attend church on Sundays and feast days — in their village the church had three altars, in honor of the holy Hierarch Nicholas, and the holy Great Martyrs George the Trophy-bearer and Nikita — and would devote the rest of their time to farming. They were gentle and merciful to the poor and to pilgrims; no beggar left their home without an alms. They loved monks and greatly desired that some of their children would become monastics. And the Lord ordained that their good desire should be fulfilled. They had a large family: five daughters — Maria, Evdokia, Anna, Alexandra and Tatiana — and a son, Alexis. The children, too, were pious. Their daughter Evdokia did not wish to marry and remained single, leading a pious life; she baked prosphora and helped her mother and relatives with housework, finding joy and consolation in prayer at home and in church. She reposed at the age of forty. Another daughter, Anna, became a nun. But the parents' holy expectations were consummately fulfilled in their son, whom the Lord showed forth as a great father of monastics in our time.

This son was that very chosen one of God's grace who is remembered with love and reverence by many, many people, both monastics and laity: the Optina Elder, the friend and co-ascetic of the great Optina Elder Father Amvrosy, and his successor in eldership — as well as the teacher and guide of the nuns of Shamordino Heritage, founded by the Elder Father Amvrosy. This was Hieroschemamonk Father Anatoly.

The Elder Father Anatoly was born on March 6, 1824, and in Holy Baptism was named Alexis, in honor of St. Alexis the Man of God. He was the eldest child of his pious parents. From his very first days and throughout his childhood the boy Alexis was under the special care of his mother. His father, besides fulfilling the duties of his ministry and his general domestic responsibilities, also took care of the little garden and the bees, devoting his spare time to these occupations. Therefore, it was the mother who looked after the little child more. She loved him greatly, and as soon as he was able to understand, she instilled in him good and holy feelings of faith, hope, love, and devotion to the will of God. His mother used to tell her little children that she desired nothing so much for them in their life as for them to be true Christians. The boy grew up quiet and meek, and was his parents' favorite. And he loved them in turn, especially his mother.

When the boy was five years old, his father, having first prayed, began himself to teach his little son to read and write. The boy was bright and gifted and soon learned the alphabet, after which they began teaching him to read the Book of Hours and the Psalter. He loved to attend God's church, standing in orderly fashion by his mother's side. His father would have liked for Alexis to read on kliros, but this did not work out as he had a very quiet and weak voice. At home, books were the boy's constant companions. Joyous and fond of learning, he was also distinguished by his kindness to others. If he were given treats or toys, he would quickly give everything away either to his sisters or to other children. In general, however, he did not like to make friends with other boys, preferring instead to remain at home with his sisters. Of course, as in every small child, there appeared in him also some bad tendencies; but his loving parents, keeping a watchful eye on him, took every precaution in time, utilizing both admonitions and chastisements as necessary. Later, on more than one occasion, the Elder would recall his childhood, as would his sisters, and several stories have been preserved about it.

Once, the little boy climbed up into the belfry; he could not get down and began to cry. On hearing him, his mother helped him down and gave him a scolding. On another occasion, while in the forest with his beloved grandmother, who also loved him, he swung at her with a branch. The old woman reasoned with him, asking, "Why are you hitting me, Leshenka?" He answered that it was because she would not let him hook the chairs together in a chain and drag them around from room to room, which he liked to do, but which his grandmother would not allow. Once, however, the boy, at already six or seven years of age, together with some other boys, climbed into the priest's garden to pick peas; the priest noticed the naughty boys and complained to Alexis' father, who punished him severely. Smarting, the boy ran to share his grief with his beloved sisters, crying and showing them his reddened ears; after this he went around with the peasant children even less. Thus, sometimes admonitions and sometimes judicious punishments consumed in him, as fire consumes kindling, the habits and propensities in which we, as children of Adam, abound from the early time of golden childhood — habits and propensities which, had they matured, would have brought forth bitter fruits. His parents' vigilance thus prepared their little child to be a vessel of God's grace.

In time the boy was sent to the Borovsk ecclesiastical academy. After four years he completed the course of studies there and was transferred to the seminary in Kaluga. The religious youth's labors began under the shelter of the Monastery of St. Paphnuty [of Borovsk], where his relics are. He studied assiduously, only at first complaining of a poor memory. Then he went on to the seminary in the city of Kaluga, which he finished third in his class. Young Alexis always successfully advanced from class to class; only once did he have to repeat a year due to illness. When he was fourteen he became ill with a fever and was sent home. During the most acute period of the illness, in a state of semiconsciousness he began to chant, "With the saints grant rest..." It pained his loving mother to hear these words. When he came to himself, she began asking him why he had been chanting this and whether he remembered doing so. The youth replied that he did remember and that he had been chanting thus because he had dreamed it. His mother, fearing that he would die soon, all but began bidding farewell to him, asking him to forgive her for having struck him sometimes. To this he replied, "Well, so what if you did — you were teaching me to do right and not wrong!" Thus, even then he had an awareness of how beneficial parental discipline can be in childhood — an awareness which is rarely met with today, not only among children and young people, but even among parents, who become foolishly carried away with false notions of excessive humaneness. When his parents saw the serious condition of their son, as believing people they hastened to summon a priest, and the sick one was given the Holy Mysteries in anticipation of his repose. But soon after this he started to improve, and he quickly recovered, remaining at home until fall in order to recover completely. Thus, he missed a year of school.

As at the academy, so also at the seminary, Alexis was successful in his studies and well liked by his superiors and instructors, but he remained aloof from them. At first, he was treated quite badly by his peers. He lived in a rented room and was always very much loved by the owners of the house. This was demonstrated with particular clarity once when he became ill with the measles. The people he was living with treated his illness themselves and looked after him without even informing his parents. Only when he had already begun to recover did they inform his parents, who visited him from time to time, especially his mother. An uncle lived in Tula who greatly loved young Alexis Moiseyevich and always sent him everything he needed: books, clothing, miscellaneous items and, in general, everything a frugal and hard-working seminarian could possibly need. The youth's health was never particularly good; while at the seminary he often suffered from insomnia. At such times, especially in spring, he would sit by the window, thinking about his lessons; his head would ache; and he would look out at the quiet moon, and even then his thoughts would more than once take him to the quiet abodes of the monastics. In spring, during his free time, he would often walk beyond Kaluga, to a hill called Vyrka; there he would sit for a long time, alone with his thoughts. True, he would sometimes go there with his companions as well. But while they would amuse themselves, immodestly at times, the future ascetic would lie on the grass somewhere off to the side, gazing at the clouds. Sometimes in a burst of enthusiasm over the beauties of nature, he would not be able to contain himself and would say to one of his companions, "Look at that cloud coming straight at us — it looks like a bear!" But the answer would be, "Ok, you lie there and philosophize — we don't have time for all that!" — and again he would immerse himself in his solitary thoughts. Once he nearly fell under the influence of his companions: he began to have milk during the Apostles' Fast, but then he became seriously ill. His sensitive conscience suggested to him that this illness was a chastisement for breaking the fast, and he immediately stopped doing so, strictly observing the fasts from that time forth. He did have friends among his companions, but very few. He did not like to go visiting either. For Nativity, Pascha, Cheesefare Week, and the summer, Alexis Moiseyevich would come home, where his family had already long been anticipating his arrival; at this time, he was a joy and a consolation to his family. He was a respectful and loving son, and a friend to his sisters. He loved to read and shared his learning with his sisters. He even taught one of them to recite the troparion "Christ is risen" in Greek.

The youth's monastic impulses were at times so strong that once he was all prepared to leave secretly to go to the anchorites of the Briansk forests, and he got as far as several versts[1] past Kaluga. However, a

---

1. 1 Verst — 3500 feet (about 2/3 mile).

violent thunderstorm came up and heavy rain began to fall. He turned back, seeing in these threatening natural phenomena a manifestation of God's disapproval of his journey. And so he finished the seminary third in his class, being given the new surname of Zertsalov there.[1] Before him there opened up the broad field of life, so attractive to young souls which have not yet known the terrible storms and hidden dangers and sorrows in which it abounds. But this youth, who had already long before come to love nature, that great book of God's wisdom; who had spent much time in admiring the starry sky and the moon, which evokes a quiet sadness in the impressionable soul — this youth was not allured by the charms of the sinful world of society. He was drawn by another realm, the realm of eternal life, of unwaning light; the spiritual sky with its spiritual stars of holy life was drawing him to itself. They holy wish of his pious parents, who desired that their son should become a monk, became his own ardent desire — and this desire was fulfilled, for it was pleasing to God.

Upon finishing the seminary, the future ascetic was offered several positions as priest, but he declined these offers, and for some time he lived at home. He went on pilgrimage to St. Sergius with his mother, who loved to visit holy places, and his sister Anna, stopping at Khotkov[2] on the way. They liked Khotkov very much, and the young man talked his sister into entering this convent. The young eighteen year old girl obeyed her brother. Her mother joyously gave her blessing, and she stayed, but it was not easy for her to adjust to the monastic life. After some time, she thought of leaving the convent. She was all ready to leave one evening, but she fell asleep and dreamed that beyond the convent gates there was a terrible darkness, while inside the convent it was bright and joyous. She awoke, and she stayed. Later Father Anatoly, who highly esteemed such obedience on the part of his sister and continued to show solicitude for her all his life, transferred her to Shamordino, where she reposed in the schema with the name Augusta, five years after the death of her brother and teacher. Such was the strong and beneficial influence of the brother upon his sisters. He himself did not immediately enter a monastery but worked for awhile in government service. Receiving a salary, he shared it with his family, remaining as before modest and strict in his manner of life, being loved and respected by all. Handsome in appearance, tidy in his clothing, and even-tempered, he was a consolation to his family when

---

1. At that time changes of surname were quite common, especially in the seminaries, one of the purposes being to eliminate confusion resulting from too many similar names.

2. I.e., at the Convent of the Protection located there.

he would come to visit them. His mother also visited him often and would always hear people praising her son. He avoided social functions, and if he did visit people, it was very selectively, and he would bring with him a beneficial influence. Once he visited a friend at whose apartment strange things were happening: objects would fly around, etc. He was heeded, and the phenomena ceased. At that time various new notions were already in the air, and a new age was at hand. The word "progress" was continually on the lips of intellectuals — but the future monk was not drawn by this movement. He saw all the negative aspects of progress, that steel monster, and he feared it. His soul was occupied with another world which he thirsted to enter; but being a thorough person, he did not make an immediate decision.

He continued working for several more years in government service, thinking all the while about monasticism. He would go often to pray fervently in the churches, and when his mother would come to visit him in the morning, she would never find him at home; he would be at the early Liturgy. He liked to go to the cathedral. He would stand in front so as to hear better, but as more people came, he would gradually move back, always ending up by the doors as he continually yielded his place to others. Seeking enlightenment in prayer, he also awaited a more evident indication of God's will, which indeed came about. And it happened naturally, unnoticeably, as it always does — even as the Lord appeared to Elias not in storm and tempest but in the gently blowing of a small breeze. So here also, God's will with regard to his entering a monastery unfolded from the ordinary circumstances of his life. He became ill, as did two fellow workers of his. The doctor diagnosed tuberculosis. Then Alexis Moiseyevich vowed that if he did become well, he would not put off entering a monastery any longer. Both of his fellow workers soon died, while the future Optina Elder recovered. After he became well he resigned from his job, journeyed home, and went on pilgrimage with his mother. He came to Optina, and there he decided to leave the world forever. His parents joyfully blessed him for this struggle which was so close to their hearts and which they had so long desired for him.

As a leader in Russian monasticism, Optina Hermitage is under the special guidance of God's providence. Unsearchable are the ways of the Lord. In the days of the three great Elders Leonid, Makary, and Amvrosy, with their disciples and co-ascetics, the monastery was sheltered from excessive pressures from the world. Its pressure and the attention of the masses were diverted by the glorification of the Akhytrskaya icon of the Heavenly Queen and that of the memory of St. Tikhon — through these same Optina fathers themselves. Meanwhile, a monetary surplus was diverted by the establishment of Shamordino. In turn, our Lord marvelously strengthened the monastery, drawing thither souls who were worthy to be vessels of His grace. And when the great Makary was already nearing the end of his life, the Lord, by the prayers of St. John the Baptist — the heavenly protector of the skete, that great cradle of eldership — brought thither also the one whom He had chosen to be first an assistant and then a successor of the great Elder Father Amvrosy.

The young man, educated, well-mannered, meek, and diligent, was received with love by Father Archimandrite Moses.

The young seminarian Alexis Moiseyevich Zertsalov was enrolled among the Optina brethren on June 20, 1857, and soon became the monk Anatoly. He was tonsured on November 17, 1862, with the name of St. Anatoly, the Patriarch of Constantinople (whose memory is celebrated on July 3). He was ordained hierodeacon on June 5, 1866, and hieromonk on September 7, 1870. On February 13, 1874, he was appointed Director of the Skete and Confessor of the brethren. Having been awarded the nabedrennik on July 28, 1876, he was awarded the pectoral cross on April 20, 1880. On April 14, 1893, he was appointed to be consecrated to the rank of Abbot, but he was not consecrated due to illness. He reposed on January 25, 1894, at 4:25 in the morning.

Such were the main events of Father Anatoly's monastic life. With entire devotion to the will of God, he entered the great Russian monastery — that worthy successor and perpetuator of the testaments of the great Elder Paissy Velichkovsky and his ever-memorable disciple Father Theodore, and Father Theodore's co-ascetic Leonid, the founder of eldership at Optina — and he gave himself over wholeheartedly to the guidance of the Elder Father Makary. The Elder came to love this new pilgrim from the vain world, and his experienced spiritual gaze foresaw his future zeal for salvation. Thus, he began to guide the new monk with special love. When Father Anatoly's mother came to see him, the Elder Father Makary received this devout woman with love, and she was profoundly comforted by these words of this teacher of monks, "Blessed art thou, good woman — upon what a good path thou hast set thy son!" The Elder himself instructed Father Anatoly in the Jesus Prayer, and he would go far off into the forest, where he would pray in solitude. Since the Elder was very busy, he blessed Father Anatoly to turn also to Father Amvrosy, Father Makary's successor. Thus, by the unsearchable ways [of God's providence] these two monks, who later labored so much together for Shamordino Heritage, were brought into the most intimate contact. In considering whom he should refer Father Anatoly to, the Elder Makary, as he gave Father Amvrosy his first disciple, explained his choice simply by saying that he was "quite bright," in order to safeguard his future successor in eldership from conceit. Before this, whenever Father Makary would temporarily leave the monastery on business, Father Anatoly would turn for spiritual counsel to Father Abbot Anthony, Father Moses' brother. This dual guidance of a monk quickly attracted the attention of the other brethren. Some saw it as being wrong and began reproaching Father Anatoly, expressing the opinion that probably he himself had insisted upon it. Thus it was that this good work, which had come about not at Father Anatoly's insistence but simply in accordance with his heartfelt desire which he had frankly expressed to the Elder — this good and richly fruitful work was not accomplished without tribulation. Father Anatoly was very troubled on hearing of such talk among the brethren, and he told the Elder Father Makary of his grief. The Elder quickly put an end to his confusion and also to the talk among the brethren itself. He said that such dual guidance would have been bad if it had been the result of self-will, and if one Elder were saying one thing and the other something else. However, both were saying the same thing, and so it turned out that the guidance of the two was essentially one and the same.

But while Father Makary showed special love and concern for Father Anatoly, he led him along the rigorous path of monastic struggle, and Father Anatoly had to endure not a few of the afflictions and difficulties of the anchoritic life. Every lot in life has its afflictions, including the monastic life, and the wise teacher did not deprive his zealous disciple of these afflictions. On the contrary, he lavished them upon him. But this was done for a good purpose: in order to build in him a good monastic constitution, and temper it for future time. Father Anatoly's first years at the monastery were very trying. The skete is particularly strict in its monastic typicon. To this austere manner of life was added yet another burden. His first obedience was in the kitchen, where after unaccustomed heavy labor he could not even get much sleep, and that, directly on top of the wood pile. Later he was frequently transferred from cell to cell. He was very neat and liked cleanliness. The moment he moved to his assigned cell, he would wash it, clean it, and begin living there — going daily to disclose his thoughts to his Elder,[1] reading ascetical books (this being the continual occupation assigned to new monks by the Elder) — and again Father Anatoly would be transferred to another cell. He would

---

1. Rooted in ancient Christian and monastic tradition, the practice of "saying one's thoughts" (or "disclosing one's thoughts," or "revealing one's thoughts") consists in the confession of one's sins — including and especially one's sins of thought — and of one's perplexities, to an elder or eldress for the purpose of receiving spiritual counsel. Absolution is not given.

just have time to settle in, and again he would be transferred to a new one: again the cleaning, again the washing — and again he would have to leave. Without a murmur he would pick up his belongings — his little icons, his rough wool coverlet, his paper and ink — and go where he was told. Later he lived in the tower. First he lived with the monk Father Makary (Strukov), and then with another monk who had been a monk for forty years and who did not recognize eldership.

From not being used to sleeping little, and due to the uncomfortable living quarters and to his unaccustomed labors, Father Anatoly began to have severe headaches. Sometimes he would be laid up for days at a time with a headache, and there would be no one around to bring him water; often he would remain without food as well, when he was unable to come to trapeza.[1] Moreover, under the tower there was a place for chopping wood. The noise of the chopping would further aggravate the ill one's condition. He asked to be transferred from this cell, but his request was refused. When he told Father Amvrosy of his distress, the latter advised him to come to Matins without fail but to leave after hearing a few prayers. The ill one did in fact make use of this dispensation for some time — but not for long. Once, his cell-mate noticed his absence, came to their cell, found him sleeping, shook him awake and sent him off to church. And so he did not even have a chance to take advantage of this concession to his infirmity. When he was late for trapeza, he would be glad if someone sitting near him happened to have a small piece of black bread left with which he could satisfy his hunger, for this nonacquisitive zealot of the ascetical life kept nothing in his cell. He went about in old clothing. Once, his cousin, a priest, visited him with his young and fashionable wife. Father Anatoly came out from the skete to see them in the same clothes he wore at his obediences — in old clothes with his sleeves rolled up, wearing an apron. This greatly astonished the guest, and they always remembered this visit...

Later in his conversations with nuns, the Elder would often recall this period of his life, and when some would complain about the difficulty of the monastic life, he used to say, "Why, what are your problems — now, we lived in a tower; you'd come from your obedience and have so far to climb, being so awfully tired — and here you'd have to fetch water too, and wash everything; the doors were low, and often you'd bump your head..." Not infrequently, Father Anatoly would come to see Father Amvrosy, and the latter would be busy but would not tell him to leave. The monk would endure this lesson in patience, but because of this

1. Trapeza — Communal meal, and in monasteries also the refectory.

would often return to his cell after midnight. He would not have a chance to lie down, and already they would be waking everyone up for Matins. After the menial obediences, he was given the obedience of chanting on kliros, but did not remain in it for long. The dull-witted choir director became angry with Father Anatoly for giving him practical pointers now and then (Father Anatoly was an expert in chanting), and he complained about him to the Father Superior. So Father Anatoly was sent to the black-smith's forge. This obedience was hard for him. The little bench was small — narrow and short — whereas Father Anatoly was tall. He would lie down, cover his head with his cloak — and his feet would be cold; he would cover his feet, and his head would be cold. During the time he chanted on kliros, because he was tall, the choir director would send him off the kliros so that he would not block the music, telling him that he could look on and chant from there; and Father Anatoly would obey. By means of these seemingly minor and yet extremely trying adversities, there was formed in him a spirit of humility, patience, meekness, and steadfastness.

Once Bishop Ignaty (Brianchaninov) visited Optina. He wished to meet and speak with a monk who had applied in practice the teaching of the holy Fathers on the Jesus Prayer. He was referred to Father Anatoly. The Bishop spoke for a long time with the monk and was very pleased with his conversation. As he bade farewell to Father Anatoly, the Bishop could not but express his esteem and surprise, saying that he was glad to have met a monk so educated and experienced in spiritual matters, and acquainted with secular learning as well. Returning [from his conversation with the Bishop] (and he had gone only after being invited twice, and even then only at the bidding of the Elders), Father Anatoly, joyful, met up with Father Makary, who was walking to the skete, surrounded by nuns and other people. The Elder asked Father Anatoly, "Well, what did the Bishop say to you?" Father Anatoly told him everything in all sim-plicity. Then Father Makary began in front of everyone to hit him with his stick, saying, "You good-for-nothing — you've taken it into your head that you're something, that you're so very good! Why, the Bishop is an aristocrat, he grew up on compliments, and so he said all that to you out of politeness — and here you swallowed every bit of it,[1] thinking it is true!" Father Anatoly went to his cell, ashamed. But as soon as he had gone, the Elder Makary said to those who were with him, "Well, how not to scold him? He's an attentive monk, intelligent, educated — and here he's respected by such people, too. Can pride be far off?" At this time

---

1. Lit., "you spread out your ears [to take in everything he was saying]."

Father Anatoly was already a hierodeacon.

When he came to the monastery, Father Anatoly liked to drink tea, but he was not allowed to drink more than three cups. So he bought a bigger cup. But when he told the Elder Makary about this, the Elder told him to bring the cup and show it to him. Father Anatoly showed it to him, and Father Makary bade him drink only two cups that size. When Father Anatoly was still a novice he, like the others, was assigned a permanent place in the refectory. Once the senior brother in their section was away. Father Anatoly, who liked salty food and who until then had not often eaten food the way he liked it, was very glad and salted the dish according to his taste. His brethren were displeased by this and began to reproach him, saying, "Would you just look at that, he even goes to the Elders [to disclose his thoughts] — and here he deprives everyone of their food!" From that time forth, even when Father Anatoly became the senior brother at table, he never salted the dishes according to his taste again but conformed to the wishes of the others. Father Anatoly patiently bore all these difficulties and endeavored in every way to fulfill all the precepts of his Elders. In accordance with their precepts he not only did not visit the cells of others, but would not even receive anyone in his own. A newcomer to the skete, who had previously been in the military, took a great liking to Father Anatoly. Once he wanted to visit Father Anatoly in his cell. He brought him jam and tried to talk him into it, but Father Anatoly would by no means agree to violate the injunction of his Elders, and he did not let him in.

Zealous in attending God's church, a man of prayer, an excellent reader and chanter, Father Anatoly fulfilled all his responsibilities with exactitude and patience. Under the wise guidance of the Elders Father Makary and Father Amvrosy, he progressed rapidly in his spiritual development through vigilant and tireless spiritual activity, edifying himself by reading the word of God and ascetical writings. Even then, one could see his future moral greatness. Thus, at that time there was living at the skete one Abbot Anthony (this was another Abbot Anthony, not Father Moses' brother), who said once to Father Anatoly, "Labor, brother — you will be a good director, only preserve humility." Father Anatoly's outward appearance was grave and stately. Even then, when he was still a hierodeacon, some people would mistake him for a hieromonk. On meeting him one woman began to confess her sins. He only just managed to get away, as she would not believe him when he said that he was just a hierodeacon. When it was his turn to serve, he would serve reverently in church and give himself wholly to prayer; when he read the Gospel during Passion Week, he would read with profound compunction and with tears.

When the Elder Father Makary reposed, a great consolation in this heavy loss for Father Anatoly was that there remained to him his other teacher, Father Amvrosy. Their great loss brought them even closer together. Later, on more than one occasion, Father Anatoly suggested to people that they pray for Father Makary, saying that this prayer would benefit the one offering it. The Elder who had reposed in blessedness would obtain God's mercy for the one offering the prayer as an expression of love for him.

The Elder Father Amvrosy saw that through patient endurance of afflictions, the reading of ascetical books,[1] and exemplary fulfillment of all his monastic responsibilities, Father Anatoly had already begun to reach a high measure of spiritual attainment and had matured sufficiently to be a teacher of others. Thus, Father Amvrosy began gradually to introduce him to the labors of eldership, making him his fellow laborer, just as Father Makary had once guided him. Even when Father Anatoly was still a hierodeacon, Father Amvrosy would send him to comfort the afflicted and sorrowing, and Father Anatoly would go to the guest house and speak with those thirsting for a word of consolation. Father Anatoly always deeply revered the Elder Father Makary and venerated his memory. The reposed Elder Father Makary had sometimes called Father Anatoly "His Highness," on the one hand as though indicating his tall stature, and on the other hand the loftiness of his spiritual attainment. It

---

1. Father Anatoly also participated in the publication of spiritual books by Optina Hermitage. After Father Makary's repose, Father Amvrosy continued his work of publishing the writings of the holy Fathers, assisted by Fathers Clement (Sederholm), Leonid (Kavelin), Anatoly and Agapit. Father Anatoly, together with Father Clement, prepared a new edition of St. Abba Dorotheos for publication and translated twelve homilies of St. Symeon the New Theologian; and with Father Clement and Father Agapit he worked on a translation into Russian of the instructions of St. Theodore the Studite. These books, as well as many others, were published by Optina Hermitage in the 1860's and 1870's (see *A Biography of the Elder Hieroschemamonk Amvrosy of Blessed Memory* by Protopriest S. Chetverikov, printed by Shamordino Hermitage, 1912, pp. 127-128).

was in view of this spiritual attainment that Father Amvrosy soon requested Father Anatoly to be at first his assistant, then proctor,[1] and finally Director of the Skete. Father Anatoly was appointed proctor soon after he was ordained a hieromonk. Father Amvrosy requested Archbishop Gregory, on one of his visits to Optina, to confirm Father Anatoly as his assistant; and Father Anatoly's appointment as Director of the Skete followed upon the death of Father Ilarion:[2] in accordance with Father Amvrosy's wish, the Archimandrite presented Father Anatoly for confirmation in this position. The Elder Father Anatoly accepted all these assignments out of obedience to his Elder and fulfilled them humbly and diligently. Later he himself would relate that for a long time after his appointment as proctor, many did not even know about it. Once as he was walking by, he saw that some of the brethren were doing something wrong. Father Anatoly reprimanded them but was met with the question, "And what business is it of yours?" They were very embarrassed when a passerby told them that this was the proctor, and began asking him to forgive them and not tell the Archimandrite. Father Anatoly did not tell the Father Archimandrite, just as in general he would always ask Father Amvrosy's advice before informing the Superior of misdemeanors on the part of the brethren. Generally he did not like to be ostentatious or to demand honor for himself. And for a very long time after he became a hieromonk he continued to receive the hierodeacon's portion of tea. Even after he was made Director of the Skete, he continued to relate to the Elder Father Amvrosy with the same respect as before; in particular, he would kneel when he went to see the Elder, like everyone else. Once Father Amvrosy spoke with him as he was kneeling, then called a certain individual and said, indicating Father Anatoly, "I recommend this one — he is my Director," thus offering an instructive lesson in humility.

Father Anatoly was a great and selfless laborer as Confessor and Director of the Skete, and he was truly a worthy successor of his ever-blessed predecessors in these positions. Nothing escaped his observation, and he both showed zealous concern for the spiritual progress of the brethren, and took care of their well-being, ordering well their skete life with its generally uncomplicated and strict observances.

In fulfilling his duties and showing every concern for the brethren, Father Anatoly took every convenient occasion to exhort each one to ful-

---

1. In Russian, blagochinniy. Corresponding to the Greek "periodeutis," this was in monasteries a position of superintendence in disciplinary matters.
2. The former Director of the Skete.

fill his obedience, explaining how an often apparently menial and difficult obedience nevertheless served to benefit others. Once when he
noticed that during a fast, the bread at the skete was poorly baked, he
sternly censured the negligent baker and explained to him how much distress his negligence was causing the brethren, who were exhausted from
fasting and work, and thus he corrected the careless one. At the same
time, Father Anatoly made use of every available moment to be found
alone in prayer and reading somewhere far off in the forest, or late at
night, or early in the morning.

When after a noisy day the quiet moon rises in the evening sky, one's
gaze, tired from the bustle of the day's changing impressions, often
pauses lovingly on the bright stars which twinkle in such a friendly way
in the infinite abyss of the heavens, and not infrequently its attention is
drawn by stars which are always seen at the same time and in the very
same place, twinkling together side by side. Our two Elder-friends —
Father Amvrosy and his ardent admirer and disciple Father Anatoly —
were two such close and inseparable stars, for many, many seekers of the
celestial world. Together they bore the burden of the spiritual guidance of
the monks, and together they also labored for the establishment of
Shamordino Hermitage. No matter how much Father Anatoly fled from
the world, no matter how much he isolated himself from the society of
woman — yet it fell to him to spend his entire life and to die amid many
people, and to labor much for women's monasticism. His labors for the
good ordering of the inner life at the newly founded Shamordino Convent are not only of profound general interest, but they will also be
instructive for very many monastics, both monks and nuns, in time to
come as well.

As soon as this convent began to be organized, the great Elder
Amvrosy, experienced in the spiritual life and endowed with many gifts
of grace, contributed much love and concern to this endeavor. However,
fettered as he was to his bed of sickness, he could not travel there often
himself to directly supervise everything. It was this work of the immediate guidance of the young convent that he laid upon Father Anatoly, who
was his most faithful and devoted fellow laborer. His labors embraced
every aspect of the life of the convent and its inhabitants.

The Elder Amvrosy's co-ascetics and the ever-memorable first Superiors of this convent were Mother Amvrosia, Mother Sophia, and Mother
Euphrosynia. The first two reposed while both Elders were still living,
while Mother Euphrosynia buried both Elders and reposed after them.
Matushka Abbess Euphrosynia was also the constant co-ascetic of Father
Anatoly after the death of Father Amvrosy. Father Anatoly was a direct
person, as was Mother Sophia, and they profoundly esteemed one

another. Mother Sophia always spoke of Father Anatoly with profound respect. She used to say that a good monk is indistinguishable in his manners from the most well-bred aristocrat. But there is a difference between the two, and a big one: the aristocrat shows tact for the sake of propriety, whereas the exemplary monk does so out of conviction and love for his neighbor. And Mother Sophia would indicate Father Anatoly as a model to imitate in this respect. When Mother Sophia became the Superior, she would say to Father Anatoly, "Batiushka, to me have been entrusted the practical concerns — and to you the care of souls." Mother Sophia liked Father Anatoly very much and always rejoiced when he would come for a visit. Sometimes in order to console sisters who were grieving for one reason or another, on such days she would say, "How can you be sad? Batiushka Father Anatoly is coming today." If he happened to be at Shamordino and the sisters would come to her for a blessing to ring for a service or for trapeza, she would send them to him. She would call Batiushka Father Amvrosy "great," and Father Anatoly "esteemed,"[1] or "our apostle." Father Anatoly and Mother Sophia were amazingly alike in their views and acted unanimously. Batiushka Father Amvrosy was as it were the head, while they were the unanimous disciples who in everything submitted to the Elder and agreed with one another. When to the inexpressible joy of the sisters, the great Elder arose from his bed of sickness and travelled to Shamordino, he would often go for walks in the woods to a certain grassy knoll, together with his faithful co-ascetics, surrounded by the sisters. In the course of these walks they would carry on edifying conversations, and sometimes the sisters would chant something from the church hymns. These walks were for all an unforgettable consolation which brightened the difficult life of the first residents of the convent, a life spent in hard work and toil. The sisters recall one such walk with the great Elder and his co-ascetics, and the conversation in which they were engaged. Among other things, Mother Sophia said to the Elders, "Now, what would Mother Sara say to us, who did not come out of her cave for thirty years in order to have a look at nature?"[2] By way of answer, Father Anatoly expressed this view, "People save themselves in diverse ways. I identify more with those saints who loved nature, like St. Sergius, St. Savva of Zvenigorod, Sts. Anthony and Theodosy. They chose the most beautiful locations for their monasteries because nature

---

1. This word (bolshoi) may also be translated "great," but in this context it would mean "less great."
2. "They used to say that Mother Sara, who dwelt above the river and was sixty years old, had never looked out [from her abode] and seen the river." *The Paradise of the Holy Fathers*, trans. E.A. Wallis Budge, (London, 1907), Vol. II, p. 46.

raises man up to God."

Father Amvrosy used to say concerning Father Anatoly that he had been given a special gift for comforting the young. The nuns would turn to Father Amvrosy as to an Elder, and to Father Anatoly as to a father who always looked out for all their needs; it was rare for him not to ask upon meeting one of them, "Do you have everything you need?" Father Amvrosy more than once told the inhabitants of Shamordino, "I rarely see you in order to speak with you because I am at rest concerning you, knowing you are with Father Anatoly." Father Anatoly loved and revered Father Amvrosy, who in turn loved him as a son or as a brother. Father Amvrosy's word was law for Father Anatoly. When people would turn to Father Amvrosy with requests having to do with the skete, he would always send them to his Director, as he called Father Anatoly. And Father Anatoly would send his spiritual children to Father Amvrosy for advice in all important matters, but on such occasions Father Amvrosy would always ask, "And what did Father Anatoly say?" And if he found out that he had not advised them to do as they were requesting, he would not give his blessing either. When Mother Sophia became ill and was at Optina, the sisters would come to see her and confided their sorrows and their fears lest Matushka should die. Father Anatoly sympathized with them and would say, "Yes, we still need her very much. It is hard to inspire such trust as she does. Sometimes I will say to someone to do it this way, and they will say to me, 'I'll ask Matushka, too, to see how she blesses.' " And as Father Anatoly said this, he spoke with visible joy and consolation. However, seeing her spent and close to death, he pointed out to the sisters, in order to calm them, that if the Lord were to take her, it would mean that she had ripened for eternal life — for when someone ripens for that blessed lot, the Lord does not delay a minute in taking that person to Himself, no matter how needed he may be here. He cited the example of St. Basil the Great, whom the Lord took very young, at only 44, despite the fact that the Church needed him.

Like Father Amvrosy, after Matushka Sophia's death, Father Anatoly had faith in her boldness before God in the other world, and sometimes he would advise the sisters, at difficult moments in their life, to go and pray at her grave. Once during a fast, the sister who was the bell ringer overslept past the time to ring for the Liturgy. The Abbess scolded her and promised to punish her after preparation for Communion. The frightened sister went to Father Anatoly to confide her grief to him. He told her to say the Jesus Prayer, to say "Our Father" twelve times, and to go to Mother Sophia's grave. The sister did so, and when after the preparation she came to the Abbess to receive her epitimia,[1] the latter meekly forgave her.

Mother Amvrosia deeply respected Father Anatoly. She herself spun the wool from which the muhoyar[2] for his rassa was woven. When at Father Amvrosy's bidding, Father Anatoly began driving to Shamordino and serving vigils in the house there, the moment he arrived, Mother Amvrosia would always send the sisters to him for his blessing and for counsel. Before her death, Mother Amvrosia experienced severe depression, and at this time Father Anatoly's visits and his conversation greatly comforted the pious Eldress.

Father Archimandrite Isaaky and Father Anatoly also performed the laying of the foundation of the Shamordino church. The principal holy object of the convent and the church is an ancient and revered icon of the Kazan Mother of God. The Elder Father Amvrosy always prayed before it, and Father Anatoly also had a veneration for this icon. Often when the sisters were ill, they would serve molebens before it, and the sick would receive relief from their ailments. One sister was very ill with encephalitis, but they brought this icon to her, served a moleben — and she fell asleep and soon recovered. Both Elders, whenever they arrived at or departed from Shamordino, would always pray before this icon and bless the nuns with it. An ardent venerator of the Mother of God and an inspired doer of the Jesus Prayer, Father Anatoly loved the great feasts of the Lord and of the Theotokos and the divine services of these days. Both at the skete and at Shamordino he liked on these days to provide some special consolation for the brethren and the sisters. He also liked the sisters to partake of the Holy Mysteries often on feasts. Of the festal hymns he especially loved those of Pascha. His nameday, July 3, he usually spent at the skete woodlands, where he would go early in the morning with one of the monks of the skete who was closest to him, and there serve a moleben to his saint and to St. Philip of Moscow.[3] On this day, a special treat would be provided for the monastics at the skete and at Shamordino. During Cheesefare Week, blini[4] were prepared at the skete; this was not done at the monastery. Many brethren would come to the skete, and they would be served blini at the Elder's bidding; this greatly comforted his kind heart.

---

1. Epitimia — A rule given to a penitent to help in correcting some sin.
2. Muhoyar — An ancient Asiatic fabric made of cotton with silk or wool, used routinely for making monastic rassas.
3. July 3 is also the feast of the translation of St. Philip's relics.
4. Blini — Pancakes, a traditional Cheesefare Week food in Russia.

When a church was established at Shamordino, Father Anatoly himself taught the sisters the order of the divine services and brought them a copy of the Typicon. When the trapeza was ready, Father Anatoly himself came the first time, blessed the food, and when everyone had sat down, himself began the reading at trapeza, afterwards passing it to the reader. When the reading of the Psalter was instituted, again, he himself inaugurated it; and when he would come, staying at first in the vestry, sometimes he would come out even in the middle of the night to make sure the Psalter was being read. After the church was consecrated, he stayed for two weeks and served, accustoming the sisters to the order of the services and teaching them to chant. He attended every service each day and himself taught the sisters to perform the Rule of Five Hundred;[1] and standing on the right kliros, he would observe it being performed. He required that the reading at the services and at trapeza be distinct, precise, and unhurried. He also taught the sisters to honor the royal days[2] as great feasts, and impressed upon them that it was essential to pray every day for the Sovereign. When he was teaching one sister to read the Psalter and she complained that it was hard for her, the Elder consoled her by saying that that which is difficult for us proves later to be of lasting value, whereas that which comes easily is also easily forgotten.[3] He bade them to read the Twelve Psalms[4] every day, and even more often the psalm, Ready is my heart, O God...[5]

He also exhorted them thus, "Ceaselessly say the Jesus Prayer, and no one will bother you. Even when there are many people, you will not notice. Do not go around to other cells; do not start conversations unnecessarily. In the church stand like an angel, without talking or looking around: the church is an earthly heaven. As you leave the church, say the prayer, 'O Theotokos and Virgin, rejoice,' and do not speak with anyone, lest you be like a vessel that was full but spilled on the way. When you are preparing for Holy Communion, say the Jesus Prayer with special diligence. When you are going to partake of the Holy Mysteries, at this Lit-

---

1. This Rule is cited in full in Appendix A of *The Elder Joseph of Optina*, trans. Holy Transfiguration Monastery, (Boston, 1984).
2. That is, the yearly feasts of the Royal Family.
3. See *The Ascetical Homilies of St. Isaac the Syrian*, trans. Holy Transfiguration Monastery, (Boston, 1984), Homily 3, p. 24.
4. An ancient service of psalmody and prayers chanted by the anchoritic Fathers both during the day and during the night; the order of this service is sometimes included in editions of the Psalter.
5. Psalm 107.

urgy watch yourself especially: do not speak with anyone and do not let your thoughts wander. Approach the Holy Mysteries with a peaceful soul, invoking the prayers of your spiritual father. When it is crowded in church and you approach the Gospel or an icon to venerate it, be careful not to push anyone. That would disturb your peace. You are coming to ask mercy from God, but how can you ask His mercy if you have just offended your neighbor in His own church? When you come to a person to ask him for something and you start fidgeting and laughing, he will get you wrong and will be hurt. All the more must we approach the Lord with reverence." Concerning prayer he said, "One must pray to God in such a way that nothing and no one would stand between the praying soul and anything else save God, or the prayer will be imperfect. When you pray being moved by nice chanting or reading, that is not yet true prayer. True prayer is this: the Prophet Elias laid his head on his knees in prayer, and in a few moments he moved the Lord to change His wrath to mercy."

Himself a man of prayer and an ardent doer of the Prayer of Jesus, Father Anatoly always encouraged the sisters to frequently say the Jesus Prayer. And he often reminded them all of the need to say the Jesus Prayer constantly while preserving purity of heart. At the same time he would relate something he had heard from the Elders Makary and Amvrosy. When Father Lev was at Valaam, a certain devout monk, Father Evfimy, learned the Jesus Prayer from him. Saying the Jesus Prayer greatly comforted his spirit, and when Father Lev left Valaam, Father Evfimy sorrowed greatly because he had no one to talk to about this prayer, as the brethren did not follow the Elder's counsels. Once, however, he met a little shepherd girl and taught her the Jesus Prayer so that she became a great doer of prayer. When the Elders Father Makary and Father Amvrosy found out about her, they invited her to come and asked her to teach them to pray as Father Evfimy had taught her. Father Amvrosy on more than one occasion called Father Anatoly a great Elder and doer of the Jesus Prayer.

Listening to Father Anatoly's exhortations on the Jesus Prayer, one sister wondered, "Isn't the Heavenly Queen, to whom I am accustomed to praying, left out in this prayer?" In answer to this, Father Anatoly explained that he who prays to the Saviour with the Jesus Prayer does not neglect the Mother of God, either. The very name of the Saviour reminds one of the most pure Virgin who gave birth to Him, and she, too, ever abiding with her Son, hears all who call upon Him. Sometimes, depending on who was saying the prayer, the Elder would advise them to say it with the addition of the word "through the Theotokos" — that is, "Lord Jesus Christ, Son of God, through the Theotokos, have mercy on me, a sinner."

When one nun said that her eyes were bad and that she could not read, he answered, "Say[1] the Jesus Prayer, and you will be saved." On another occasion — this was during his final illness — he indicated, in speaking of the Jesus Prayer, that there are also other short prayers, but that this is the best one, the chief one, and the sure path to salvation. To explain his words he often also cited examples from the lives of the saints and from the prologues. And during his final illness, his attention turned more than once to the Jesus Prayer; he would give exhortations concerning it, and then his head would fall limply to his chest from exhaustion, while his enfeebled lips continued whispering that same Prayer of Jesus.

In teaching the sisters the Jesus Prayer, he worked with them as with little children; in this regard, the following simple but moving narrative of one of the conversers with and pupils of our great Elder is most instructive. She says,

"I was twelve years old when I conceived the desire to enter a convent, and I ran away from my parents. They found me and wanted to take me home, but I did not at all want to go, and they let me stay on as a visitor. After six months my mother, not having the money to pay for me to remain at the convent as a guest, but mostly afraid to leave me at the convent at such a young age, came to take me home — but I wanted to enter the convent. So my mother decided to go with me to Batiushka Father Amvrosy for a decision. When we arrived at Optina and came to the skete, we heard that Batiushka Father Father Amvrosy was going somewhere, and in fact, he soon did come out to the gates, looking just like an angel of God, and drove off to the country. Everyone went their ways. My mother started talking to a nun; as for me, I couldn't sit still, and seeing that some nuns had gone through another door on the other side of the gates, I asked, 'Matushka, where are they going? Who lives there?' She said, 'Batiushka Father Anatoly, the Director of the Skete.' I asked, 'And why are they going there?' She answered, 'To ask about whatever each one needs to.' I decided to go there too, and see; for some reason this name impressed itself on my soul. I went into the hut. There was a nun there. Batiushka was busy with someone. I asked, 'Can I see Father Anatoly?' At that moment the one who was with Batiushka came out, and they told me to go in. When I saw Batiushka, I became very frightened and even screamed — I had never seen such a tall person in my life. Batiushka was wearing a white cassock and was radiant like a saint of God. Batiushka asked me, "Whose girl are you?" I said, 'I want to enter

---

1. Lit., "Read."

the convent, but my mother won't let me.' Batiushka said, 'Where is your mother?' My mother, noticing that I had been gone a long time, came looking for me. Batiushka asked, 'Whose girl is this?' My mother said, 'Mine, Batiushka!' Batiushka said, 'So why don't you let her enter the convent — she wants to enter the convent.' My mother began to cry, saying, 'She's too little, I can't let her go.' Batiushka said to her sternly, 'I will take her into the convent and be responsible for her.' Then my mother said, 'I entrust her to the Heavenly Queen and to you, Batiushka!'

"And so from the time I was twelve until I was 40, I spiritually grew and was nurtured by the great Elders Batiushka Father Amvrosy and Batiushka Father Anatoly. They were always kind to me, the sinner, and they watched over me like a child. It seems to me that a father or mother could not have so watched over and felt for their children as the Elders would care for us. Batiushka Father Anatoly used to speak to everyone out of the *Philokalia*, and although I listened attentively, at first I did not understand. Batiushka would begin to explain how one must learn to live, to love God, to pray — to say the Jesus Prayer...

"When Batiushka would begin talking about prayer, he would become radiant, his face would light up. He said much, only I did not remember anything because I was so young. He used to say, 'I'll give you treats, only say the Jesus Prayer without ceasing.' He would pour you a whole pocketful of cookies and other treats and tell you to pray for the Tsar; he gave me a prayer for the Tsar to read morning and evening. When we would visit Optina, Batiushka would not bless us to go to church often saying, 'Pray at home.'

"He also would not bless us to sit in church during the First Kathisma (at the beginning of the Resurrection[1] vigil) and would say, 'Father Abbot Anthony strictly bade us to stand. He had a leg ailment, wounds on his legs, and he would never sit down.' Batiushka Father Anatoly also enjoined us not to leave church during the kathismata, saying, 'There are wolves running around — they could drag you off. If you have to leave, go earlier, or afterwards, but not during the kathismata.'

"Once Batiushka said, 'When I entered the monastery, if I saw a monk with a ruble I would think, "How rich he is." ' I asked, 'But what did you need money for?' Batiushka answered, 'We would have liked to have some bagels; now we have both money and bagels, but we are not wanting for them any more.' Batiushka was very kind and merciful. He would forgive everything, only he would sternly reprove you for talking in church.

---

1. Or, Sunday. The word for 'Sunday' in Russian is 'Resurrection.'

"Batiushka also said, 'When bad thoughts disturb you in church, pinch yourself hard to remind yourself where you are.' Once I told Batiushka that I was very much afraid that I was going to have temptations. Batiushka said to me, 'Just live peacefully, do not condemn anyone, see only everyone's good side, do not judge people — and God will cover you. And I will add that one who says the Jesus Prayer has no temptations.' Batiushka would begin to teach us how one can accustom oneself to saying the Jesus Prayer, 'God comes to dwell in the heart of the person who says it. The Father, the Son, and the Holy Spirit are there, and the holy angels, and the saints are never separated from thence.'

"Sometimes Batiushka would explain to us for two hours at a time about how to say the Jesus Prayer. He was such a man of prayer. Batiushka Father Amvrosy once said, 'Father Anatoly has been given such prayer and such grace as is given to only one in a thousand — that is, prayer of the mind and heart.' Only Batiushka concealed everything — you would never know that he was such a great man. And few people, in fact, were aware of it. His kindness and love for his neighbor are impossible to describe — he was ready to lay down his life for others. He endured much from people, but he was never afraid of being maligned. In fact, he would rejoice on hearing an unfavorable word, saying, 'As long as God sees the truth.'

"I asked what prayers to say when I did not go to Matins. Batiushka blessed me to say 3,000 Jesus Prayers, and if I did not go to a vigil, the prayer 'O Theotokos and Virgin, rejoice' 100 times.

"I once said, 'Batiushka, our dear one!' Batiushka answered, 'They used to value me pretty dearly before, too: "Alyosha, you're not worth a cent." '[1]

"After entering the convent, I became ill. I was fifteen years old. The doctors found I had a heart ailment and tuberculosis of the throat, and said that I would soon die. But I did not want to die. Batiushka said to me, 'Say the Jesus Prayer in whatever way you can — sitting, lying down — and everything will pass.' I did so, and by his holy prayers became well. 23 years have passed since then, and I am alive, and I perform an obedience according to my strength, and I do everything for myself in my cell; although I am not in excellent health, previously I could not even walk about my cell.

"By way of comforting me in various sorrows, Batiushka would often say, 'Be patient, M. — it will be nice for you, you will have your own

---

1. This rhymes in the Russian: "Alyosha, stoyish dva grosha." Alyosha is a nickname for Alexis, the Elder's name in the world.

cell.' His words were fulfilled, and I have my cell, only now our dear Batiushka has departed this life."

While requiring the divine services to be performed strictly according to the typicon and sometimes copying out the Optina rules for Shamordino, the Elder, at the same time, would not approve of those who, being worn out to exhaustion from their obediences, would still try to fulfill their entire rule. Seeing this as a bad sign, he would say, "If you can't go to church, don't go, only do not grumble." To those living in obedience at the convent cottages, he would give this advice, "Living out in the country, you may sleep [all you need to], only do not grumble, and do not eat on the sly. Otherwise, [the habit] will establish itself like a snake, and no matter how much one eats, one will never be satisfied. Why, it is not by your own choice that you are living out in the country. So just live there peacefully and you will be saved." In order to comfort them, the Elder used to say to sisters who were ill and were grieved because they could not be at the church services, that their former prayer would be accounted to them, and that for now, prayer at home was sufficient. Only, they should pay careful attention to their heart to make sure they were not staying home more because of slothfulness than because of illness.

Viewing the monastic life as the one most conducive to serving God with entire dedication, the Elder would take every occasion to clarify for the sisters the lofty meaning of this life in all its details. He saw the cenobitic life as a wonderful school for the cultivation of humility and patience. He used to explain the concept that the cenobitic life mortifies the passions thus, "Even a snake will sit quietly in its hole — but just try touching it, and it will hiss. So it is also in a community. Take a variety of pebbles, put them in a sack and shake them for a long time, and they will become round. So it is also in a community.[1] The nails on the ceiling are dark. But the ones on the floor are bright, because they get stepped on, and so they become shiny. Thus also a monk who is cleansed by adversities becomes radiant. We see people sinning, but we do not see them repenting." "A virgin," the Elder said, "who has consecrated herself to

---

1. "As a hard stone with sharp corners has all its sharpness and hard formation dulled by knocking and rubbing against other stones, and is made round, so in the same way, a sharp and curt soul, by living in community and mixing with hard, hot-tempered men, undergoes one of two things: either it cures its wound by its patience, or by retiring it will certainly discover its weakness, its cowardly flight making this clear to it as in a mirror." St. John Climacus, *The Ladder of Divine Ascent*, trans. Holy Transfiguration Monastery, (Boston, 1978), 8:10.

God must by every means refrain not only from evil deeds but from evil thoughts as well. Her soul should shine with purity, and she should stand blameless before Christ her Bridegroom. And to this end, one must more than anything else guard one's eyes. Wherever you may be, keep your eyes lowered, calling to mind your sins and looking down at the earth into which you must return. As you walk about the convent, do not wave your arms or look out of the windows. Do not go into the cells of others without need. Sit at home, and you will be at peace." The Elder greatly valued remaining in one's cell and used to say, "Sit in your cell, try more than anything else to stay there. By doing so, a monastic can escape many temptations. If a rock is lying on the road, everyone drives and walks over it, but if it somewhere off to the side, it lies in the grass and becomes overgrown with moss — no one will touch it. The same with the monastic. If he stays in his cell, he will begin to progress in the spiritual life and in the Jesus Prayer, but if he goes about from cell to cell, he will lose his spiritual peace and be fit for nothing." When the first group of sisters were appointed to be clothed as monastics, the Elder instructed them at length concerning the monastic life. He was very reluctant to permit the sisters to go home, and sometimes he would say, "We had a girl here and she went home — no matter how much I told her not to go, she would not obey, and she never came back. I am very sorry for her."

Holding monasticism in high esteem, he held eldership in even greater honor (that is, the training of a nun in the monastic life by an elder). Concerning himself, he used to say that he could not let a day go by without seeing his Elder and disclosing his thoughts to him. He greatly loved monastics who were zealous in this work. He would encourage frequent and thorough confession, explaining the value of repentance. His world and his consolation had such power that many sisters remained at the convent solely thanks to the strength of the Elder's influence. He exhorted them to continually offer repentance to the Lord from the heart, and to hide nothing from their spiritual father. He ascribed the benefit of disclosing one's thoughts in part to the fact that it develops a consciousness of soul and pain over one's sinfulness, from which in turn there develops the humility so essential for salvation.

When people did not follow the Elder's advice or did the opposite, they would not find spiritual peace and would receive harm instead of benefit. One sister, against the Elder's advice, travelled to Zadonsk on pilgrimage, and did not have so much as a minute of joy or peace. Only later, when she asked the Elder's forgiveness, did she feel peace and find consolation in her memories of the trip. The Elder gave special attention to those who were still spiritually weak and spoke with them most. When a sister once began to be annoyed with him because he spent more time with one sister than with the others, he said, "I see you less because even if one drives you away, one can't make you budge — whereas she will leave the convent before you know it." This in fact happened three years later, to the sincere grief of all at the convent. Father Anatoly intended to tonsure another sister into the mantia, but for some reason she kept refusing. The Elder became grieved, and when in answer to his question, repeated three times, about whether she had come to be tonsured into the mantia, she kept replying, "No, but I trust something will still come of your words," he answered, "No, it won't." And in fact he soon died, and that sister was never tonsured by him into the mantia, which she later lamented many times over. The Elder also used to say that the Jesus Prayer aids very much in disclosing one's thoughts well. When the prayer has become firmly established by practice, it passes into the mind and heart of itself. A young tree is easily uprooted, but not so an old one, and so it is with every sin and every habit, he would say. With regard to asceticism, the Elder would say to the sisters, "Keep to the middle way — do not run ahead, and do not lag behind." He would especially encourage those who were working at obediences to be diligent in saying the Jesus Prayer, in the stead of other prayer rules. One sister would mention the following in her narration of how the Elder Anatoly guided her:

"I entered the convent at 33 years of age. Even while I was still living in the world, I was almost continually ill. After entering the convent I was not at all well and often broke down under my cross of continual illnesses. Then I would go to Batiushka Father Anatoly and he would strengthen me spiritually.

"Once I was very sick. Batiushka came to me and I said to him, 'Batiushka, I won't be saved — I have various thoughts.' Batiushka answered, 'You can't catch everything that swims in the sea. The same with thoughts — they come and they go. Just do not become engrossed in them but drive them away. They attack you because you received the tonsure early.' Later I said to him, 'Batiushka, bless me to confess my former sins.' He said, 'If you start confessing your former sins, they will be accounted as sin, because you received the tonsure — you confessed them earlier, and they are forgiven.' I said, 'I do not perform any obedience. Bless me to undertake the struggle of living alone so as to fast, pray, and sleep on bare boards.'

"He said, 'No matter how much you may sit in your corner, involuntarily the thought of your struggles will enter your head. The evil one, you know, neither eats nor drinks nor sleeps, but for all that, he lives in the abyss because he has no humility. That is the enemy tempting you. What kind of struggles can you undertake? Just your illness is enough for you. Endure patiently what the Lord has given you. Submit to God's will

— there you have a struggle. Say the Jesus Prayer. Struggles are the leaves, whereas the Jesus Prayer is the root and fruit of everything. Humble yourself, reproach yourself in everything, endure illnesses and afflictions with gratitude — that is higher than fasting and struggles and all obediences.' Once I said to him, 'Batiushka, I have a temptation: I do not want to confess to you.' He answered meekly, 'Confess several times to Batiushka Father Amvrosy.' Batiushka left that same day. After three days I came to feel so easy, and my temptations all disappeared as if they had never been. I awaited Batiushka impatiently so as to confess my sins. Soon he came; I was very glad, confessed to him, and asked forgiveness. He forgave me and consoled me, exhorted me from the heart and strengthened me."

While awakening spiritual interests, attunement to spiritual things, and cultivating sensitivity of conscience, the Elder trained the sisters in bodily labors as well. He understood every obedience as a form of service to the Lord and taught them to patiently bear the afflictions which are inevitably associated with the honest fulfillment of any task. At Shamordino there were at first a little over twenty sisters, all of them young. There was much work, many afflictions, and moreover, anxiety would creep in as to whether a convent would in fact be established there. The sisters worked the land themselves, doing all the labor, and would often become discouraged. When Father Anatoly came, he would lift their spirits and often inspire them by his own example. Once the sisters were breaking up manure and crying, exhausted by the unaccustomed labor. Father Anatoly came, picked up a pitchfork, and began himself to shovel it — and it was as if their despondency had never been. Sometimes he would bring the workers soft mint cookies or bagels from Optina, and thus the Elder-ascetic would offer consolation to these young seekers of the life on high. When he would come to where they were working, he would bless them all and comfort them; and it is not surprising that when the sisters would find out that he was coming, they would run joyfully to meet their beloved Elder. When sisters who were living out in the woods became lonely and frightened — it would seem to them that someone was walking around the house, wailing — the Elder served a moleben and advised them to say the Jesus Prayer often. The sisters followed his advice and were calmed. When sisters would bring forward complaints against an older sister or would not get along together, the Elder would compassionately sympathize with them in their grief, analyze the situation, reconcile them, and admonish them concerning what they should do to avoid discord in the future. One sister was burdened by various obediences at various times and complained about this to Father Anatoly. He comforted her, persuading her to be patient. Once, when she asked,

"When will they transfer me from my obedience?," he said, "When you correct yourself." Another sister asked his blessing upon entering the convent to buy a Gospel and a Psalter. After giving her his blessing, he said, "The main thing is to diligently perform your obedience. Let it be higher for you than fasting and prayer..." To a sister who grieved at living out in the country [on obedience] he would say, "Be patient, everything will pass, and then how nice it will be. So do not grieve, but be patient and humble yourself, and the Lord will save you." In sorrow and grief, he would counsel them to have recourse to remembrance of God and thus to gladden their soul.

To those who were ready to decline difficult obediences he would say that it was needful and better to endure patiently, because in time everything would turn out for the better. One sister found her obedience difficult and complained to him. The Elder said only, "Be patient for just a little." After a short time she became ill, and when she recovered she was given a new obedience and freed from the difficult one. That same sister once came to Father Anatoly grieving and said bitterly, "Oh, why did I come to the convent?" In answer to this he said to her, "If people in the world knew how hard it is to live in a monastery, they would not come even if they were compelled with a stick — they would sooner go barefoot so long as they could stay in the world. But if they knew what a reward is laid up for monastics in Heaven, they would drop everything and go to monasteries." He was much displeased if anyone wished for death in adversity, and he would reprove them. He frightened one sister when she spoke thus by replying, "Want me to pray and you will die?" Of course she objected, "No, no," and began asking forgiveness: she realized how unprepared she was for death, which she had so lightly asked for. Possessing an excellent knowledge of the *Philokalia*, he would often give those who were experiencing sorrows the discourse of John of Karpathos to read. "All our temptations will pass," the Elder would often say, "only one must endure patiently, and then you will receive consolation — if not here, then certainly in the future life." "Just live peacefully," he would say, "do not grieve one another, bear one another's burdens, do your obediences, and you will be saved. Why, we came for the Lord's sake, we left father and mother, and thus we must patiently endure everything." During the chanting of "Make steadfast, O holy Theotokos... all them that form a company and gather for to praise thy name... deem them all worthy of glory's crowns"[1] during a service, one sister got the idea that only chanters will receive a reward, and she became grieved that

---

1. The Third Ode of the Katavasia to the Mother of God, which begins, "I shall open my mouth."

she was not a chanter. With these thoughts she went to see the Elder. Upon meeting her, he asked her three times, "Do you chant?," and on receiving a negative response, he said, "That's what the problem is — there's no chanting down here," and he indicated the heart, thus signifying that everything depends upon the inner disposition of the soul as one performs an obedience, and not upon the obedience itself. He would also say, as an instruction in patience, "Take a rock — hit it, then praise it. It will remain silent — and you should do the same when people grieve you." To console those who were distressed because of their obediences, Father Anatoly would sometimes relate something appropriate from the lives of the saints, or recall something he had witnessed. To one sister, who was burdened by her obedience in the garden, he related how a certain ascetic, fleeing the praise of men at his monastery, went to another and there was constrained to dig in the garden as an ordinary worker. He wished to find out whether this work of his was pleasing to God, and he dreamed that he had died and the judgment was taking place. When there remained nothing to his credit to counterbalance the weight of his sins, the angels threw in the spade, and it outweighed them. To another sister who found it hard being called to all kinds of obediences, the Elder said only, "They

Saint Anatoly

call you — that means you are needed." To a third, who found it hard picking potatoes, he said that he had once enjoyed this job. All three were comforted, and each went at her task with renewed vigor.

He admonished the sisters not to give in to despair, and to this end always to preserve a readiness to endure afflictions. As an illustration of how displeasing to the Lord murmuring is, the Elder would relate the following, "At the Belev convent, there lived a schemanun, Mother Paulina's sister. She had many sorrows in her life. She lived an exemplary life, and after some time she reposed. Some time later, a nun who loved her and wished to know her fate in the next life, after earnest prayer, saw her in a dream. The reposed one was sitting in a lovely room, in unusually bright light, but nevertheless looked unhappy. When asked why she was not happy, she answered, "It is well with me, but it would be incomparably better if I could see the face of God, and this is not permitted me. I did not bear afflictions without murmuring, and in order to see the face of God, when the rod of afflictions pierces one's heart, one must carry one's cross unmurmuringly to the end.' " While abhorring flattery, the Elder valued people's labors and would by every means encourage the diligent, often remarking, "I couldn't possibly have done it so well myself." When everyone was expecting Mother Amvrosia's heirs to come and take all her belongings, and especially the icons, the sisters grieved; but with Father Amvrosy's blessing, Father Anatoly would visit them, and they would take the Kazan icon and serve molebens, and he would comfort the sisters. And the heirs took nothing that was of value to the sisters. Likewise, when the buildings in the country burned down and the sisters were temporarily reduced to poverty, Father Anatoly hastened to console them by his presence, by words and by his assistance. The Elder often had to drive to Shamordino in bad weather, in spring when the river was flooding, and on more than one occasion he was in danger of drowning when the carriage broke down. Several times people tried to persuade him to abandon these labors, but the Elder remained faithful to his teacher and to his testament of serving Shamordino, and he would not even think of leaving the sisters without Confession and preparation for Holy Communion, or in general, without the consolation of talks and exhortation. He would say, "I will never abandon Shamordino and my spiritual children. The Elder gave me an obedience, and I cannot refuse it."

The Elder took care that the sisters' living conditions should be good, but he would not cater to weaknesses. At first at Shamordino tea was held in common, and he would absolutely forbid the sisters to have samovars in their cells or cook anything in their cells. In his understanding, humility was everything; he used to say that salvation depends not on the place where one is found but on one's inner state.

An orphanage was soon established at Shamordino.[1] The Elder greatly loved these children, just as he greatly loved little children in general. Sometimes he would go for walks with the children, throwing candies in the grass and watching them search for these treats. Sometimes he would also send apples to the orphanage. Once when he was staying at Shamordino, he showed special concern when a fire broke out in the orphanage. The Elder came with the Kazan icon to where the fire was, and as others tried to put it out, he labored with them in bringing an end to the calamity by his ardent prayer. Father Superior Moses of Tikhonov Monastery, a renowned ascetic and friend of the Elder, carried the Kazan icon around with him, as he also happened to be at Shamordino at the time. Sometimes the children would write the Elder sins they had forgotten in confession, and he would answer. Once he gave them a general epitimia for their sins in a letter he sent. Explaining to one sister his special concern for the children and for the young, the Elder said, "You came to the convent at a mature age, and you are not in such need of consolations as the young. A young tree has to be dug around and watered, it adjusts and begins to grow, and no longer requires attention, and can be left without such care as before."

There was no detail, there was nothing at the convent which remained untouched by the Elder's loving hand. Everywhere he brought peace and calmness, acceptance of one's lot, diligence and zeal for salvation. At one point, with Father Amvrosy's blessing, he declined a position of superiorship which was being offered to him,[2] consecrating his entire life to his monastery and his Elder, as well as to the convent founded by the latter. Always warmhearted and thoughtful toward his relatives, he was no less loving toward everyone else: already all were his near ones, for his heart burned with the love of Christ. When he would serve the Liturgy, after attentive and careful preparation, and stood during the Cherubic Hymn with his hands raised on high, this venerable Elder truly

---

1. After the Shamordino Convent was founded by the Elder Amvrosy, people seeking, sometimes quite desperately, to arrange for the material and spiritual welfare of poor orphans would entrust them to the Elder and the convent, and thus the orphanage came into being.
2. "...He was assigned by the Synod, beginning on August 3, 1871, as abbot of the Spassky-Orlov Monastery and elevated to the rank of archimandrite. Out of obedience to Fr. Ambrose, and for the sake of the labors of eldership, he refused this career." See "The Life of Hieroschemamonk Anatoly (Zertsalov) of Optina," *Orthodox Life*, Sept./Oct. 1989, p.8; translated from Optina Monastery and Its Era by I.M. Kontzevitch.

seemed already to be a citizen of Heaven to the brethren who held him in honor.

As a sickle cuts off an ear of grain, so his determination to fully surrender himself to the guidance of his Elders Father Makary and Father Amvrosy cut off at the root in Father Anatoly everything from which there could have developed sinful habits and the ways of an ordinary, sinful man. Every infirmity and weakness withered in him under the influence of fasting, obedience, and the general strictness of his manner of life, just as cut grass withers under the sun's burning rays. And the fire of prayer, which blazed so strongly in the reposed one, inflamed his spirit, and having first cleansed it, strengthened it, so that toward the end of his life, Father Anatoly had the same gifts of spiritual counsel, clairvoyance into the innermost recesses of the human soul, and knowledge of the future with which his teachers, the great Elders Makary and Amvrosy, were so richly endowed. He foreknew the deaths of his close spiritual children, their illnesses and adversities, and carefully warned them of approaching trials. The recollections of his spiritual children are full of descriptions of such incidents. We will mention a few. To one nun and one monk he predicted long in advance their future callings of superiorship; to a young girl he revealed that she would soon die; and to a nun he foretold an illness of the legs. He informed people beforehand of impending trials, and likewise of deliverance from afflictions. The Elder's very appearance reflected his spiritual height and his lofty prayerful disposition. His striking humility was evident even in small details; his zealous spirit and his modesty were foreign both to ingratiation and to visible severe asceticism.

Batiushka had an extraordinarily kind disposition and was very merciful. Our Matushka Abbess used to say concerning him, "He's not a father, but a tenderly loving mother to his children." One visitor said of Batiushka, "He is an extraordinarily intelligent, extraordinarily kind, and thoroughly Russian man."

He could not abide hypocrisy and flattery. He liked directness and openness, and he himself was very direct. Batiushka Father Amvrosy used to say of him in the words of the Gospel, "He is an Israelite in whom there is no guile."[1]

The Elder Anatoly was very trusting. Preserving simplicity himself in his relations with everyone, he never suspected anyone of falsehood or deceit. Often after listening to someone's story of their troubles, he would take it much to heart and grieve for that person. Sometimes someone

---

1. Cf. John 1:47.

would say to him, "Batiushka, are you sure they told the truth?" Batiushka would answer, "But why would they lie to me?" He was compassionate in the highest degree: when he would learn of someone's misfortune, he would remain upset for a long time, until he got a nervous headache. It was this, according to the doctors, which caused his heart ailment, which in turn caused other illnesses. Sometimes after reading in the newspapers of some sorrowful event in some other country, he would talk about it and grieve over it for a long time. We remember how he grieved over the shipwreck of the "Rusalka." His simple manner very much reminded one of Batiushka Father Lev, whom he faithfully emulated. Sometimes he would come to those awaiting him in the hut and begin relating something gaily and jokingly; there was always an edifying meaning behind his stories. Sometimes he would bring up human failings. Those who were close to him, seeing that people would sometimes get a mistaken impression of him, would grieve and say, "Batiushka, some people might not like what you just said, and they will think you were talking about them." He would reply, "I don't care what they say about me — truth is the most important thing. In St. Makarios of Egypt it says that he entreated God for twelve years to grant him simplicity. As for me, I have been asking for it for seventeen years, and I can't forego it for the sake of public opinion." Batiushka did not like it when people would express their fervent gratitude to him for every trifle, but neither did he like insensibility and ingratitude in people who would not appreciate anything.

He cherished the most sincere love for all, especially for his spiritual children. To those in whom he saw special attachment and devotion to himself, he was himself the more well-disposed, and he would not renounce his fondness for these people and would defend them. Sometimes people would say to him, "Batiushka, why do you cover her — they say such and such about her, and it is true." He would answer, "Let them say what they like — I know her soul." If someone caused him grief or trouble and he could see that that person had done it from inexperience or without thinking, and sincerely regretted it, he would forgive him and never remember the incident again. However, when under the pretense of devotion to him, someone would take advantage of his trustfulness and candor to do him an injury, and on discovering that Father Anatoly knew of it would ask his forgiveness, Batiushka would forgive him, but would no longer trust him as before. And events would in fact show afterwards that this person had only a superficial attachment to him. When he found out something bad about one of his spiritual children, he would never scold them but would wait for the person to repent on his own — as he liked for people to sincerely acknowledge their faults — and would never attach importance to every trifling thing. By his manner, he would give the person to understand that he was displeased. If the person noticed that Batiushka was no longer the same as before and asked what the matter was, and would only begin to acknowledge his fault, then Batiushka would begin to speak — and as he had a very ardent temperament, he would sometimes very sternly come out with things he had known for a long time but had never reproved the person for. However, the moment the person humbled himself, asked forgiveness and repented, Father Anatoly would forgive him immediately and try to comfort him afterwards. Sometimes he would come out for a general blessing and say something — and of course those who were standing close to him could hear better, but if you happened to be standing further back, sometimes you would become sad, thinking he didn't even see you. It was just as if Batiushka felt this, and he would come up to you and ask, "Where have you been?," or he would look at you in such an affectionate and fatherly way that your heart would rejoice. Sometime you would go into the hut and there would be several people sitting there; everything would be quiet. Then in the hall there would be heard the quiet creaking of shoes and Batiushka's steps, the door would open, and he would appear on the threshold in his white cassock, girded with a belt, and would say affectionately, "Who's here?" As he blessed us, he would say something or would just look at us, and one would feel happy and joyful.

His food at Optina, from his first year there and almost all his life, except for the last two years, was at the common trapeza; here he would go together with the brethren. He ate very little. During the last years, when he did not go to the trapeza, his entire dinner, prepared on the hearth by his cell attendant, consisted of a piece of salted fish with horseradish, or a piece of pressed caviar, followed by fish soup and buckwheat kasha with kvass[1] and green onion. His supper consisted of the same. He had tea twice a day, with neither bread nor jam. Sometimes we would say, "Batiushka, will you bless us to serve you some tea?," and he would say, "Again this tea, always more tea — isn't there some nice water?" Water

1. Kvass — A fermented drink made from rye or barley, and having a dark color and sour taste.

was his favorite drink. He drank coffee, too, but very rarely.

When Father Anatoly visited Shamordino, he would be brought more varied fare, but to everything he preferred grated radish with kvass,[1] and when it did not appear at dinner, he would say, "Everything's fine, but I miss that nice radish." And he would recall how he had had a great liking for herring, but Father Amvrosy had blessed him to eat grated radish instead. The sisters would ask, "Batiushka, why do you eat radish all the time?" And he would answer, "You sillies don't understand anything: our life is bitter, and so we have to eat bitter things." During Great Lent he would bring with him dried bread prepared from the black bread made at the skete, bid them to pile it in a dish and pour kvass over it, and he would eat it. Long before the beginning of Great Lent he used to say, "Good times are on the way — we'll grate up some radish, soak us some dried bread..."

Batiushka was merciful even to the birds. In winter he always had a cage under his window with hempseed. Only, he did not like the greedy, grudging sparrows, and he had a wire rigged up: when a sparrow flew in, you were supposed to jerk the wire, scare him, and make him fly away. Batiushka greatly loved flowers, and there were always bouquets in the vases. He would always bring flowers to Shamordino when he came, and many visitors to Optina would be given flowers.

The Elder served his children, the inhabitants of the young convent, for 21 years, and it is not surprising that everyone became used to him as to their own father. And he, as the faithful co-ascetic of the great Elder and founder of the convent, devoted himself entirely to the holy work of the guidance of souls to salvation, and applied all his strength to this endeavor.

On October 10, 1891, the Elder Father Amvrosy reposed, and this grievous loss, mourned by the Elder Father Anatoly along with the two monasteries, Optina and Shamordino, severely affected Father Anatoly's health. Not endowed with a strong constitution by nature, it having been overtaxed also by struggles, and having suffered from severe headaches for thirty years, after Father Amvrosy's death, Father Anatoly began to fail rapidly. Pensive and sad, he acutely felt his spiritual orphanhood and himself quickly drew near the end of his life. To Father Amvrosy's repose there was added yet another sorrow: the local bishop, who was not well-disposed toward Father Amvrosy and his work, temporarily forbade

---

1. Bitter black radish is proverbial in Russian. The expression for being thoroughly sick and tired of something (or someone) is, "He is more tired of it than of bitter radish." Also, the very word "kvass" denotes sourness.

Father Anatoly to travel to Shamordino. Although this prohibition was soon revoked, it had a lasting and profoundly severe effect upon the Elder's health. At the end of 1892 he travelled to St. Petersburg and Kronstadt to see Father John, whom he had revered for a long time, and to consult with doctors. Together with Father John, Father Anatoly served on October 10, the day of Father Amvrosy's memorial, and was comforted by conversation with him. The doctors found that Father Anatoly had a weak heart and water in his lungs. In accordance with their advice, he prepared to begin treatment; however, this treatment, requiring walks, was soon discontinued. The Elder's legs began to swell, his shoes no longer fit, and so he became unable to walk. In the fall of 1893 his final illness began. For three months he had to sit day and night in a chair — and this after having been ill all fall. On September 7 and October 10 he was able to summon enough strength to serve on these memorial days of his unforgettable instructors,[1] but in general he was failing quickly. When his strength began to diminish, he visited Shamordino one last time, prayed fervently before the Kazan icon and at Mother Sophia's grave, looked around at everything, blessed everyone and comforted everyone by his greeting and affection. For the residents of Shamordino, these were the final gleams of this bright, dear star of piety which was being extinguished.

The Elder's final illness was grievous, and especially difficult were the attacks of hiccoughing which occurred at times. But he meekly and humbly endured his illness. On December 15, 1893, he secretly received the schema; only Father Geronty, his confessor, and several people who were close to him knew of this. The Elder confessed several times, and partook of the Holy Mysteries of the Body and Blood of Christ until the very last day. At this time there were brought to him holy wonderworking icons of the Mother of God: the Akhytrskaya icon of Kozelsk, the Kazan icons of Optina and Shamordino, and the Kaluzhskaya icon. Praying before them, the Elder found rest. During his illness, he was comforted when the Holy Gospel would be read to him, especially the 14th and 15th chapter of the Gospel of St. John. During his life the Elder had a special veneration for the holy Apostle John, St. Gregory the Theologian,[2] the Supreme Commander Michael, and the holy Great Martyr Barbara, and during his illness also, he called upon them with special frequency. To his very last days, he did not cease from consoling and exhorting his spiritual children whenever he could; among them were also lay people and monastics from other monasteries. These last the Elder always

---

1. That is, the Elders Makary and Amvrosy.
2. The Elder reposed on his feast, which is also the feast of the icon of the Mother of God "Assuage My Sorrows."

received without delay, and when sisters from Shamordino would bring this up to him, he would answer that we were the ones who could wait: we live nearby, whereas they underwent so many hardships in order to get here, and can they even come at all, except rarely? Of the ancient ascetics he most often brought to mind at this time Sts. Anthony the Great and Pachomios the Great. With reverence he would remember the Optina Elders Lev, Makary, and Amvrosy, and the Father Superiors Moses and Anthony, as well as Mother Sophia and many others, and also Archbishop Gregory in particular. During his illness, sisters from Shamordino, with the Bishop's blessing, assisted him continually, taking turns. Only a week before his death was the Elder in any condition to be transferred from his chair to his bed.[1] During his illness he was comforted also by a telegram from Father John of Kronstadt and one from Grand Duke Constantine Constantinovich.[2] A month and a half before his death, he blessed Shamordino with an icon of the Mother of God of the Sign, entrusting the young convent to the Most Pure One in his prayers. Having blessed everyone and bidden farewell to everyone, he quietly reposed during the reading of the Canon for the Departure of the Soul, on January 25, 1894, at 4:25 in the morning, in his 71st year.

Profound grief overwhelmed the hearts of the monks and nuns who were devoted to him, and their heavy loss, following so closely upon another great loss — the death of Father Amvrosy — was alleviated only by prayer and by the awareness that the Elder had inherited the lot of the righteous. Many of th sisters later saw the Elder in their sleep, sometimes in priestly vestments, sometimes comforting, sometimes confessing, sometimes healing — and after these dreams they felt consolation and joy once more, and some obtained relief from their illnesses. The Elder is buried not far from his instructors, and here prayer is frequently offered for

---

1. That is, apparently before this time bed rest had been impossible because of the water in his lungs.

2. A well-known literary figure, educator and humanitarian, Grand Duke Constantine inspired his many children with piety and devotion to their country. One son, Oleg, was subsequently killed in action during World War I; three other sons, John, Constantine and Igor were martyred with Grand Duchess Elizabeth Feodorovna and others; and a daughter, Tatiana, became a nun and later Abbess Tamara of the Mount of Olives Convent in Jerusalem.

the repose of the souls of all these benefactors of humanity.[1] Thus was extinguished the seventh great luminary in the numerous assembly of the ascetics of Optina, mighty in faith and boundless in love for people sorrowing and suffering under the burden of our sinful life. He is laid to rest amid his instructors: to the right in the Kazan church, Fathers Moses, Anthony and Isaaky are laid to rest; and in front of him, and a little to the left, Fathers Lev, Makary and Amvrosy.

In the evening sky, when the moon rises and everything — earth, and waters, and forests, and fields —is as though covered with silence, little stars shine brightly in the heavens, lost in the infinite vastness. And among them seven large stars, called the Great Bear,[2] shine with special brilliance... Our reposed Elder loved often to look up into these heavens, and at these stars. Let us look and see also — how many people voyaging on the seas have been guided and still are guided by these stars in their journeyings... And from the stars let us look down once more to earth, upon our much-suffering homeland. How many holy sons have arisen in her, great in humility! How many ascetics who have given their entire lives to serving God and their neighbor! And among them are not our seven great sons of Optina Hermitage shown forth as being like these seven great stars? And as those stars serve travellers on the deep seas, cannot their life serve also for us as a guiding star to the life on high, amid all the tempests of such a perilous and stormy sea — the sea of life...

From, *Russian Strugglers for Piety of the 18th & 19th Centuries*, ed. Russian Monastery of St. Panteliemon, Mt. Athos, July Volume, (Moscow, 1908)

---

1. Over the Elder Anatoly's grave a white marble monument was erected bearing the psalmic words, With patience I waited patiently for the Lord, and He was attentive unto me, and He hearkened unto my supplication. And He set my feet upon a rock, and He ordered my steps aright. And He hath put into my mouth a new song, a hymn unto our God (Psalm 39:1-4) (see Priest S. Chetverikov's biographical introduction to several of the Elder's letters, *Soul-Profiting Reading*, Moscow, 1902, p. 536.
2. That is, Ursa Major, the most prominent of the northern constellations; it contains the stars forming the Big Dipper.

GLOSSARY

Akathist A series of hymns consisting of thirteen kontakia (short hymns), each followed by a refrain, and the first twelve followed also by an oikos (pl. oikoi) (an intoned or chanted hymn).

Aposticha Stichera accompanied by verses taken from the Psalms.

Canon A series of eight odes consisting of troparia celebrating the feast of the day.

Exapostilarion A troparion occurring at the end of the canon at Matins.

Heirmos The opening stanza in each ode of the canon.

Hierodeacon A monk who has been ordained to the diaconate.

Hieromartyr A martyr who was a member of the clergy.

Hieromonk A monk who has been ordained to the priesthood.

Hieroschemamonk A schemamonk (see below) who has been ordained to the priesthood.

Hymns of Ascent Hymns based on Psalms 119-133 (these Psalms are called the Odes of Ascent). They are chanted before the reading of the Gospel in Matins.

Kamilavka A tall hat worn by monks and nuns.

Katavasias The concluding stanzas from each ode of the canon, often chanted together as a group.

Kathisma (pl. kathismata) Each of the twenty sections into which the Psalter is divided.

Kliros The part of the church (usually toward the front and to the side) where the choir stands.

Kontakion Originally a long poem; now a stanza inserted in the canon at Matins.

Little Schema See Mantia.

Mantia (Gk. mandias) The outer garment of a monastic, a wide garment, very long, and without sleeves, worn as a cape over the other monastic garments. This is given at the tonsure of a rassophor into the lesser schema, at which one pronounces vows and becomes a monk (or nun) proper.

Moleben A special service of prayers of thanksgiving and petition offered on the occasion of some special occurrence in the life of an individual or of the nation. A moleben may be requested at a time of special need or at a time of special thanksgiving. Somewhat equivalent to the Paraclesis.

Nabedrennik A rectangular article of the priest's vestments, suspended by a shoulder strap, worn at the side hanging down from the waist. This article is bestowed by a bishop as an ecclesiastical dignity.

Oikos The stanza which immediately follows the kontakion.

Paraman The name derives from the Greek "paramandias" meaning "something besides, or added to the mantia." This is a square of material on which is depicted the Cross of Christ with the lance and reed and the inscription, "I wear upon my body the wounds of my Lord." By means of cords or ribbons tied to each corner it is fastened around the shoulders and waist of the monk. This is given to monastics at the tonsure into the mantia.

Philokalia A compilation of exalted texts on prayer and the spiritual life which span from the fourth to the fifteenth centuries, compiled by Sts. Macarios of Corinth and Nicodemos of the Holy Mountain, first printed in 1792. An abridged translation into Russian, the *Dobrotolyubie*, by St. Paisius Velichkovsky, appeared in 1793.

Prosphora The specially-prepared bread stamped with the Eucharistic

Seal which is brought by the faithful to church to be used at the preparation of the Holy Eucharist. The faithful submit with the prosphora names of the living and the reposed to be commemorated at the preparation. The priest, having commemorated the names and having removed portions, placing them on the holy paten, returns the remainder of the prosphora to the one who submitted it. Prosphora so used may be kept and distributed afterwards as a blessing from the Divine Liturgy.

Prothesis table The table used in preparation of the bread and wine to be used in the Holy Eucharist.

Rassa Monastic robe with wide sleeves, worn by monastics who have been tonsured.

Rassophor The name derives from the rassa, the robe with wide sleeves, and means "wearer of the rassa." A rassophor monk has been tonsured into the monastic estate, but as yet has pronounced no vows.

Schema A piece of material decorated with many crosses and inscriptions, also called the analavon, worn by the highest state of monastics. The Greek word "schema" (form, shape, figure), and its Slavonic translation "obraz" (which in addition means image, manner, way) are also used to designate the habitual dress of monastics in a general sense, and sometimes their manner of life as well.

Schemamonk (or nun) The highest state of monastics; a monastic tonsured into the great schema takes vows of complete renunciation of the world. In place of the paraman he wears the analavon, or schema, which is ornamented with many crosses and suspended from the shoulders.

Stichera Hymns usually inserted between verses from the Psalms.

Triodion The liturgical book containing the hymns and the typicon for Great Lent and the weeks preceding it. Also, the name for the period itself.

Troparion A stanza of hymnology; this word is also more specifically used to indicate the main troparion of the day (the dismissal hymn).

Typicon The book that contains the rule or order for the daily offices chanted in church. In the monastic context, it signifies also the Rule adhered to by a monastic community.

INDEX OF TOPICS

TABLE OF LETTERS